Es'kia Mphahlele

Es'kia Mphahlele was born and raised in Marabastad, Pretoria. This town is the setting for his first autobiography, *Down Second Avenue*. Mphahlele attended school regularly for the first time at age 11. He grew up to become a teacher, and became active in resisting the implementation of Bantu Education in black schools. Together with two colleagues, Mphahlele was banned from teaching in South Africa. He then went to work for *Drum* magazine, writing mainly short stories. In 1957 Mphahlele and his family left for Nigeria, where he worked as a teacher. Over the years he lectured in universities in Nigeria, Kenya, Zambia and the United States. He also travelled widely in Europe and Africa. He obtained a PhD in English in the United States. After returning to South Africa in 1977, he became professor of literature at the University of the Witwatersrand. He retired in 1987 and went to live in the Northern Transvaal, close to the site of his childhood village. *Afrika My Music* is the autobiographical sequel to *Down Second Avenue*. Mphahlele has also published short stories, a novella, critical essays and three novels, *The Wanderers*, *Chirundu* and *Father Come Home*.

Afrika
My Music

An Autobiography 1957–1983

Es'kia Mphahlele

Ravan Writers Series

We carried the song across countries
over oceans
over snow-topped mountains
Afrika my music.

You carried us across countries
over oceans
over desert and savannah
Song of Afrika.

How could we not return
when this is where
the afterbirth was buried for rebirth? —
Afrika my music.

For the family, sacrifice the individual,
For the community, the family;
For the country, the community;
For the soul, all the world.

— Sanskrit poem rendered by Rabindranath Tagore.

for Khabi

& the bonds that make us

for all who have faith in African Humanism

for all who have granted me the privilege

to pursue the Humanistic Dream

Published by Ravan Press (Pty) Ltd
PO Box 145 Randburg 2125
South Africa

© Copyright Es'kia Mphahlele 1984

First published 1984
Second edition 1995

ISBN 0 86975 484 X

Typesetting: Opus 61
Cover painting by Eli Kyeyune
Cover design: Insight Graphics, Pretoria

Printed and bound by Galvin & Sales, Cape Town
(0575)

I

The Sounds Begin Again

I am sitting out on the stoep of our house at Lebowa-kgomo, fifty kilometres south-east of Pietersburg. A city in the making. In front of our row is bush. Pitch dark. Not more than six kilometres to the north, beyond the bush through which the Tudumo river cuts, is the hill. A narrow valley away from the hill is the Mogodumo mountain range. Further on, out of my line of vision, Mogodumo is severed at Chuene's Pass for the road that runs from Lydenburg to Pietersburg. Mogodumo-tona (masculine in Sesotho) is the huge, imposing part of the range to the left of Chuene's Pass. The part in front of us is Mogodumo-tshadi (feminine). Partly because the name itself suggests a superhuman rumbling within that sheer bulk of rock heaving against space, I like to think of Mogodumo as the mountain of the gods.

Twelve kilometres to the east is Maupaneng, the village in the Mphahlele district where I spent seven years of my childhood, looking after cattle and goats. The mountain dark and its boulder-heaving rivers has since those days held some enchantment for me. In all the years of our exile we did not encounter such a river as the Hlakaro is on its journey through Maupaneng. Apart from the Congo in parts, and the Zambezi at the famous falls, the rivers have been placid, heavy-bosomed.

Every so often I jog in the Mphahlele district and trace the goat-and-cattle trails we maintained in my herdboy days. I still remember them vividly. On these excursions I try to recapture the smells of the place. So often I am jolted out of my reverie by the birdsong of my youth. I pick up *morula* fruit and berries, and the taste travels back forty-seven years. I left these haunts in 1930 and did not return until July, 1976.

Pitch darkness, riotous moonlight, night sounds, boulder-heaving rivers, orchestrated by stories about giants and huge snakes before which man humbled himself — all these filled my life as a boy with terror. Now I drive home from Pietersburg in the moonlight, and approach the moon-blanched length of rock on the feminine side of Chuene's Pass. Suddenly I am startled by the overhanging shadow of the male on my right. I can't help feeling the protective embrace of the silence as I make my passage, the male and female reaching out towards each other through moonlight and shadows.

Philadelphia, Pennsylvania, is a long way off now. In the months since our arrival on August 17, 1977, it has become a sporadic memory. We shipped back all we owned, but the real investment required of us was the emotional and spiritual energy it took to accomplish this return from twenty years of exile. Problems of re-entry, political decisions and psychological readjustments have simply pushed America into some corner of the mind.

For four full months I waited for a reply from the University of the North, Sovenga. I could not see why

I should not be given the professorship of English, and yet I was apprehensive. So was Rebecca. They gave me the run-around for it, too. There was an interview at Pretoria University, after which I was advised to meet the Personnel Officer at Sovenga to discuss conditions of service. I might well have had the feeling that I was in — the only candidate to come up for an interview, they said.

The reply came. Curt and cold: 'Your application has been unsuccessful . . . .' The official crap and all. The muck and the smell of it . . . . I felt bitter. The South African Consulate in Washington D.C. had read out to me a letter from the Department of the Interior stating that I would be allowed to return to South Africa, on condition that I came to reside in Lebowa and sought employment at the University of the North. To get that far had required a five-year negotiation with the government through the good offices of the Chief Minister of Lebowa, Dr. C.C. Phatudi. I could taste gall in my mouth . . . .

Before we left South Africa in September, 1957, to teach in Nigeria, I used to sit on the stoep of my house in Orlando West, Soweto. I looked out towards the lights of white suburbia, Northcliff especially, across the darkness. Lights that always enchanted me. I was waiting for my passport, waiting for the exit gates to open. After fifteen months of harrowing speculation attended by doubts and forebodings, the passport came, a day before my departure.

This time, in 1977, I was waiting for the inner gates to be opened. After twenty years in the international community, where merit counts most in my line of work — where, after my application for the first Nigerian job, I had always been *invited* to academic positions — I had returned to a country where the black man has learned to wait, endure survive.

I was indeed back home.

Tonight, a week before 1979 breaks upon us, as we sit out on this stoep in Lebowakgomo a few kilometres from Capricorn, Rebecca and I feel our optimism has been partly vindicated. The University of the Witwatersrand has offered me a position in its African Studies Institute as Senior Research Fellow. I have accepted, and shall begin on the first day of February. Also, the Minister of Justice has taken my name off the list of those writers who may not be quoted, whose works may not circulate in the country. Back in April 1966, I was one of a whole batch of writers living abroad who were 'listed' under the Internal Security Act. Only *Down Second Avenue, Voices in the Whirlwind,* and *Modern African Stories,* which I co-edited, may now be read in the country. *The African Image* (revised version), *In Corner B. and Other Stories* and *The Wanderers* remain banned under the Publications and Entertainment Act. The Vice-Chancellor of the University of the Witwatersrand and the lawyer, Ismail Ayob, had simultaneously petitioned the then Minister of Justice to remove me from the list of the gagged, otherwise I would not even be able to circulate my notes in class.

After my reverse at Sovenga, Rebecca took up a job as community social worker under the Lebowa Government Service. She has the degree of Master of Social Work from the University of Denver. I was employed by Lebowa's Department of Education as inspector in charge of English teaching.

During ten months travelling the length and

breadth of Lebowa, I discovered what twenty-five years of Bantu Education has done to the standard of English. Just flattened it. Not that white students entering university are much better equipped, though this is for different reasons. Among Africans there was greater competence in the use of English before 1958 — among both teachers and pupils. Progressively fewer students have been majoring in English, still fewer proceeding to the Honours degree.

These tours of duty gave me perspective, they made me long for the classroom. To make it worse, Lebowa, like other territories that are supposed to be managing their own education departments, does not have the money for a full-scale attempt to upgrade teachers and training institutions. The system is still 'Bantu Education'. Its key functionaries are whites seconded by the central government who enjoy extra pay for 'hazards' or 'hardships' because they are supposed to be working in outpost conditions.

The English-language press championed my cause when I lost the Sovenga post. Government officials refused to answer their questions. The university administration, Rector and all, let it be known that the then Minister of Education and Training had turned down its unanimous decision to appoint me. The Minister refused to give reasons. He promised, though, that he would veto any appointment Ezekiel Mphahlele might be given by any university or other institution under his control. Someone in the university administration came out with it at last: it was not the policy of the central government to let blacks chair departments like English.

I began to understand why the university had not been seen to put pressure on the Minister to take the

man they wanted — though they believed, according
to their statements in the press, that my academic
qualifications were 'unimpeachable'. What was harder
to understand was why they had staged that farcical
interview at Pretoria University in the first place.

The interview! The atmosphere is weird. The
Registrar — a Mr. Steenkamp — gives me a curt nod as
I enter the room, and motions me to my seat. The
committee is sitting on a platform, I on the floor level.
The platform is lit up, I sit in a kind of semi-gloom.
The committee consists of the Rector of the University
of the North (the late Dr. Kgware); Professor Leighton,
head of English at the Rand Afrikaans University;
Professor Sebaga, head of English at Pretoria University, Professor Mativha, head of Venda at the University
of the North; Professor Pretorius, head of History at
the same place.

Only the men from Pretoria and the Rand ask
academic and pedagogical questions. The African
professor restricts himself to one question, which
does not give rise to discussion: do I think African
languages are important enough for us to continue to
teach them?

The Rector asks what I understand by university
autonomy and academic freedom in relation to the
University of the North. Dr. History asks why I have
come back to seek employment in an institution that
is a product of a system of education I had attacked
before I left the country? Why have I come back to a
country whose whites are racist as I describe them in
the subtitle of a poem of mine? What position would
I take if the students rioted?

We tell whites at least a million lies a day in this
country. First, because we must survive, second, because they themselves already live a big lie. Lying to

the white man who employed me or who processed my life was a natural thing to do before I left South Africa. I learned to be relatively at ease with whites abroad, and I did not have to lie in order to survive. I could sell my labour on the best market. In the process I either unlearned or tucked away in some corner of the subconscious the impulse to tell a white man lies. It is no effort for me to tell the appointments committee in front of me the truth about my views on the matter raised.

It is only after I have left the Senate room that it occurs to me that I have repeatedly talked about the 'independent states north of the Limpopo river' to distinguish them from South Africa. Academic freedom and university autonomy? A university should be accorded the universal right to develop its own curricula in a way that reflects the culture in which it is operating, and in turn feed something into that culture so that it does not stagnate. An African university must express African culture even if white expatriates still teach in it. I should like to think also that a South African university will feel constrained to work towards a future that will make the concept of 'separate development' irrelevant; that curricula and syllabuses can express a culture striving towards a synthesis that will be truly *African*.

An African university should be manned by the people best equipped, in the context of today's separateness, to perceive and promote the black man's aspirations. As soon as possible we should employ an increasing number of Africans. But Africanisation should not mean merely employing more African teachers; curricula and syllabuses should increasingly be Africa-based, instead of constantly singing the triumphs of Western civilisation. For instance,

African literature should be the starting point from which we can fan outwards. The English department should become a department of literature, the integral part of which would be comparative literary studies. And the more obvious principles: a university should promote freedom of inquiry, freedom of speech.

I cannot help but read mischief in Dr. History's question about my return. It seems to suggest that I am unique. I merely answer: I wanted to return to my ancestral home — South Africa; I want a meaningful cultural context to work in; I want community. I left the country because I was banned from teaching: I did not skip the country nor leave on an exit permit. If I had continued to teach I would still have opposed Bantu Education. Who loves everything the government of his country does? My return has ultimately nothing to do with whether I like the system or not. I have always believed that the democratic ideal should accommodate political dissent. How about that, Dr. History?

Students rioting? I would not encourage it. But after saying this, I should point out that students want a representative council (I have heard of one that was banned at Sovenga) that can be respected and accommodated by the administration. Candid debate must be allowed for and listened to seriously. How about that, Dr. History?

As a parting shot, Dr. History asks how members of the Congress for Cultural Freedom will view my return to a country they have repeatedly condemned. I answer that I had not thought it necessary to institute a referendum on whether or not I should return.

Booby traps, booby traps . . . . Intellectual integrity, where is your home, where is your sanctuary? I later learned that stock questions about academic freedom and university autonomy were part of the repertoire on these occasions.

A white man from the University of South Africa was appointed. If God moves like a crab, as we say in our languages, what simile would be fitting for the way the South African government works? After this, I was invited by heads of departments at two other 'ethnic' universities to consider the possibility of joining their departments. I was agreeable. Somewhere along the line internal negotiations struck bedrock. Some top university official teetered on the edge of the cliff and then turned round to tell my promoters that he was afraid the government would not approve .... We often fail to see the strings by which the bantustan puppet moves in the floodlights, but the full-bodied dancer — how can *that* escape us?

I stop to contemplate a serenity I have rediscovered in the northern Transvaal landscape. I realise how cosmopolitan, how suburban my family's lifestyle has become; for better, for worse we have become bigger than our urban ghetto beginnings. The bonds that have held us to the original African experience, though, have remained intact during our travels. We still feel a strong identity with our ancestors: the living dead who are the spiritual dimension of our reason for returning. *Come back native son, native daughter come back!*

In the last year I have been reacquainting myself with the smell and texture of the place. A changed human landscape in many ways, one that is still changing but essentially still real to me. Pockets of

African urban life have broken into the idyllic rural
scene. Boys no longer herd cattle and goats: instead,
they go to school regularly. Women still carry water
on their heads for long distances, either from a river
or from a communal pump. Just as they used to
fifty years ago when I was a boy and, of course, for
centuries before. Field husbandry has diminished
considerably owing to the disruptive impact of the
migrant-labour system and the lack of good land.
Those who come back to live here go in for small-scale
commercial ventures or into professional and admin-
istrative jobs. What else could there be in the midst
of all this rural poverty?

Yes, a changing human landscape, but still essentially rural, though now Mirage aircraft from the
military bases further north come whizzing and
piercing through space overhead every so often.
From the southern urban complex, echoes of another
turbulence and pain come to my ears like the sound
of ocean breakers staking a claim on the shore. The
imagination is straining for the meaning of this
confluence: super-tensed birds of steel from the
north, the painful south and its turbulence down
there, and between them, this pastoral serenity and
I, who have in the last twenty years become
thoroughly suburban. So much so that, because I
could live anywhere I liked abroad if I could afford
it, I wonder now that I am back home what slum living
would be like.

A poem is straining to be born. It was Vinoba
Bhave, the Indian mystic, who said: 'Though action
rages without, the heart can be tuned to produce
unbroken music . . . . ' Supertensed jets, political
noises, the power drills of the south and their
tremors, the wanderer returned to look for a

physical, and a social and cultural commitment
. . . . My very return is a compromise between the
outsider who did not *have* to be bullied by place
in other lands (and yet wanted a place, badly) and
the insider who has an irrepressible attachment to
ancestral place, be it in a rural or an urban setting.

Like the rest, I must submit to the pull of place, I
must deal with the tyranny of time. This composition – the border between us and Zimbabwe,
Mozambique and other territories, the birds of steel
seeming to spoil for a fight, this serenity, the turb-
ulent south – let it strain at our hearts; if our hearts
be found whole, we are content.

During those highly impressionable years as a herdboy
in the Mphahlele district, I got to know fear. Fear of
the dark, fear of high mountains in which I had to
spend hours looking for lost cattle or hunting
rabbits. Fear of rivers that tumbled down, uprooting
trees and boulders. I got to know the cruelties and
benignities of nature. Then I became an urban dweller
in Pretoria, where I had been born. I came to love it, in
that mindless way a child can be said to love a place,
with all its filth, odours, terrors, poverty, death.
Because of the memory of those years, when we
seemed to grow up casually, when we were always
liable to be crushed by the life Pretoria and Cape
Town had planned for us, I cannot today help
feeling nostalgic about the sense of community we
shared in Marabastad; nostalgic even about the
smells, the taste and the texture of life as we experienced it in those days – even though I would
not want to live in a slum again. Never. Those
terrors of rural and urban life became rooted in me
so that I could never, even in my adult life, outgrow

them. They haunt my dreams today, they help define my responses to life wherever I live it, among other humans and in my books.

Some African poets, particularly the Francophone poets, have sweet things to say about night. Night as a symbol of blackness. Night 'teeming with rainbows', as Aimé Césaire would say. Night of ourselves. Black souls communing with night and listening to its mysteries, night defining black souls and their pride. Night was no longer to represent the ugly, the mysterious, the sinister, the darkness of spirit. After the terrors of pastoral life, *my* nights in the slum were orchestrated only by screams, moans, police whistles, the screech of squad car tyres. Life became a myriad burning fuses, each radiating its own dump of explosives. Explosives that seem to renew themselves by their own rubble and ashes, creating always their own fuses in the process. In our African townships we seek the day, not the night.

The tyranny of time, the tyranny of place . . . . The muck, the smell of it, the fever and the fight, the cycles of decay and survival . . . . And 'the sounds begin again'. I want daytime, I want place, I want a sense of history. Even though place will never be the same again for me, because its lights and shadows may change, I want to be there when it happens.

The tyranny of time, the tyranny of place . . . . The muck and the smell of it . . . . Back to 1941 when, at twenty-one, I took up my first job as a teacher of the blind in an adult institution, Roodepoort. Fresh from teacher training, from the protection of boarding-school life, utterly confused. I made up my mind to finish high school by private study and proceed by the same route up to the M.A. I lived in another slum fifty miles from my place of birth, and it could have been that Pretoria slum transplanted. Night screams, barking of half-starved mongrels, the rattle of wagons loaded with human manure collected from lavatory buckets . . . the smell of night . . . the throb of a life seeking at once some violent release, some affectionate contact and a corner to deal with the terrors of night, to take stock of the hurts, the buffetings, the braveries of daytime . . . .

Something strange happened to me as I studied by candlelight, listening at intervals to the throb of night out there. I found myself writing a short story. During my primary school days, I had rooted everywhere for newsprint to read. Any old scrap of paper. Our ghetto had no newspaper deliveries, no school libraries (forty years later we still don't have them) . . . . There was a small one-room tin shack the municipality had the sense of humour to call a 'reading room', on the western edge of Marabastad. It was stacked with dilapidated books and journals junked by some bored ladies in the suburbs. Anything from cookery book through boys' and girls' adventure to dream interpretation and astrology. Needless to say, mostly useless. But I dug out of the pile Cervantes' *Don Quixote.* I went through the whole lot like a termite, elated by the sense of discovery, of recognition of the printed word, by mere practice of the skill of reading. But Cervantes was to stand out in my mind, forever.

Another thing that fired my imagination was the silent movies of the thirties. Put Don Quixote and Sancho Panza together with Laurel and Hardy, with Harold Lloyd, with Buster Keaton, with all those heroes of American cowboy folklore — Hoot

Gibson, Tim Mc Coy, Buck Jones and so on. Put Don Quixote next to Tarzan the Ape or Tarzan the Tiger: a crazy world. And yet unwittingly we wanted just this kind of entertainment to help us cope with the muck and the smell and the demands for gut response of everyday life. As I read the subtitles aloud to my friends who could not read as fast or at all, amid the yells and foot stamping and bouncing on chairs to the rhythm of the action, amid the fierce clanking of the piano near the stage of the movie house — as I did all this, fantastical ideas were whipping around in my mind. I was intrigued, captivated by the age-old technique of story-telling. All we saw in the movies, all we read in those journals and books, was about far-away lands, not our own sordid setting. It was an exciting release, although we were mindless of the reasons for it.

I recount all this to indicate some of the equipment I brought to the adventure I found myself embarked upon before I knew it. I had not read any short stories before — of the artful kind we compose today. Lots of tales, yes. So I had no genuine models. I simply stacked them up without any hope of publishing what I wrote, as it would have been unthinkable for a white magazine even to consider them; nor even a white-owned newspaper circulating among Africans. Looking back on the stories now, they read hopelessly like the kind of thing that aspires to be a novel and so fails to make the incisive point it set out to, capturing only the aura of tragedy that surrounds black life. I wrote simply to depict the situation and the human beings who act it out, without the technique by which dramatic and rhetorical connections are made between real-life suffering, the socio-political system, and art. My focus was always the drama of life as lived in the ghetto. I saw 'white' life merely as peripheral. The exercise in literary compromise had begun for me, something even more profound than what is often referred to as 'writing yourself out of a situation'. And the sounds begin again . . . . Outside there, from inside this tin shack in Roodepoort location, I can hear a wedding song. The singers will stop at our corner, I'm sure, to dance. The moon is out. Its light will be trying to bounce off the corrugated-iron roofs, but rust will resist that moongame. Maybe I'll step out for a little diversion when the group comes round the corner.

Four and a half years later, I had finished my high-school course and was eligible for high school teaching. But I would have to continue with private study. I went to Orlando, 1945. And the sounds begin again . . . the gang wars, the police squad cars, the political rallies, the baton charges, cops shooting . . . high-school teaching and further self-education. A new phase for me: teaching English in a ghetto. Every teacher in my schooldays had tried blissfully and unwittingly to murder any love I had for literature. Walter Scott, Jane Austen, Dryden, Milton, Richard Steele, Joseph Addison, Thackeray — imagine this forbidding line-up in an African setting! Throughout my junior high school days, let alone before that, through the forties, mission schools allowed no one to teach English who was not of English stock. We had to pass exams; we had to succeed. Our parents had themselves little or no education: we had been told education was the key to a decent livelihood and respectability, and we wanted those — oh, how desperately we wanted them in order to rise spiritually above our sordid conditions. So we had to chew on a lot of literary sawdust and wash it down with a smile.

I had thus come out of that bludgeoning with perhaps a fragment of Dickens, a chunk of undigested Shakespeare. I resisted Milton until I ceased to care which paradise was lost, which was regained. How can I even now engage our African students in the epic sweep of that poetry when I myself do not identify with a lost paradise? Man's first disobedience — that can be a mighty big joke in Africa. Yet we keep swallowing the Hebrew myths and folklore, and their poetry escapes us. But we had to be subjected to that theology, just as we had been baptised while our infant eyes were barely open, with no say in the matter but a yell in the minister's face. Hence the name Ezekiel or Es'kia: heavy stuff, man, heavy . . . .

I rediscovered Dickens, the classics. I discovered Gorky, Dostoevsky, Chekhov, in my private studies and preparations for my classes. Somewhere along the line, my high school students and I discovered each other. I was constantly asking myself questions relating to the value of poetry for me and my students, and for the township culture we were sharing — a culture that was very much an assertion of the human spirit fighting for survival against forces that threatened to fragment or break it. Of what use was poetry in a social climate that generated so much physical violence? In a life that resisted any individual creative efforts, a social climate that made the study of literature, particularly in a foreign but official language like English, look like playing a harmonica or jewish harp in the midst of sirens and power drills and fire-brigade bells? It was the full recognition of these factors by students and teacher that conditioned the love we developed for literature. A love that had to be self-generated, given all the hostile external factors. The element of escapism also helped sustain that interest. Just as Cervantes,

Laurel and Hardy, Buck Jones had served us when I was a boy. An element of escapism that one would have been ashamed in later years to acknowledge, because a few steps from there could land you in sheer snobbery. And snobbery is the cruellest joke anyone can play on himself in an African township. For me, as one who was then writing short stories, the whole literary adventure was a compromise between several disparate drives and urges.

Underlying the questions that we grappled with about the function of literature was always the motivation to master English at the grassroots level of practical usage. English, which was not our mother tongue, gave us power, power to master the external world which came to us through it: the movies, household furniture and other domestic equipment, styles of dress and cuisine, advertising, printed forms that regulated some of the mechanics of living and dying, and so on. It was the key to job opportunities in that part of the private sector of industry where white labour unions had little to lose if they let us in.

We had embarked on an adventure. This sense of adventure explains the enthusiasm, the energy, the drive with which Africa all over confronts the imperatives of learning.

It was during this period of self-education, of teaching, trying to understand what my students wanted, that I made three discoveries, all interrelated. Things that were to change my whole outlook, my whole stance and consequently my literary style. I became sharply aware of the realism of Dickens, of Gorky, Chekov, Hemingway, Faulkner. I became aware of the incisive qualities of the Scottish and English ballads and saw in them an exciting affinity with the way in which the short story works: the single situation rather than a developmental series of events; concentration of the present moment or circumstance; action, vivid and dramatic; singleness and intensity of emotion, generated by the often terrifying and intense focus on a situation; the plotted and episodic nature of the narrative; the way in which character, instead of developing fully, is bounced off; the 'telescoping' of where the characters come from and where they are at present; the heightened moment of discovery or illumination; the 'leaping and lingering' technique in which the ballad passes from scene to scene in the narrative without having to fill in gaps, leaping over time and space and lingering on those scenes that are colourful and dramatic; the resonances. I have never, since, ceased to be moved by those ballads. They are so close to our own folk tales that depict violence and the supernatural. With so much death and violence around us in the ghetto, we seemed to be reliving those old days when life was so insecure, when nature was both kind and cruel, and when whatever force presided over human affairs abandoned us to our own predatory instincts.

Most directly related to my style and point of view was the third discovery, by chance in the late Forties, of Richard Wright's short stories, *Uncle Tom's Children* (1936). He was an Afro-American novelist who died in exile in Paris in 1960. I smelled our own poverty in his Southern setting. The long searing black song of Wright's people sounded like ours. The agony told me how to use the short story as a way of dealing with my anger and indignation. It was the ideal genre. I fed on the fury and poured more and more vitriol into my words until I could almost taste them. I would come back from work, wait for the time my family would be asleep, do my studies, and return to my short-story writing. I would go out on my Orlando porch for a break, and have a clear view of the distant lights of Northcliff, thirty or so kilometres away. More and more they took on a symbolic meaning for me, those lights, because between me and them was the dense dark, so dense you wanted to compare it with soup. Since my return from the rural north as a boy, electric lights had never ceased to enchant me. They reminded me, as they still do, of the unfriendly darknesses and riotous floods of moonlight in the rural north. Seen from a distance, the lights taunted me, ridiculed me, tantalised me, reassured me, set off in me an urge sometimes to possess them, sometimes to spray them with black paint, to eclipse them one way or the other.

In 1954, Langston Hughes and I were introduced by letter. He sent me his collection of stories, *The Ways of White Folks,* and his poetry collection, *The Weary Blues.*

We were to meet several times in Africa and the United States before he died in 1967. Although he did not have the driving diction that was Wright's trademark, in their own gentle and almost unobtrusive manner Langston's short fiction and poetry did things to me. I realised later that I had needed them both — those two antithetical idioms of black American expression, Wright's and Langston's.

II

Nigeria, France, Kenya — and the Pan-African Hop 1957-1966

The tyranny of place, the tyranny of time.... Grassroots. The muck, the smell, the fortitude, despair, endurance. Always the sounds begin again. Experience and the place that contains it .... The politics of education, the campaigning, the voices of protest. As reporter and fiction editor on *Drum* magazine in the mid-Fifties, I had found myself striving towards a sense of balance — indeed compromise — between writing as self-expression and writing as objective reporting of the social scene.

September 1957: Nigeria, first stop on my route into exile. Four years you looked for the smell and the feel of place. It was there all right: the smell of Lagos. the smell of Ibadan; the harmattan scouring the savannahs of the north, the harmattan, that dry desert wind .... The abundance of humanity in Nigeria and Ghana and their theatrical lifestyles .... First there was the scintillating sense of freedom and daytime, after the South African nightmare. You wanted to slow down, shake off the cold sweat after the nightmare had spat you out into the full glare of Nigerian daytime. You had to stop clawing around in search of opposition, of insult. But you seemed to hear, still, the distant proclamations of law and order across the Congo, the Zambezi, and the Limpopo, down in the painful south of the south. Your anger was still a sediment in the pit of your stomach waiting for Time's purgative or agitation . . . . The harmattan was nothing like the fierce August winds of the south. Down there you learned to lie to the white man in order to survive; anger and bitterness, running and fighting and running again, these seemed like vital compulsions. In Nigeria, or in Ghana, you had to stop running or else you'd plunge into the Niger or bolt into the Sahara and not live to learn your lesson. You got to know that the immigrant's journey is a long, long road, a heavy road. He tunnels through, back again beneath the pounding footsteps of thirty-seven years, the South African ground level bearing down. It took us time to unwind. Rebecca and I expected opposition and tough words whenever we met whites. None. The crutch that had given you an identity back home — anger and all — had been taken away. You had to move under your own steam. Throughout our exile, some of us South Africans were learning that. It became for us a test of independence: without the spur that oppression is, that revitalises longings and drives and purposes so that you keep moving lest you be ground underfoot — without this, could we continue under our own steam? Some of us did, others have been marking time, still others have disappeared into the larger stream of humanity, essentially anonymous.

I have known musicians who left to try and make it in the big world. They had, by local standards, cultural and economic, given us superb entertainment. Out there where other standards operated, they became anonymous. Hugh Masekela, Dollar Brand, Miriam Makeba; Letta Mbuli, Caiaphas Semenya,

Jonas Gwangwa are among the very few who have
held out. It isn't fame you want in my line of work, it
is having your shadow noticed — as we say in Sesotho,
to have *seriti* — a presence. And some of us have
developed our scholarship in a way that would have
been impossible under South African conditions.

Out of the four years we lived in Nigeria, I taught
in a high school for fifteen months and for the rest of
my stay in the University of Ibadan's extension programme. The stodgy Oxbridge clique, which dominated all West African university education at the time,
wouldn't consider employing me in the internal
English department: I did not have a United Kingdom
M.A., alas. But I loved teaching, anyhow, and travelling to various outlying districts to teach adults was a
fruitful experience. The people of Nigeria were generous, so the condition of being an outsider, a person
without a British education, was not burdensome. I had
time to write, to engage in the arts that Ulli Beier was
promoting in Lagos, Ibadan, Ile Ife, and his home base,
Oshogbo, where Suzanne Wenger, the Austrian Shango
priestess and artist, revived the Yoruba shrines.

Ulli Beier was always sniffing around and digging
up indigenous artefacts and crafts, oral literature, and
bringing them to public attention. He was always
encouraging village and urban writers and artists, and
was right there in the centre of the Nigerian literary
renaissance. Shaggy-headed, soft-eyed, always conscious of the danger that is common among Germans
who fall in love with Africa — anthropologists, missionaries like Albert Schweitzer, musicologists, literary
connoisseurs like the late Janheinz Jahn; men who all
but throw African earth on their heads, who leave
their teeth to rust because they think Africa doesn't
wash; men who crash though African doors with an

appetite for self-immolation. No, Ulli wasn't this sort, an idealist though he has always been. I do not know the circumstances of the split between him and some of the Nigerian writers and artists which led to his leaving the country. I can only surmise that he fell foul of the love-hate relationship between Africa and Europe.

I had moved out of a literary renaissance among blacks in South Africa into another — a West African one, which was in full swing, having begun with the decade of the Fifties. It was exciting to work with and be in the company of Nigerian writers, artists, actors and educators: Wole Soyinka, playwright, poet, novelist; Gabriel Okara, poet; Mabel Segun, poet, Amos Tutuola, novelist; sculptor Ben Enwonwu; painters Demas Nwoko, Uche Okeke, and so on.

In December, 1958 I was invited to Kwame Nkrumah's All-African People's Conference in Accra. As Ghana was the only African country that had been freed from the European colonialism that had swept over the continent in the nineteenth century, most of the countries represented at Accra were still colonies. Ethiopia and Liberia were also there, but not Sudan.

The Ghanaians, in their togas, walked with admirable pomp. The atmosphere was most elevating. Inspired by Nkrumah, we heard the rumble of wheels of freedom's chariot just around the corner. The late Patrick Duncan and Jordan Ngubane were present, representing the South African liberal view. Alfred Hutchinson, then in Ghana after his flight from the Treason Trial in South Africa, walked in during a plenary session. The four of us had our turn to meet the great leader and talk to him.

I found myself on the Race Discrimination Commission of the Conference, together with Kenneth

Kaunda. He was leading UNIP against Welensky's Federation. He looked frail and sickly, but it was quite clear to me that he had the beating of his rival Nkumbula (also present). Then there was Hastings Banda, resident in Ghana at the time. Frantz Fanon from Algeria delivered a fiery speech against colonialism. His calm face and manner belied the high-tension wires within him.

During this and subsequent visits to the University of Ghana, where I had been invited to conduct extramural writers' workshops, I got to know Kofi Awoonor (then George Awoonor Williams); playwright Efua Sutherland, Frank Kobina Parks, poet; Ama Ata Aidoo, fiction writer and playwright; musicologist Professor Kwabena Nketia; historian Dr. Danquah; educationalist Jones-Quartey (now dead); scholar Quaison Sackey; poet Adail-Mortty; sculptor Vincent Kofi, a big hulk of benignity who immediately set you at ease. He has since left this world. As has Dr. W.E.B. Dubois, whom I met in Accra. A truly great man.

Efua: she looks at you out of those big, rolling, watchful eyes and slender, longish face. Every movement of hers is casual and ever theatrical, graceful. Flashes a captivating, woman-of-the-world smile that belies her strong attachment to native soil and constant refusal to attend writers' conferences. Resists most offers that would enable her to travel abroad or in Africa and prefers a private but nevertheless community-oriented life.

Ama Ata Aidoo: takes no nonsense from anybody, this stocky, chubby woman. Has a sharp tongue that seems to lick you first with flattery before she whips you with it. Unprovoked she's most amicable. Listens to the words of her people keenly; creates a many-peopled atmosphere in the narration of a single incident.

In 1959 we had a conference at the University of Ibadan on the press in Africa, at which the late Patrice Lumumba turned up. A fugitive from Belgian tyranny in the Congo. Seemed to have a speech defect, reportedly suffered during a torture session. The Belgians, incompetent colonisers, ran Lumumba's country as if Leopold's ghost were still stomping up and down the Congo basin, teaching them the ABC of the thoroughbred coloniser's drive, his collecting instinct, his killer instinct. And still they bungled it. Whose heart? Whose darkness? Lumumba, trussed up and watched over by guards . . . then the final shots, eternal darkness . . . . Seventeen years later in the south, a man trussed up, and the long journey into darkness. Bizarre . . . . The hearts sinews twisted almost to snapping point. And no one had bungled, this time around. Whose heart, whose darkness this time?

When I was vacationing in England in 1959, I saw much of Doris Lessing and my dear friend, the late William Plomer, in his Surrey house. Doris introduced me to Joshua Nkomo, a refugee from the made-in-England Federation. Amiable, sociable, a political survivalist. Suddenly his face becomes stern, his bulk seems to be edging itself into an invisible fissure, heaving to make a wider passage for itself and his people. Those, too, were the days of Welensky's federal foolishness, when the white man was shooting his mouth about African nationalism being poppycock.

I was a guest of Sylvester and Jenny Stein who had also moved from Johannesburg. Sylvester was writing fiction and a play here and there. Afterwards I moved to Anthony Sampson's — former editor of *Drum*, and

Sylvestor's predecessor.

Black Orpheus, edited by Ulli Beier with an editorial
board including Janheinz Jahn, which I subsequently
joined, was publishing African, Afro-American and
Caribbean critical writing. it was not until I joined it
in 1958 that it began to publish fiction as well. Our
Alex la Guma's short stories appeared in the journal,
as did those of James Matthews and Richard Rive.

Wole and his 1960 Masks were producing plays in
Lagos and Ibadan, among which were his own *The
Lion and the Jewel, The Swamp Dwellers, Brother
Jero,* Sarif Easmon's *Dear Parent and Ogre,* J.P.'s
Song of a Goat.

When Rebecca and the children, Anthony (10),
Teresa Kefilwe (7), and Motswiri (4), joined me in
December, 1957, I had in three months already tasted
enough of the heat, the rain, the harmattan, and the
classroom, to be able to tell them with conviction
what a good life it was.

Yes, Nigeria and Ghana gave Africa back to me.
Ghana had just celebrated her independence, and we
were three years away from Nigeria's. We found a
people walking with self-pride in spite of colonialism.
We found here formidable cultures in spite of Christ-
ianity and Western education. True, I had to work
under Nigerian bosses at the C.M.S. Grammar School
(Lagos) and the University of Ibadan who wanted me
to ingratiate myself with them because Nigeria was
giving refuge to a bedraggled runaway slave from
South Africa. But all my colleagues, and the numerous
Nigerians whom we befriended with great ease, were
most generous and warm.

There we were, urbanites who had not yet shared
in the full urban life of the white man in South
Africa — where we had felt police terror as children,

Rebecca and I; where missionary and government authorities had been tugging away at our souls, each claiming our loyalty, and to hell with the ancient traditions of our people, their humanism. The bonfire — so much for your traditions: the Christian god be praised; Ezekiel is now his name, his sins have been washed away . . . .

You the parents of this child, and his godparents, this child must walk in the light of Christ: God be praised he's no longer a heathen, teach him to love Jesus because Jesus loves him: he shall carry a pass, but Jesus loves him . . . . He shall have no permanent abode in the city's precincts, but Jesus loves him . . . . He shall pay heavily for his schooling, he shall sit with two other children at a desk made for two only, but if he has to sit on the floor he must understand . . . . You his mother, you his father, shall strip yourselves and go hungry so that he receives the white man's education, but Jesus loves him. He shall have no room of his own at home in which to do his lessons, but Jesus loves him . . . . Disease and malnutrition will ravage his people, but Jesus loves him . . . . He shall lose his African soul to buy a ticket to the Kingdom of God where a beautiful carefree life awaits him, because Jesus loves him . . . .

We had continued to believe these things, until most of us were over twenty-one. We believed what they told us: that to be Christian was to be civilised, to be civilised was to be Christian, like the European . . . .

We were coming into a Nigeria that itself had been and was still going through missionary education. So we were the same in this respect. But Nigerians had no migrant-labour system to worry about. Their cultures were still relatively safe except where desperate missionaries had hacked their way through and planted a station. The African rulers retained much of their traditional grandeur and esteem, unlike our South African traditional rulers, whose pejorative title 'chief' had become appropriate to their supervisory role: mere shadows of a great past, mere policemen for the government.

And we flourished in Nigerian freedom, even while it was still a colony. And we were drawn into its life by the people, who were at ease with themselves. And we loosened up in the real tropical-African milieu of Nigerian cities like Lagos and Ibadan, which were nothing like white cities such as Johannesburg and Pretoria. Nigeria restored Africa to us. We had come to think of ourselves as urbanised in South Africa — those of us who were located in ghettos on the fringes of towns and cities as a work force to serve the white man. Of course we had been uprooted from our traditions: we used modern means of travel; our eating habits had changed; families had been broken up and discovered new arrangements permitting the extended family to survive; commerce and industry had created new desires and wants in us, and our modes of dress had changed accordingly.

We had to survive ghetto life, deprivation, a 'civilisation' that beckoned to us from across the colour line but at the same time resisted us, denied us full participation in its life. We had fashioned our own ghetto culture out of the bits and pieces of what was available to us in western culture, and the stubborn sediment of the indigenous that could still be stirred up from the depths of our collective personality. Having come from diverse ethnic backgrounds, we had regrouped in the ghettos, and the ancient sense of community had reasserted itself and found expression in our togetherness. Ghetto life reinforced this, as well as the desperate need to survive the destructive elements of urban life: slum dwellings, the muck and the smell of townships, the physical violence, the erosion of family life, poverty.

In a sense we had taken that solid sediment of Africanness for granted in South Africa, and yet, ironically, we had also tried to suppress it in order that we might deal with the cruelties of the present. Especially when the Afrikaner had attained political power and set out to revive our ethnic groupings in order to destroy the nationalism that had built up since the African National Congress had been founded in 1912. We came to believe that to reassert our traditional humanism, in other words our indigenous personality, would promote the Afrikaners' political interests.

Now here we were in Nigeria, surrounded by an exuberantly theatrical lifestyle, shrines, religious festivals, masquerades and so on. It was here that we came full circle. We knew that we had begun the Panafrican odyssey: shades of Orpheus.

I was stationed at Offa, on the boundary between the Western and Northern regions. I had just spent four months in England — July to October, 1959. Rebecca had gone back to Johannesburg for the birth of our fourth child, Chabi. They joined me in February, 1960. March 20th: the news about Sharpeville came to us on the BBC news programme. Makhudu Rammopo was staying with us after his arrival from South Africa, where he had been principal of a school in Atteridgeville. He was due to take up a teaching post in the mid-west. We had been school-mates in Marabastad, Pretoria. The two of us, as well as Moloi, the boy who lived next door to

us, were very close. Moloi, the singing boy, was
always so cheerful and full of bounce. Sharpeville
rocked us out of bed. Rebecca, Makhudu and I were
stunned, speechless. And the harmattan continued to
whip around outside.

Exile, Sharpeville, dum-dum bullets. Death. Some
seventy corpses. The image was unbearable. Guilt.
Why aren't we there? Nothing. Just to be there, to be
physically with those who felt the muscle of power
inflate the atmosphere. To be among the mourners,
to belong, to express commitment . . . .

In the Department of Extra-Mural Studies, University of Ibadan, I travelled to Ilorin in the north, to Jebba
further north, and to another point eastwards, ending
the week with Offa itself. Each day I taught an adult
class from 5 pm to 7 pm. You were supposed to stay
at the university level of teaching — British style —
but you soon realised that most of the students
wanted to finish the 'O' level of the Cambridge Certificate of Education, and so you had to split the class
into two — one with a tangibly utilitarian motive, the
other with a purely cultural motive.

For three years I chewed dust. I got high on the
harmattan as it deposited its Saharan silt in my nostrils,
sucking them dry in the process. But enough of the
travels of an extra-mural donkey. As I couldn't reach
my director in Ibadan — figuratively speaking — with
suggestions to change the stock format of outpost
teaching, I jumped at a cabled message from Professor
Mercer Cook, the retiring director of African Programmes, Congress for Cultural Freedom, Paris. It
asked me if I would be interested in succeeding him.
If so, could I come to Paris for an interview with
John Hunt, then Executive Director.

France

It was clinched and done. August, 1961, the second major move. We trooped into Paris. Just as we were later to troop into London, New York, Denver. At the time of the Paris move, Puso, the last-born, was only three months old.

Richard Wright, whom I had hoped fervently to meet in Paris, had died the previous November. I had lost a golden opportunity.

We knew no French. All I knew was the conjugation of the verb *être*. The Congress paid for a practical course in French at a technical institute where the government sends foreign technicians who are on a study tour. Five hours a day, for six weeks, of seeing screened images, listening, talking, looking, listening, talking . . . . I came out speaking French with reasonable fluency and the ability to read *Le Figaro, Le Monde, France-Soir,* and other papers, plus Camus' *L'Etranger.*

The older children picked up French easily — even Kefilwe, who rejoined us later after trying British schooling. Tony stayed on at a Quaker boarding school at Middlesborough, Yorkshire. As I had a French secretary, my French improved immensely with the passage of time.

France. You look around you for a spiritual anchor. You feel strongly un-European. French intellectual life is beyond reach. The Africans you meet move casually and with a *savoir-faire* kind of ease. Plastic bombing is on the increase, with French rebels in Algeria trying to stage a coup — the kind Ian Smith was to try with greater success four years later.

Algerians in France are vengeful. The air is thick with
guerilla wrath. But because De Gaulle is on the
Algerians' side, it is the white fascists, not the Algerians who are the subversive party.

Jean-Paul Sartre's dwelling is plastic-bombed. A section of the Congress for Cultural Freedom's quarters on
Boulevard Haussman has been hit by the fascists . . . .

Meanwhile we are still straining at the tether which
ties us to the centre of the South African experience.
The tyranny of place, of time. This took on a symbolic
meaning: the inner compulsion to hold on to the
smells, the images of much, the texture of southern
life.

We lived on Boulevard du Montparnasse, just off
St. Michel, a few blocks from the Le Select and La
Goupole restaurants. Our apartment was to become
a kind of crossroads for writers and artists: Ethiopian
artist Skunder Borghossian; Wole Soyinka; Gambian
poet Lenrie Peters; Richard Rive; South African poet
in exile Mazisi Kunene; Bob Leshoai, who was running
a travelling theatre from province to province in
South Africa; B.M. Khaketla, grammarian and poet
from Lesotho; the late Soas Jones-Quartey, Ghanaian
scholar; Kofi Awoonor, Ghanaian poet and a beloved
friend; J.P. Clark; Nigerian scholar Abiola Irele;
Nigerian broadcaster Emmanuel Omasola; artists like
Julian Beinart, Peter Clarke, Dennis Duerden, and the
South African *emigrés* Gerard Sekoto and Breyten
Breytenbach, both of whose paintings hang in my
house. Both were the most regular visitors at Du Montparnasse, and Breyten stayed there with our children
for a week while we were vacationing in Geneva. My
friend Ed Miles, professor of international marine law
at the University of Washington, Seattle, has great
admiration for Sekoto's paintings, but thinks Breyten's

are flippant — 'just horse-shit'. And Ed is an art connoisseur of no mean sensitivity and judgement. He is one of the best read scholars I have met, with a voracious appetite for imaginative literature.

I was invited by Ulli Beier and the Nigerian writers to help form the Mbari Writers and Artists Club in Ibadan, that vibrant city of African culture. Wole, Christopher, J.P., Demas Nwoko and Ulli were at the helm. The Congress was most willing to give initial funding. I was sent to Ibadan and asked to be first president of the club by the members. The premises were modest: art gallery, small intimate open-air enclosure for experimental theatre. The gallery also served for art and writing workshops, I being involved in the latter. One of the first non-Nigerian artists Mbari exhibited was the late Vincent Kofi, the Ghanaian sculptor.

The Congress raised money from Merrill Foundation in New York to finance Mbari Publications, a new venture the club undertook. Work by Wole, Christopher, J.P., and Lenrie Peters was first published by Mbari, before finding its way to commercial houses. *Black Orpheus* continued in full force, the most vital little magazine in Africa at the time.

With a Congress sponsorship, *Black Orpheus* organised a literary contest for black African writers. I administered the contest from Paris. Alex la Guma, still under house arrest, ran off with the first prize for his powerful novella, *A Walk in the Night,* accompanied by Dennis Brutus's volume of poetry, *Sirens, Knuckles and Boots*. He was also still in the Cape. Mbari published these works. There were noises in white liberal quarters in South Africa about racism in reverse because I had insisted on the contest being restricted to black Africans.

Admittedly Sharpeville was still rankling inside me, and I had begun to be disillusioned by non-racialism which I had embraced in the ANC throughout the Fifties. Rivonia was finally to put it to sleep. Disillusioned by it, that is, as an immediate goal. But the main reason for the contest restrictions was that I did not want to see South African blacks (Africans, Africans of mixed descent, Asians) intimidated by white competitors, brought up cosily and privileged, even before they began to see themselves as part of the larger continent of Africa. I wanted us to see ourselves directly in competition with fellow-Africans. I wrote a letter to a South African paper to this effect.

I went on to help set up an Mbari centre in Enugu, eastern Nigeria, under the directorship of John Enekwe, the poet.

Makerere University, Kampala (Uganda), 1962. The first African Writers' conference to be held on the continent north of the Limpopo. Under the sponsorship of the Congress in Paris I and my secretariat brought together a lively group of people who were not in the least what you might call a 'school', not even those from Nigeria who were caught up in an upsurge of creative writing, by then institutionalised at the Mbari centre.

The only Africans from South Africa who could attend were Bloke Modisane and myself, who were already in exile, and Bob Leshoai, who was on a tour. Neville Rubin, who was editing a journal of political comment in South Africa, was there too.

There were Afro-Americans who were touring Africa: the late Langston Hughes, and literary critic and historian Saunders Redding. Other participants included the West Indian playwright Barry Reckord. Rajat Neogy, editor of the Kampala-based *Transition,* like Ulli Beier as editor of *Black Orpheus*, became a vital link between the conference and his readers. *Transition* became a strong East African centre of cultural activity, organising as it did, especially after the Congress had adopted it for financial aid, several writers' meetings in Kampala. Rajat was later to be hounded out of Uganda by Dr. Milton Obote, then Head of State, because the journal opposed intolerance towards the growing number of intellectuals who were critical of the government.

Against my counsel, the Congress and Rajat decided to move house to Accra, under the regime of Dr. Busia. I foresaw a similar crackdown on intellectual freedom when this was not in agreement with government policy. Rajat was again hounded out. That was the end of *Transition*.

More Kampala conferees: Wole Soyinka — volatile, with a voracious zest for life. A restless bundle of energy, just raring to go at any time. Razor-sharp wit, quick as flint, written all over his face. Has an instinct for fields of green, succulent corn. Knows the ways of political predators, was to be their captive sooner or later. Has a gigantic sense of the theatre. Takes an epicurean interest in wines.

If Wole can be compared with lightning and thunder, trailing clouds of fury and indignation, Chinua Achebe is like the soft, warm rain of the Nigerian climate. While Wole's prose diction evokes an image of high-tension wires, word after word seeping belatedly into the reader's consciousness because of their difficulty, Chinua's prose sings and abounds with echoes of human voices. Sees more into the human scene than he'll let on, eyeball to eyeball. His sense of humour is gentle, where Wole's has the fullness and speed of fierce waterfalls. Chinua shows a love of people, even in his comic view of life, whereas Wole is more often harshly satirical, in the best sense of the phrase.

Christopher Okigbo. Who would have thought in 1962 that he would become a Major five years later and die in active service in the Biafran war! The lyricist *par excellence*. A brilliant intellect, like Wole's. Highly disciplined poetic idiom, if often difficult. Self-assured, and yet he did not try to dazzle his audience with the products of his training in the classics at Ibadan, even though he said at Kampala that his poetry was meant for poets.

But Chris's *Path of Thunder*, published posthumously, proved that he had begun to care about who was reading his poetry during the Nigerian crisis — who stood to gain by giving ear to Okigbo the town crier prophesying war, pleasure domes and sacred rivers and sunless seas aside. Showed verbal facility in his earlier poetry, but was, like Wole the poet, difficult. Wole the playwright has always been comprehensible. Chris's public poetry, the kind you find in *Path*, opens up. Like Wole's prison poetry and *Ogun Abibiman* (1976). It all opens up like a big, generous dawn, so that reading it is like walking into daylight. Indeed I see public poetry in Africa and in the African-American world as poetry-turned-theatre. The poet feels the presence of an immediate audience.

J.P. . . . . Loud-mouthed, belligerent. His spoken language breathes and charges like a bull. J.P. talks as if he were always straining at the leash, demanding immediate release. Loves to be unpopular, even among fellow-writers, as long as we give attention to what he says and writes. Or was it that he always felt constrained to do something brash and brave, to assert his presence, like campaigning for the headship of an

English department? Another writer whose diction
sings. Writes verse drama in which one cannot but feel
the tension between the lyrical and the dramatic. The
latter is often sacrificed — for better or for worse?
I'm not sure. I still think he writes better poetry than
drama.

Kofi Awoonor, Ghanaian poet. A beloved friend.
His dark complexion the very sum of Africa's blackness. You read a fervent lust for life in his bright eyes,
his nose, his mouth. Can sit on a discussion panel
right there on stage with a cap on, dressed up like a
West African at the market-place or bus terminus-cum-
workshop. Like the African-American, too, who just
wants to dramatise a defiant non-conformity, An
amiable person, Kofi, a man with a passionate sense
of political commitment. Great admirer of Kwame
Nkrumah. Like Wole, has known the isolation of grey
walls as a captive of those who seek to mutilate the
mind. Another lyricist *par excellence* — I think the
best in Africa. Has a natural grasp of his people's
spiritual rhythm of life, which in turn breathes exquisite energy into his own poetry.

Camara Laye, novelist of Guinea, now no longer
with us. Shy, had a serene, dreamy look on his face.
Lived in exile for a while in Senegal. Paulin Joachim,
poet originally from Dahomey (now Benin) but living
in Paris. Met him at subsequent conferences. A
strong pillar of *Présence Africaine* in Paris. Knows the
picture magazine business from A to Z, was then
editing *Bingo*. Since his early poetry that spoke of
African roots, has been maintaining a low profile as a
poet. But his poetry plunges deep into the African's
predicament. Mild mannered, soft face, a tolerant
smile, an intense listener.

David Rubadiri. A Malawian exile now living in

Uganda and teaching English in Makerere. Lithe and
easy as a cheetah. His face could have been a carved
mask, but his smile spreads tenderness and warmth all
round. Speaks with a low voice that constantly seems
to be soliciting the listener's confidence.

James Ngugi (now Ngugi wa Thiong'o) had only
published short stories in journals then. He was with-
drawn, spoke haltingly, like a man looking for words.
But he was intense. I spoke to him, to poet Joseph
Kariuki, also Kenyan, to another compatriot Jonathan
Kariara, and to a Tanzanian painter, Elimo Njau who
was living in Kampala but was preparing to move to
Nairobi. I had asked the Congress to release me
after the second year, about September 1963. I wanted
to return to teaching. I broached the idea of setting
up a a creative centre like Mbari in Nairobi, and they
all agreed it would be most welcome. They would
help launch it. As the Congress acted only at the
invitation of an accredited group of writers and artists
in any country, they would need to write a formal
letter to Paris. We would take it from there.

Kampala was planned as the beginning of a four-
month tour of African countries, during which I was
to study existing cultural projects and assess the needs.
I was accompanied by my secretary, Francoise
Robinet. The tour took us to Brazzaville, Congo;
Leopoldville (now Kinshasa); Yaounde, Cameroon;
Accra; Abidjan, Ivory Coast; Freetown, Sierre Leone;
Dakar, Senegal. Then I proceeded alone to Nairobi,
Dar-es-Salaam, Zomba and Blantyre in Malawi;
Lusaka, Salisbury (now Harare) and then back to
Ibadan, where I joined my family for a vacation.

Still more writers, actors, theatre producers, artists,
educationalists, politicians, labourers, students. These
peopled my African beat. Lenrie Peters, Gambian

poet: tall, black, warm, with an aristocratic poise. Has the steadiness and reticence I have come to associate with surgeons, he being one himself, British-trained. His poetry does not boast any exuberance. Has a tight ascetic diction which has a strong intellectual appeal. Emotion is very much subordinated to the intellectual content.

Léon Damas, poet who died recently in Washington D.C. A man with gaunt features and an easy, relaxed manner, he lived in Paris for several years, like Aimé Césaire, until he became a professor at Harvard University.

Tchikaya uTam'si: although we usually place the former Brazzaville-Congo (People's Republic of the Congo) as his country of origin, he is a world citizen. A dynamo. A brilliant but complex poet. Like Wole. I saw much of him in my Parisian days when he was with UNESCO. Vociferous, but most entertaining. His ample gestures and eager voice often made me feel he could appropriate the right to say, there is UNESCO my friend, take it, I give it to you. And Paris too. Take it, *mon vieux,* I've more where they come from . . . .

Bernard Dadié, Ivory Coast: a good-humoured, gentle personality behind those dark glasses. Alas, has gone the unhappy way of so many of our African writers and artists who cannot resist the call — external or internal or both — to enter government service. Then a gentle separation begins between the man and the muse. Though I can't imagine that for him it could possibly have been a violent boarding up of the muse. The theme of those haunting lines from one of his finest poems — 'Bullets still behead the roses/in the mornings of dreams' — is taken up again by Soyinka's 'Where/Are all the flowers gone? . . . Death alike/ we sow' — written during his imprisonment. I have had the opportunity to write an introduction to the English translation of Dadié's *Climbié* and the folk-tale *Le Pagne Noir*, both rendered by a former Denver colleague and friend of the family, Karen Hatch of California State University.

Abioseh Nicol, Sierre Leone: a stately and calm presence you have there. His intellectual pursuits cut short his impressive literary productions: from bio-chemistry to top university administration to United Nations development programmes. The return of the native: from studies abroad sets out to rediscover Africa — what is the meaning of Africa? A theme taken up also by Lenrie Peters, another second-rounder, landing on African soil like a parachutist . . . coming through condensed time, hitting the ground with a jolt, then lugging his paraphernalia across the field — his new cultural equipment . . . there, you're at the starting point, you're *always* at the starting point.

In February 1963 Francoise and I, under the auspices of the Congress, organised two conferences at Dakar and Freetown (Fourah Bay College), then headed by Dr. Davidson Nicol (alias Abioseh Nicol). The aim was to throw into open debate the place of African literature in the university curriculum. We wanted to drum up support for the inclusion of African literature as a substantive area of study at university, where traditionally it was being pushed into extra-mural departments and institutes of African studies. Heads of English departments suddenly woke up one morning to see an ugly duckling in the coop and cackling noises began about 'English classics', 'the great tradition', 'the novel is still an infant genre in Africa', 'these plays are derivative', *'déja vu, déja vu!'* Why not a department of African literature to avoid embarrassing the 'great tradition' in English, while still teaching the literatures of the continent in extra-mural and African studies? Indeed, the University of Nairobi's English department, under the chairmanship of Ngugi wa Thiong'o the novelist, was later to go one better. He established a department of Literature in the place of the department of English, in which African literature was central, other world literatures fanning out from it.

For purposes of establishing a rough academic framework, some of us proposed that African literature should include all writing, imaginative and expository, that was created out of African experience. This would include in turn the Conrads, Joyce Careys, Huxleys, Blixens, Henleys, Lessings, the South African whites. Students would in time sort out what, in this literature, was an act of commitment to the African soil and an expression of a cultural identity shared by the majority of our indigenous peoples; and conversely, what was an imposition of European sensibility on African materials and human landscape.

This proposition raised some snide remarks from certain quarters, where some writers were denying any writing as African literature that was not in in-digenous languages! All the same, more Africans were to continue writing in English and French, and more and still more of this literature was to be introduced into university studies.

At the conference, which had been opened by President Senghor, a black American teaching in Dakar at the time decided to dramatise his 'African Identity' He knew, he said, that some people like myself, who were critical of nègritude, would want to exclude from the syllabuses literature inspired by this concept. He touched the wrong chord inside me. That evening I stomped up and down in my hotel room composing a reply for the next day's first session. Intellectual dishonesty cranked up by the desire to be politically 'with it' sticks in my gullet, and I felt the juices swooshing up and down my whole body.

Next day, a sleepless night constantly nagging me to pay up, I said my piece, 'Remarks on Nègritude'. Sleep, my creditor, kept well outside the auditorium. I was wide awake, deliberate.

Francoise Robinet arranged for me to meet President Lèopold Sèdar Senghor at State House. This was to be our second meeting: I had met him first in April, 1962. But my heart still butterflies inside as I enter his palace. I've privately rehearsed my French, but it comes out haltingly in his presence.

Put at ease by his unassuming gentle manner and soft eyes — this man of culture, poet and statesman — I loosen up, my conversational French relaxes and he condescends to its level. We speak culture, culture, CULTURE. Here is the confluence of the rivers Sine and Seine. For so long he has walked up and down *le chemin de l'Europe, chemin de l'ambassade* — the road to Europe — as the envoy balancing loyalties to France and Senegal. Been back to Africa several times before he entered formal politics, to listen to the voice of his forebears. Felt like an exile, a prodigal come back to the shrines where the dead breathe their essence.

I can't help but leap to October 1976 — Senghor's 70th anniversary celebrations. Another visit to Dakar at his invitation, Rebecca with me. A week's fanfare, junketing, speechifying. We're appalled at the number of Europeans invited to read papers on African culture and development. What would Europeans have to tell us about ourselves? Haven't they done this long enough — explorers, missionaries, administrators, scholars — when we were too dumb and captive to challenge their stories? Could this be Senghor's demonstration of *La civilisation de l'universel?*

State House cocktails. The splendour of African womanhood, in native regalia: the elegance, here in a European building with formidible pillars, high ceiling, chandeliers — Europe in Africa: *le chemin de l'Europe, le chemin de l'Afrique* . . . the weight of Europe in Africa . . . .

Wole was fêted by the President in grand style. They sat together on the evening of the performance of Wole's comedy, *The Lion and the Jewel*, done in French. *Les dieux comme je les aime* . . . the gods are here, the way I like them . . . that's what was running through my head that evening.

During my visits to Dakar, I had the good fortune to meet also the novelist Cheik Hamidou Kane, shy, unobtrusive; the poet and folklorist Birago Diop; historian Cheik Ant Diop. I came to love this savannah country and the easy, casual dignity of the people's movements; the feminine elegance in places where formalities are traded; the tall, slender men with intensely eager faces; the music of the balafon and the kora. My friend Gerard Sekoto was to come to Dakar in the early Seventies to spend some time painting Senegalese scenes. He has some superb paintings of that period.

Our paths interwove in Africa, in Europe, in America — Alioune Diop's and mine. This Senegalese scholar has continued in steadfast commitment to the promotion of African culture from his Paris stronghold at *Présence Africaine*. It is often argued that Africans communicate more easily from Paris, London, Bonn, New York, even Lisbon, than from any African capital. Hence Alioune's protracted stay in Paris, managing only a branch office of *Présence Africaine* in Senegal. Still, there are men like Professor Joseph Ki-Zerbo of Upper Volta and Hampate Ba of Mali who have consistently operated from home ground. Certainly, for a publication to circulate widely in Africa, it requires a metropolitan European base.

Sembene Ousmane, Senegalese novelist. Labourers' settlements are his beat. Casual in appearance and manner. Down to earth, has been in the labour movement in Marseilles. Combines an epic vision with a microscopic portrayal of the poor man, of the labourer — all God's bits of wood, i.e. people who must all be accounted for, because they *are* human beings.

Now working in the medium of film, his talent as fiction writer is paying off. He has always been too busy exploring humanity at the market-place and street level to concern himself with philosophical questions debated on the public platform, often just so much intellectual horseplay.

From Dakar I jet to Nairobi. I renew contact with Joe Kariuki, Jonathan Kariara, Elimo Njau. Ngugi is not in town. Their minds are set on a creative centre in Nairobi. Indeed nothing of any cultural interest for Africans is happening in Nairobi at the institutionalised creative level. There is the Donovan Maule Theatre, a white-expatriate private institution that imports British and American musicals and British Shakespearian players. Then there is the National Theatre (sic), a colonial government-backed affair that even has a conservatoire of music. Both highbrow theatres and beyond the reach of the Africans in the locations — in more ways than one.

I meet Okot p'Bitek, the Ugandan poet. Social rebel through and through. Laughingly and like a trumpeting elephant he pushes his weight through a city to — no, not to demolish it, but to warn the once-been-to-school Ocol and his ilk to expect a stampeding herd any time. For a start, the gentle beast lets them have it — a powerful spurt of water from the trunk. Okot is a gay, laughing rebel. To look at him you would never imagine that he cared that much about society, about the false self-image colonial education has cultivated in us. Unlike the traditional satirists of western literature, Okot really loves humanity. From his workshop where he hammers out a fresh new idiom, he spits venom and hisses at our foolishnesses, at political tyranny.

My autobiography, *Down Second Avenue*, the latter half of which I had finished after my arrival in Nigeria, was doing well. Foreign translation rights were being solicited from several quarters: German, French, Serbo-Croate, Bulgarian, Swedish, Czech, Japanese, Hebrew, and Portuguese were to follow. *The African Image*, started and finished at Offa, Nigeria, had been published early in 1962, the year of my African tour. A small volume of short stories, *The Living and the Dead,* had been published by *Black Orpheus.*

My younger brother, Baasie (Solomon), was ill with throat cancer. As I had surrendered my South African passport in 1959 (Rebecca in 1960), to take advantage of a British passport before Nigeria became independent, I had to apply for a visa to visit my brother, his family, and my sister. I did this through the consulate in Nairobi. My application was turned down. I had written a number of articles for the Nigerian press in which I attacked white racism in South Africa . . . so it figured.

To Blantyre, Malawi, then to Zomba. David Rubadiri received me there. He was later to become ambassador for Malawi in Washington D.C., before he eventually settled in Kampala. David did everything possible to obtain an interview for me with the man who was destined to become life President of his country — Dr. Hastings Banda. It didn't work out.

Instead, the Minister of Education, Kanyama Chiume, received me. He made it clear to me who he was. Quite officiously, hardly opening his mouth. Walked and sat as if his spine had been reinforced with a steel rod right up to the nape of his neck. It *had* to do, this meeting. Other cabinet ministers like Chipembere and Orton Chirwa had refused to see me. I wanted to meet intellectuals and politicians to find out about the state of culture in their countries — culture, of course, as an educational process and as the amalgam of creative activities and spiritual values. Throughout the tour I was dispatching reports to John Hunt, Executive Director of the Congress, to give him a sense of the potential in each country.

So here I am with Chiume in his large office. The pictures on the walls give me an eerie feeling. I am surrounded by colonial ghosts, who peer out to remind me that *they* had steered the caravan of history across this country.

Chiume is trying to show me that my visit is redundant. Why do I want such information, he asks stiffly. I repeat the purpose of my mission. The men of culture in Malawi may, for instance, want to plan a creative project, in the interests of pan-Africanism. We may then all co-ordinate our cultural efforts under a pan-African umbrella. My organisation in Paris would consider assisting such a project.

'There's no need for that here,' the Minister says, heading me off.

'How's that?'

'My President has sent six candidates to learn journalism in Ghana — President Nkrumah's generous offer.'

'There's no school of journalism in Ghana,' I remark, with a sense of uselessness.

'You can learn journalism on a newspaper, and our President is a dear friend of President Nkrumah. Never forget that, my friend.' 'My friend' tastes like a crumb I've picked up from the floor.

'Of course, of course,' I say, 'how stupid of me.'

What I am really thinking is what goddam journalism can one learn from Basner (former 'Natives' Representative' in the South African Senate). He was editing one of the newspapers and dominating the Ghanaian press in general, cracking the marxist whip against African teachers from South Africa, who, he charged, were 'bourgeois'. The teachers eventually left Ghana.

When the Minister is about to dismiss me, I remember quickly that I want to grab the opportunity to ask, 'Tell me, Mr. Minister, why is your government so hostile to South African exiles and refugees, especially Africans? There was a most displeasing editorial in *Malawi News* that launched a bitter attack — a violent attack — on our exiles and refugees for leaving South Africa. Let them return home and engage the forces of apartheid there, so the editor says. He doesn't seem to be aware, I mean, that our people have been engaged in this process for three centuries. My people are not lazy, put them to work and you'll see for yourself.'

'We've hardly enough work for many of our own people, understand!'

'Yes, — er — well — it's just a manner of speaking. Anyhow, what if the South African government decided to send away all the Malawian mine and kitchen workers — would that please your government?' He lets that pass, with a snort.

Instead he says: 'You left on a South African passport, I presume. If South Africa's so bad, why did they give you the education you have and even a passport? Supposing you're a spy of the South African government?'

'Why should they trust *me*, Mr. Minister, when they have so many brilliant people of their colour in your country, Zambia, Rhodesia? I met you in London, Mr. Minister — remember? — fighting Welensky's Federation. You travelled on a Federation or Malawian passport issued by the colonial government. Would I have dared to suspect you of being a spy for Welensky?'

'I'm a busy man, Mr. Mphahlele, you'll excuse me.'

With that and with a face like a mask, the Minister stands up abruptly. The hind legs of his chair do not move back as abruptly because of the carpet fibre, and the chair tilts back, front legs off the floor. He almost topples backwards, bang against the wall behind. I rush forward, but he raises his hand imperiously to stop me. He regains his balance. 'A good morning to you,' he says, obviously unsettled, as he leaves me in the hands of his secretary. His words trail behind him, so speedy is his exit.

When I related my interview to David, he gave me his coy, tired-looking, wisdom-threaded smile. 'He's the old man's most trusted minister. As literal and prosaic as they come — even if poetry came charging towards him like a buffalo.'

Seven years later: 1969. I stop in Dar-es-Salaam to see Bob Leshoai and his family, on my way from Lusaka to give a series of lectures on African literature in the United States — I have a short leave of absence from the University of Zambia, where I am senior lecturer in English. I also know that Chiume, Chipembere (now deceased) and other top men from Banda's government are refugees in Dar. I'm keen to talk to Kanyama Chiume as I want a little enlightenment on the state of affairs in his mother-country. And on Banda, after whose image I am planning to cast the character of a hero in a satirical novel.

Recently, a goodly number of Malawian officials have fled Banda's tyranny. Chiume receives me in a downtown café. We talk a long time. He's affable, subdued, and has a glint of wisdom — no irony, just fact — in his eyes in place of the steady, almost unblinking stare I remember from our 1962 meeting. His face moves with passion. He's eager to tell me something . . . shades of Coleridge's Ancient Mariner.

Something about the trust old Banda had in his now-exiled ministers. Here's a man (Banda) who came from England after forty-three years. Had no connection with Malawi or Federation politics before. They call him to come and lead them. They put him on the throne and now he starts scattering them like a serpent among goats. Chiume tended him whenever he was ill at home and abroad, on and on. I keep playing the fellow-exile with questions so that we should not find ourselves looking at each other across the silence of the café, tacitly remind-

ing each other about 1962. He must surely know
that I have not forgotten, that I'm telling him not to
worry about it . . . to think nothing more of it. . . .
that it doesn't matter any more . . . .

'I'm bitter,' Chiume says finally. 'Tyranny stalks
our land, people disappear in the night and never
return, *never*. Our river teems with crocodiles,
there's no crossing over for us, if you see my meaning. And to think that everywhere we went, in
Africa or in London, I had to look after him during
his attacks of whatever it was that brought him to a
standstill.' After a brief silence he says, 'I'm writing
a book about Malawi — it will be translated into
Swahili.' I reply that it is a good thing for these
times to be recorded by the chief actors of the
drama.

I left him in the café.

I had been vaguely toying with the idea of writing
an allegory set in Malawi on a theme suggested by
the folk-tale about the stork that was asked by the
frog community to be their king. He had a frog
dinner every day. The idea took hold and bugged me
even more after my conversation with Chiume.

I'm at the Caravan in Dar the following day drinking a beer. A fellow joins me. I can see he's ahead of
me by a long stretch. Belches and sits opposite me.
His head talks for him, nodding and turning away
from my eyes alternately. Rather like the toy dog
people like to place under the back window of a car,
its head nodding endlessly, as long as the vehicle is
in motion. Maybe something is in motion inside the
man.

He's clearly not of this place. Indeed: 'I greet you
strangerman,' he says, 'stranger to stranger.'

'Greetings, brotherman.'

'I'm not drunk — hic — excuse me please strangerman — hic, you do not know me I do not know you
but shit — hic — shit you're African and I'm one —
Malawi, you?'

'South Africa.'

'Oh-oh. No difference.' He giggles.

'Mphahlele, Es'kia Mphahlele, and you?'

'Chisiza, Yohanese Chisiza. I'm pleased to make
your acquaintance you — hic.'

'Refugee?'

'Guess — hic.'

'We do not carry badges.'

'Don't try to get smart with me — waiter!' Waiter
comes and collects his order and returns with a
bottle of lager.

'You see, I'm not drunk — hic.'

'No you're not.'

'But you think I am.'

'Forget it.'

'Refugee — you?'

'Exile.'

'All the same — no difference.'

'You like levelling all things, right?'

'Getting smart with me again?'

Must have heard it in a movie, this 'getting smart'
idiom, I thought.

'Well, you'll meet many of us here from — hic —
Malawi — hic. Some big nobs too — or — hic — fellows
who used to live high on the old man's favours —
government you know — hic — shame!'

'What shame?'

'What shame? — hic. There's a man here who used
to carry — hic — towels and handkerchiefs in a bag
whenever he and the old man went abroad or into
the country on business — hic.'

'I hear you.'

'Old man froths at the mouth whenever he speaks in public. They say — hic — he once had fits — who knows — may be everlasting.'

'I hear you.'

'Now where's the minister today? In shitstreet, I tell you — here in this very — hic — Dar. Er — on your way to?'

'America.'

'Where whites are shooting blacks?'

I blow my pipe smoke through my nostrils into the air.

'Old man chased us out like — hic — village mongrels. *We* might have helped the old man to chase others out when we were still — hic — loyal to him — instead he runs us out. All the same — no difference who chases, who runs — hic — Mother died, my brother was murdered and they say no one knows — hic — he was — he was one of the old man's advisers. The crocodiles are hungry — when the old man says that, people disappear in the night — hic — it's bye-bye — *no more* — you can do what you like — *no more* — the crocodiles are hungry . . . .'

As I leave him I try to piece things together . . . . The political men and women I stumble into in the years of exile. Faces. Power. Tyranny. Faces. Power. Benevolence. The army. One-party government. The CIA. Africa. Sycophants, O sycophants, what is your final reward for belly-crawling, for wiping the froth off your master's mouth, for erecting statues and buildings in honour of your masters, painting the land with their names? Crocodiles are always hungry . . . . You end up here on this steaming Dar waterfront and look at the ships sailing in and you know your ship is not coming home for maybe

a long time. And each time you write that prop-
aganda tract to whip up feeling among fellow-exiles,
each time you write that article for the local paper
to tell your host country how insatiable the monster
back home has become, your apocalyptic tone
waxes more and more strident. In the long run you
seem to hear your own tape-recorded voice over
and over again. The truth hits you: you're going to
be out in the cold a long, long time, relief is not in
sight. Political crocodiles take nothing for granted,
never go to sleep. They stay stubbornly on the trail
of pursuit, like the law man in Victor Hugo's *Les
Miserables*. Even scented, hanky-waving, flyswish-
waving crocodiles . . . .

And Chipembere left for Los Angeles. And he
wrote me a letter saying how sorry he was that he
couldn't come out of his bedroom to see Bob and
me in the living room, because he was preparing to
leave for the U.S., so please don't think I meant to
be rude to you because you must have waited for me
for forty-five minutes at least and I'm sorry.

Chipembere wouldn't even come out for five minutes to tell us he could not see us. He died two years
later after protracted illness. I had never met him,
never known what kind of a person he was.

Back to 1962. The African tour. After arriving in
Salisbury I tried again for a visa. I had the silly idea
that as the journey would be just across the Limpopo, a visa should not be that difficult to obtain.
No luck. I was never going to see my brother again.
If ever again I hear someone say bureaucracy is
impersonal, I shall scream. Because that says nothing
about what I felt then. Still less about what I feel
today . . . of that, later.

I was the guest of Dr. Stanlake Samkange in his

Harare home. He and his African-American wife, Tommy, gave me a most pleasant week. He is a historian who was later to write novels with incredible ease and speed. Son of a former church minister, he abhors violence. Has a peace-loving exterior, too, doesn't look like a man who knows the joy of swearing and its fulfilment. We were to see more of the family in the United States, where he was professor of history at North-Eastern University, Boston. Stanlake later entered Zimbabwean politics, through Bishop Muzorewa's camp. Reports had it that he had brought to Zimbabwe his Rolls Royce. Stanlake takes such tremendous delight in his material acquisitions that he is quite at ease with his status, where someone else would dread to venture out in public lest he appeared outrageously different. And yet this ease, this love for the expensive things in life, is not offensive in the least. Because he has a tender interior and is benevolent.

Back to Ibadan to join my family. We also opened the Mbari Artists and Writers Club in the centre of that immense sprawling city. There were hardly any high-rise buildings in Ibadan in those days. You stood on the promontory on the northern side and saw corrugated tin roofs, some rusted, some shooting out lines of silver in response to the bounce of sunlight. And the roofs gave you a sense of abundant humanity.

I was appointed first president of Mbari by the writers.

I had a long chat with Cyprian Ekwensi, at the time the most popular African novelist — popular in the best sense of the word. Stylistically the most accessible fiction writer in West Africa, his narratives straddle the urban and rural proletariat: thieves, prostitutes, cynically corrupt politicians, the razzle-dazzle of Lagos. Ekwensi was read widely no matter what the pedants said about his 'journalistic' style. Because he is a good story-teller. The people of his fiction can be seen at any street corner, bus stop, market place, and so on. He also contributed stories to the West African edition of *Drum* magazine, some of which were thrillers set at the Yaba Roundabout, Lagos.

'It was a nightmare, bra Zeke. Hell, a nightmare. I arrive at Lusaka Airport. One immigration coon says all the people with foreign travel papers should hand them over if we're in transit. We can go into the city if we like until we have to catch our next flights. So, whoopee, I zoom into the city, such as it is — see what I mean? I'm from Botswana you see, where I was doing my research for my degree in Fine Arts, and on my way back to the States via London. I slug down a double Scotch on the rocks and sleep like I'm being paid for it. Like a good nigger who's used to international travel I'm in good time at the airport the next day for my flight.

'Another immigration biggy says, "You ara under-a alesiti."

"Under what? Arrest?" I feel my eyes are straining to take leave of their sockets.'

'Gee, Wally, your eyes are *lekker* froggy anyhow under normal circumstances, what must they have been like *then!*'

'You're laughing at me, so I'll shut up Bra Zeke, okay?'

'No please, I'm just chicken-shitting as they say.'

'Well, the IB says I went to the city without a transit visa. Me, I tell him how another Immigration

said we could go. "Who's that?" he wants to know.
' "The other officer," I say. "There he is." The
bastard denies — "Hei man, *ka mmago*" — he just
says he never told us such a thing. "So?" I ask immigration B. "So you go into the airport cell," he tells
me. "*What!*" "No noni-sense," he says. "I know
you, you South-i-Africans, you think you're smart
even-ing when you're refugees. Come with-i-me."
Bra Zeke I'm just too baffled to argue, but meantime *kea fufulelwa* — just feeling murderous I tell
you. I feel I can pee in the concourse to let off
steam. Pee on his shoes too.
' "Can I speak to the big man?" is my question
when he locks the cell gate. Kind of question you
ask for no reason except you can't simply shut up.
' "The big-i-man is out-i town. When-i he is-i not-i
here I am big-i-man myself."
' "The shit you are," I say in Tswana. "How long
do you want to keep me here?" "When-i I finish-i
inivesitig — eiti you."
' "Damn zombies!" I blurt out in English, sure he
won't understand. Investigate, I think aloud, *investigate* . . . . The word sinks into the base of my block.
It brings back memories of another time. Three
years ago down there. The jingling of keys, the eyes
of indifferent authority. Power. And you know Bra
Zeke, what happens to a nigger when he gets power.
He's just a mess. The walls. The porridge they bring
for lunch. I hear the London plane take to the
sky . . . . Well, Wally, son of Khunong, you're in the
cooler. Memories. They bear down on me like a
toothache that makes you think it's only kidding and
that greater things are still to come. And yet, you
know Bra Zeke, funny thing is — do you ever think
this way? Funny thing is even at that time I longed

to be back home. A dark stockade at home is always brighter than the one in a foreign country. Talking to a man in authority when you understand each other is easier than having to talk to zombies you have no way of reaching even in the English they can dig.'

'I know what you mean, Wally.'

'All that hot afternoon I'm trembling with anger, you understand — feeling feverish. By the way, it's a Saturday. I know it won't be till Monday that someone will find a report about me on his desk. All night I half dream, half dramatise in my head, zombies with power. Niggers with a badge. And I'm scared of I-don't-know-what. Just scared hollow. Well, Monday afternoon comes. "Here is-i your travel-i document-i," jailer says and opens the gate. "Your plane is-i here. Take it-i and leev-i the count-lee. You are lucky my friend-i."

' "*Ke mmago! Ek sê dis jou ma daai!* Go ef yourself." Again I simply want to pee in the concourse. Just hose the damn shining floor.'

We may be together in exile but we all know that each one of us must be the master of his own dark alley. You learn the ways of the alley cat before you know it, and colonise the backyards. And yet you also know you've got to clear that fence to re-enter broad daylight away from the garbage cans. It's got to be done.

My dear Mother,

Yesterday I heard Dikeledi is in London to attend a conference on child care. I cannot tell you how my heart jumped to hear this. I know I shall hear all the news

about you, although I don't know if she still lives in
Alexandra, if she still visits you often as in the old days.
She always wrote to me to tell me news of you and Tau.
He must be big now, after all these ten years. I cannot
imagine that he must be 20. It is about six years now
since Dikeledi wrote for you to me. So I must meet her
and give her this letter.

I am not going to lie to you, Mother. I have not been
myself these past years. I have just come out of hospital
where they treat you for the sickness you get when you
drink too much. I lost one job after another. The ancestors are punishing me — yes, punishing me for not
sending for Mantwa and the children as I promised to.

I left the political movement long ago. They are just
playing marbles. They grow fat on moneys given by
many countries and rush about in and out of expensive
hotels, rush all over the place like rain that refuses to
fall. We Sotho and Xhosa and Zulu and Machakane marry
one another and we speak all the languages. And here
these monkeys come out and play tribal politics with us
who speak Sotho or Tsonga or Venda.

Yes, I did not write to Mantwa and the children for a
long time. The longer one waits to write the more difficult it becomes to do so. Out of shame. Now I cannot
speak to her across the dark river that is between me and
her grave. I tell myself that she is happier with the ancestors now, happy with my late father, and is safe from
the misery of this world. I'm glad her parents took the
children. What should I say — that I hope Tau is taking
care of you? Me his older brother who should have been
doing that?

Funny thing, Ma, every time I think of you I seem to
hear bells. Not church bells, just a mixture of bells, you
know. Will you ever forgive me? But that is not the important thing — not really. Only if I can forgive myself

will things come right. And I cannot. My heart is heavy with guilt and shame, it's like I'm dragging a heavy chain to which my heart is tied.

I kept drinking and losing jobs. What use am I to myself? Several times I have gone to the sea to walk into it so that it could put an end to my torment. But I returned long before getting there. I'm a coward that cannot even face himself. Look, Ma, I promise that I shall write when I have heard how you are. I promise. If I do not, let my father and my living ancestors cut my tongue out. I'm not touching liquor any more. The doctor says if I keep away from it I'll be all right. I was sick for so long I don't want to travel this road ever again. Pray for me. I never learned to pray, as I used to tell you. Because the god they led me to over there never showed his face. But I remember how you and father used to say you have your own picture of him and it is enough that you saw him to be different from the one we were all taught about. Pray for me, Ma, to the one you saw and understood. Greet Tau. Hei Tau, remember I'm still your brother. Don't turn your back on me. Ma will tell you everything. Soon I shall be strong and will find work and send you some money.

This room is cold, I never have enough money to buy heat. I miss you, Ma. I'll see you again, Ma, just wait and see. Let the ancestors keep us for each other.

Goodbye for now, Ma.
Your son, Lekau.

Next day at the conference.
Who am I looking at?
It's me, Lekau. Have you forgotten me, Dikeledi?
This is Lekau. My father alive! It is you, Lekau!
Yes, you have not changed much, Dikeledi. Look, I

shan't waste your time. I've a letter I'm asking you to deliver to my mother. Give it to her in her hands, please. I wonder why you stopped writing for her.

Come to this little bench and let's sit down and talk a little while; we have a tea break.

How's the old lady?

I — I thought you knew, Lekau. I've long left Alexandra. I'm in Springs. My husband was transferred.

Oh, I see. I wonder why she did not tell Tau to write.

I don't know. Lekau, after I left Alexandra — I — I heard your mother died. I heard long after she was buried. I went to Alex to add my word of sympathy. Tau said he could not find any of your letters. Thought she burnt them for fear of the police. He could not remember your address. I could not either. Let me see — it's three years — yes, three years now.

Tonight I'm thinking of you, Sekoto. The Paris nights we crawled from one night club to another until the wee hours of the morning. It's — what — fourteen years now. And you had already been there for fifteen! Why do I think of you? Your large painting of an African head hanging on the wall opposite me. A young woman's. The most precious of my art collection. Remember how, as you told us, it was the first few years in Paris. How very sick you were? After nights of slaving in night clubs playing the guitar to keep yourself in food, clothing and shelter? How the proprietor used to throw wine into your mouth constantly just so you wouldn't tire, to kill that sharp and nagging pain in your soul. Only a little so that you'd enough left to feed the notes from your guitar. How you survived the Parisian cold cuts, the cole-slaw and salami of the *charcouterie* . . . . Then

you had to live in hospital so you could come to a
self-realisation. The memory of Pretoria, of your
painting and the crumbs of recognition from white
liberals.

The memory of your departure to brave the cut-
throat life of Parisian salons and galleries. How blood-
sucking it was to be, you would not have known. You
had come into your own by the time we met, but you
were still hacking your way through the forest just to
be in a group show. One-man shows were beyond your
reach, you had to keep sending work back to the home
country and to American galleries.

Yes, this African maid you painted. Tonight, as so
often, she seems to take on a different life. But I
know it goes according to how the lights dip and
beam inside of me. And tonight the sounds I hear
from my stereo help paint the mood. You must
remember, of course, the blue that is dominant in
your painting, varied by patches of white, toned down
by dim artificial lighting in my living room — Nairobi,
Denver, Philadelphia, Lebowakgomo (Northern Transvaal), Johannesburg. Big eyes, big lips, firm, youthful
jaws, a handkerchief casually but elegantly worn. A
stylised straight neck, a collar-bone pulling with a
horizontal tension.

Sounds. Tonight I am playing music on the stereo
that plunges deep, down to my very crotch. And she
continues to stare obliquely out of the wall, now part
of the scene, now aloof from it. I began with the late
Errol Garner (you know of course that he died a day
after the beginning of 1977) and took in Oscar Peter-
sen, Coleman Hawkins. Can you imagine a crystal
stone sculptured by the elements with carefree pre-
cision? Then, looking more deeply, you come to the
tinges of black and blue in the very heart of the

stone, giving it warmth — lyrical warmth — and sweetness such as never cloys. That's how Errol's and Oscar's piano comes to me. Hawkins's tenor has been saying other things to me. Not quite the simple if bold story line from Hodges. But still basic.

I came to Miles Davis's 'Kind of Blue', with the late Cannonball, Coltrane, Evans, Kelly; then Miles Smiles. And the maid kept staring obliquely out of the wall, out of the grassmat decor we have provided for her to serve as a backdrop.

Am I boring you with all this stuff — this recital? I don't care. I just need to talk to you. We come through Stanley Turrentine's 'Mister T' and 'The Blue Hour', Sonny Rollins's 'Bless this Child' and 'Good Morning Heartache', and 'The Freedom Suite'. Talking about 'Good Morning Heartache' brings to mind Diana Ross. Remember how she used to miaow her part in the Supremes? And then she found herself acting Billie Holliday's life in *The Lady Sings the Blues*. Whatever critics may say about some lapses in that movie portrayal of Billie Holliday, it did Diana Ross plenty of good. Learning to sing the blues gave her voice depth and the sadness that echoes African-American history. She wouldn't have got that any other way. The feline composure and gaiety is gone. She's a full woman with a full voice.

And the maid keeps looking that way with her large this-is-me eyes.

'The blues ain't nothing but a woman' the tragic Dinah Washington sings to me. 'Georgia on my mind', Billie says. 'I want a little sugar in my bowl', pleads Nina Simone. Bessie Smith's 'Jailhouse Blues' comes through again, travelling on Dinah's voice. And Roberta Flack's 'I don't want no tears anymore'. How they link up with Miriam Makeba and Letta Mbuli and take me back to the real and only blues voice I have ever heard in South Africa — Dolly Rathebe's — is more than I can say. But I feel it in my spine. All the thrills that come from art always register in the nape of my neck and travel down the spine as far as the shoulder blades. Enough.

I stay on a sustained blue note, you'll observe. Long, painful, solitary. What women! Maybe what accentuates my mood is that it's raining outside. Philadelphia is in the Delaware Valley. When it rains here, spring, summer *and* winter, it feels as if life is one long, dripping, weeping, drizzling siege. And you coil into yourself, gather up your reserves of warmth and faith and hope. And all you can do is indulge yourself, hang on that blue note as you play one record after another.

Uncanny the way events throw you this way and bounce you that way, isn't it? Here I am among blacks who long, long ago came here, as slaves, from our continent. Life is rough for them up here in the northern cities, where whites will give them at best an inch at a time. An inch which they must fight for. Whites hardened by their own ethnic-immigrant complexes — Irish, Jewish, European continentals of all kinds. Northern white racism hits you suddenly. So often African-Americans prefer to return to the south — that territory which we tend to think defines the savage prehistory of racism.

'I'm goin' back,' one keeps hearing in the African-American blues, goin' down south to shake the dust of this town off my feet.' And I find myself pulled into the mood, find myself returning to my own south. And it's T-Bone Walker's 'Funky Town'

blues all over again. It's way back to the 1920s when
Walker worked with Ma-Rainey. Leadbelly, Light-
nin' Hopkins? Of course.

I'm back to Dinah. *Blues ain't nothing but a woman
crying for a man . . . when she wants loving . . . a
feeling that will get you down . . . feeling bad . . . dis-
gusted and feeling sad . . . a common heart disease . . . .*

For a moment I hear only the line about loving a
married man: just one of the many heart diseases.
Because suddenly she seems to be singing about the
woman in *our* deep south. The woman who'd wait for
a man, a son, who may never return, ever. Or will
return from jail when she is wasted. Or will return
dragging a corpse of a mutilated something inside
him. And she starts to work on him, to try to mend
him. How long has the train been gone? And she cries
all night long.

Your African maid still does not flinch. Never will.
The arrested, contained beauty of Keats's 'Grecian
Urn' . . . unheard melodies . . . . Just thought you
should know where I'm coming from Gerard, as they
say over here.

What about you, Gerard? You always wanted to go
back to Africa in those days. But not South Africa,
not *our* deep south. When I said wouldn't it be
better for your painting you said, yes. But something
in those soft eyes told me you were a little afraid.
Perhaps plain scared. You had been so long in Paris,
you said, but not in so many words. I knew you
weren't lonely any longer. You could handle Parisian
life. Fourteen years, since 1948, you had been
through a baptism of fire. Why not settle in Africa? I
asked, when you were fighting so hard, bleeding so
much, just for a group exhibition? The galleries, you
said, belonged to a select group: what was a black

painter worth in a European city glutted with artists?

You settled for a brief visit to Senegal. For purification, for a spiritual renewal. You returned with fascinating, exquisite paintings of the Senegalese human scene: the tall, delicate-looking figures, the women in sweeping garments, with stately headgear, the men in their long *bubus*. The texture of savannah air is all there. Spare grey colours . . . . My good friend Ed Miles showed me what he had bought from you in Paris when he arrived back in Denver — before he left us for that fat post in Seattle, Washington.

A South African gallery failed to sell your Senegalese collection. Couldn't understand the art, you said, or some such thing. I remember there was a time in your early art life in Pretoria when white liberals boasted a Sekoto on their walls. The provincials! The Africans, for their part, couldn't afford the prices, of course, and hanging works of art on walls was not part of our tradition. The African exile and his audience . . . which audience? The eternal question: white liberals who can pay but whose interest has short legs, or blacks who *can* tune in but haven't the money? If it's any comfort to you, the African (and I mean all who are not officially called white) writer in exile has the same dilemma. For him it's not so much the economics as the almost total absence of his works in South Africa. They are not available down there. You know the reason . . . .

Tonight as I sit and look at your African young woman on the wall I shudder to think that a man can grow old outside Africa. Until he loses interest in returning. Someone — his name escapes me — reporting to the United Nations Refugees Commission, says that twenty years is the limit. Beyond that, the wish to return pales into rationalisations for staying out —

to paraphrase him. I'm sure he's right. My ancestors
have been on my mind these past ten out of twenty
years. To refuse to do their bidding or not to have it
in your power to . . . . And how do you tame the
malignant pain, knowing it's terminal?

I had a theory that for some of those who refused
to return there was a frightening spectre out there on
native ground. They believed they wouldn't be accepted because they had no cargo to bring back — some
object of substantial value or some achievement that
speaks for itself. Like the protagonist of Ayi Kwei
Armah's *Fragments* who resists that cargo cult his
fellow-Ghanaians — been-tos and their extended families — are constantly acting out. He dares return
without any cargo. Then he cracks up. I'm not sure
any longer about that theory — I don't know, Gerard,
I don't know. But always Khalil Gibran's words return
to me:

> *Of what value*
> *Unto them is the lamentation of an*
> *Absent poet?*

Unsinkable Rebecca. On September 6, 1961 the
Mphahlele clan trooped into Orly airport. Winter was
in the air. The Nigerian heat was still in the blood-
stream, but we knew that soon we would be singing
another tune. Puso, the youngest, was four months
old; Chabi 2; Motswiri 8; Teresa Kefilwe 11; Tony 14.

Francoise, my French secretary, was there to meet
us and escort us to our flat, off Boulevard du Montparnasse. This was to be a temporary place until a
better one should be ready for occupation on the
Boulevard itself, off St. Michel.

But before this happened I was sent by the Congress

for Cultural Freedom to Venice, Italy, to represent it
at a conference of the Society of African Culture,
publishers of *Présence Africaine*.

Owing to disorganisation in flight schedules, and
delays, I had to return by train, from Milan to Paris.
The longest train journey I had ever taken. Gave me
something like an eternity to feel guilty and anxious
for having abandoned my family when they had
barely shaken off the Nigerian sun and dust and sweat.
A long, long, elastic night it seemed. I dreamt I was
dead, and remembering that I had not left a note in
the compartment to direct the officials to my Paris
address, I willed myself to return to the compartment.
As if to comply, death spilled me out, in order to
come and write the note. I decided then that I wasn't
going back inside death's abode.

Then I heard voices surging from under the train,
as if the wheels were minting them: voices rattling
and breathing, talking by turns — *where are you
going, where are you going?* The screeching of metal
brakes at a station tore open the flimsy cocoon of
sleep, death let go of me. Dream dissolved. I was still
in the compartment. I was soaked in sweat.

And the train tore through the timeless, placeless,
nameless night at a really frightening speed. I imagined
high bridges, knife-edge bends, mountain tracks, so
many dangers that often bring a sad end to this kind
of (to me) silly show — away with the mastery of
machines . . . .

Then I lived through a series of vignettes. Crazy,
weird. Yet I was not asleep. I was riding a fast billy-
goat that started bucking like a mischievous donkey
or horse; then I was entering the stem of a fat tree
and closing myself in; then cattle were running on me,
leaping from a monstrously high wall, and I was run-

ning to avoid being crushed; then police were chasing
after me, back in South Africa; then I was in a garden
where all the vegetation was a yellowish-green, and
yellowish-green animals shaped like dinosaurs, as we
see them in pictures, moved past me, utterly indifferent. The colour was overwhelming, dizzying.

I was not asleep. I thought I was going out of my
mind. I was seized by a sense of foreboding. And the
orchestration provided by the wheels underneath
accentuated this feeling. I was also remembering things
I thought should have happened, but recall of which
was impossible when my head wasn't playing tricks.

Only nine years later — 1970 — when we returned
to the United States from a two-year period in Zambia
— were these happenings tracked down to low blood
sugar — hypoglycemia. The dreamlike drama never
occurred during my working time. Only when I lay
down in bed, and then only when I had eaten the
wrong foods. Then it was, too, that I recalled a night
at Oxford in 1959 when I suddenly seemed to op-
erate on two levels of consciousness — this fake
remembrance of things past, concurrent with awareness of the present. I had then thought it was a wholly
psychological response to the objectionable intonation
of a white South African visitor into whose company
I had been thrown. The subsequent medical diagnosis
applied also to the English experience.

I came out of St. Lazare station into the chilly,
slender morning light to catch a bus to the Left Bank.
My nerves still tingled from that horizontal terror. A
good thing if it happens when you are, I thought,
securely housed somewhere. Could have been worse,
too, maybe, than in a train streaking somewhat ir-
responsibly along the very spine of a dark-dark night.

I found Rebecca had moved to the flat on Boulevard

du Montparnasse during the week I was away. She
had organized the operation competently, as always.

'Well,' she said to me, laughing over it all, 'it's
already happened.'

'What has?'

'French.'

'What French?'

She made wild gestures with her arms, lifted her
shoulders, puffed through the mouth as the French
do when they speak. 'First, your kids start yelling for
Weetbix and Rice Crispies, the lot. The French in
the shops don't know what you're talking about.
There's no sign language for cereals. And their con-
tinental breakfast — *basadi!* We and our African or
English breakfasts, we're doomed. Then I go to the
chemist downstairs and ask for disposable napkins.
Nix. No French, no English, no nothing. Then I point
at Puso's backside and tug at his napkin and say
dis-pos-able. And the little brat? Just gazes and waves
his hands as if he were not the subject of this discussion. We all give up. Francoise came to the rescue
the next day. What a darling she is — can't imagine
where we'd have been without her.'

A few days later Rebecca, coming out of a bakery
shop, sees a small group of people clustered under the
window of our apartment, six floors up. Other people
across the street are also gazing fixedly at our window.
Wild apprehensive gestures and excited predictions
animate this street-theatre audience. When Rebecca
looks up, it is to see Chabi and Puso throwing all the
Mphahleles' clothes, pillows, and linen out of the
window into the street. The pavement is already litter-
ed. Recklessly gleeful noises can be heard from up
there as things hurtle downwards.

A chilly awareness that she had inadvertently left

the glass door giving on to the balcony open sends
Rebecca up in a state of panic that renders the knees
decrepit. The Mphahleles have arrived.

We learned to handle that time-honoured institution,
the French concierge or caretaker of the building.
A character one reads so much about in literature.
A short little man with a strangely broad nose, Monsieur Aumont lived on the ground floor. He delivered
our mail when he was in the mood and also wanted
pity, which he welcomed only when a handful of
franc coins made a jingling noise. He would report
a headache, a backache, *infection de poumon* — some
bronchial ailment — pains in the body. If it was the
chest, Aumont coughed with a show of effort when
he announced it.

The concierge was responsible for keeping the fire
going in the basement to heat the building through
pipes in the winter. The furnace ran on fuel called
mazout. The day it was finished and he couldn't
reach the manager, we froze. We had to make fire in
the grate with newsprint. But never for more than
two days at a time, a period sufficient to remind us of
our dependence on him. When he replied curtly to
your question about fuel, '*C'est finit, tout á fait*' —
finished, altogether — his face was a veritable picture
of contemptuous boredom, indifference, pointless endurance, all in one; which in turn seemed to say to
me: kill me if you like, you murdering middle-class
pig!

Several times when Monsieur le Concierge came to
the door, Motswiri, who was in a French school and
was trying out the language, would say, *Qu'est-ce que
vous desirez monsieur?* — what can I do for you,
monsieur? The old man's face would smile indulgently
and ask *ta mama?* — your mother — where is she?

Or Motswiri would peep into the concierge's front room. *Qu'est-ce que vous desirez, monsieur?* The old man would think the boy was being solicitous: any errands I can run for you — cigarettes, bread . . . ? Then we discovered that the boy was playing his own game. He had invented a tune to go with his *que'est-ce que vous desirez, monsieur.* Even danced to it with Chabi and Puso. Rebecca administered a light but insignificant whack, and another, and another, and the picnic stopped. 'Show respect for your elders, hear me! You've been enjoying teasing the concierge, haven't you!'

Motswiri's French became fluent, as did Kefilwe's, who also started at the Lycée. I was busy learning the language at the government technical institute. I visited *Présence Africaine* more frequently when I could converse with ease.

For her part, Rebecca, always busy with the kids, survived by her own ingenuity and native practical sense, by her outgoing temperament. She has always been able to bulldoze into a new community, let people know what her intentions are, openly tell them what she likes and what she doesn't, without being either rude or patronising. People become her friends or don't, and she is not going to agonise about those who she reckons are difficult. In her social work she shows — to my mind — excessive compassion, and tends to absorb her clients' woes to a degree that can hinder good relationships in present-day capitalist societies where welfare is relief and compiling of records — always patchwork, never a radical onslaught on social ills and root causes. She is the extrovert, I the opposite, the dreamer. If she says we are going to build a house, I'd better believe it. I'm going to present buts and ifs and howevers, but I'd better believe it, because she can manage the whole operation. During my travels, in the course of my work with Francoise, whenever we came to Africa to organise one or other literary or arts or educational conference, or went to Sweden, Denmark or Germany for lectures, Rebecca held the fort in Paris.

Tony was in boarding school in Great Ayton, a Quaker institution in Middlesborough, Yorkshire. Two high schools in Nigeria had had disciplinary difficulties with him, so we arranged for him to try a *very* good boarding school without his having to deal with a new language, a new system.

Although Gerard Sekoto was not having much luck with one-man shows, he lived moderately well. He had a patron who housed him — at rue des Grands Augustins, St. Germain de Prés. He had a small studio he worked in at one corner of the apartment. He was doing much better outside Paris — in other European cities and in the United States. He was a frequent friend-guest in our apartment.

Breyten Breytenbach, on the other hand, was flourishing, both in Paris and outside. His satirical style, parodies, neo-surrealism, seemed to appeal to European sensibilities. It was not only Ed Miles who thought it was all 'horse-shit'. Mazisi Kunene, who was often in Paris, also thought Breyten was wasting his talent, that his work was all a dead-end joke, a sign of decadence. Certainly Breyten's deformed shapes are impossible to live with, with the exception of one painting that I possess: a frog parodying man or the other way round. Ed and his wife Wanda thought the artist was being most unkind to the frog kingdom.

We saw much of each other – my family and Breyten

and his wife Yolande.

Gerard, Breyten, K.P. from Nigeria, and I, all go bistro-crawling one night. Every time a joint closes for the night we go on to another. From St. Germain de Prés, up St. Michel, then back, and across the Seine. And we tear through the market area, stumbling over boxes. Three South Africans and a Nigerian in Paris at dawn. We throw down some more booze on the Right Bank as if to marinade ourselves. Then we have nothing to do but return to our territory across the river.

Out of the grey dawn Breyten says, 'Zeke, deep down I'm sober as a square Calvinist, but the other self says I'm drunk. Which am I to believe, eh?' Gerard says, 'Zeke, Breyten, K.P., I'm drunk as a hobo, and my arse is itching. In my boyhood days I'd use a dry maize cob.' I say, 'Speak for yourselves, boys. Me — shit, I'm drunk also.' And K.P.'s contribution is, 'Gerard, Zeke, Britain — you son of a Woortracker — why do you write such fuckin' good poetry in a language no one can read except yourself — if Zeke didn't paraphrase it in English how would I understand the damn thing? Why don't you write English paraphrases?' 'K.P.,' Breyten replies, 'you mouse in a china-shop, why do you write poetry as if you were taller than me?' 'China?' says K.P., then shouts, 'China, who be China, where be China, where be shop? Abi you tink I'm drunk-o.' And then he hollers up the Seine, 'CHINA! WHERE'S YOUR SHOP?'

We stop at K.P.'s hotel on St. Michel to make sure he's where he's got to sleep. He straightens up, tries to square his shoulders, to become a foot taller than he is. All we hear as K.P. makes his grand entry is an eloquent *whaaaa!*

'The bull is sick in the chinashop,' Breyten observes, 'but don't worry, the porters are helping him up. Now

Zeke,' he continues, as if he were the very personificat-
ion of a conjunction between two sentences, tomorrow
— I mean today — as I promised, Yolande and I will
come and stay with the children for you, hear? Don't
worry about a thing. You and Rebecca just fuck off
to Geneva for your holiday. This Voortrekker and
Vietnam will take care of things.'

We see Gerard to the door of his apartment.

Up St. Michel, all alone, in the grey of dawn. Every
so often I all but run into one of the trees growing in
a row on the pavement. A strategy pushes through
my thick brain and takes matters in hand, quite independently, as I reflect later, of the brain. I stomp
up the boulevard, hitting the pavement heavily, like
an African warrior. My shoes make a clatter that
resounds in the hollow belly of a Sunday dawn, but
the weight I put on my feet keeps me steady. Past the
Luxembourg Garden I know I'm almost home. A
small voice comes through to ask, what about Geneva?
What the hell does he mean *Geneva!* I say aloud,
'Geneva's next Sunday, dummy, not today!'

Madame Gomet, our *femme de manage* — occasional
domestic help — was an amiable person with a
chubby face. She would come on the eve of one of
those wild-cat strikes that characterise French life.
There is a series of them throughout the year, workers
laying down tools for a day. Madame Gomet would
try to explain to Rebecca what she should expect.
'Demain,' she would say in single words climbing
towards a sentence, 'grève — électricité, gaz (for
cooking), water, the buses, trains — there will be a
stoppage of all these, everywhere.'

She was very gentle with the children. Rebecca,
always adventurous in these matters, would ask
Madame Gomet for French recipes. The French-

woman always obliged and would even help Rebecca prepare some.

That was France in the early Sixties.

Africans — from West Africa, Madagascar, Mauritius, the Comores, the West Indies — converge in France. In Paris you see them mill around on the Left Bank, at ease, some hand in hand with white female friends. Paris in the spring: you should walk from the Right Bank, along the river to the left, past Place de la Concorde, past the Louvre. Paris was made for walking. It has a lot to tell you, and asks for nothing in return, no confidences, no commitment. Only one thing can sour a walk for me: dogs and their owners. They leave their obnoxious waste on the pavements and their owners indulge them all the same. Cats and dogs — the bane of my life . . . . It's more than enough to contemplate the way dogs and cats walk in and out of the human condition in western society . . . . Man alive!

Blacks in Paris. You take the French in small doses — they don't allow more than that, anyhow. You're all right if you understand that your friendship or acquaintance with them will go as far as the café or bistro, and rarely into their homes. Not because you're black, people will tell you, but because they keep that area of their lives secluded, even in their relationships with one another.

So you strike your own level and coast along and relax, understanding that you are still an outsider, no matter what. They have a streak of cruelty, too, the French. Their former colonies can show you the ravages of the French personality. But in their own country, too. So you take them in doses, to avoid hurt. I don't know to what extent, if any, the traffic in any big city reflects a national character. To see drivers skirt round a blind man crossing the street (rather than wait) appalls me.

Paris teems with exiles, ex-colonial blacks, which gives you the illusion that racism is minimal. Deep down in the French psyche it is expected that you, the outsider, should allow yourself to be sucked into its 'superior' culture, into a language that is the ultimate idiom of gentility and aesthetic enlighten- ment, one that you can't possibly resist if you are tuned into the charm and wisdom of western civil- isation. It is expected that you should know that this assimilation is only possible on the Frenchman's terms. Deep down in such a psyche lies a calculating racism.

By the same token, the British with their studied aloofness and traditional laissez-faire attitude lead you to believe that you're all right with your indige- nous culture, as long as you learn enough English to understand that it is the idiom of a superior culture with a long and rich literary tradition. There's the rub: you can't learn a language without assimilating its thought systems and therefore its culture. Thus the aloofness implies a racist mind: you can't make it to our level, the Englishman is saying.

I ask myself if I may not be making a journalistic comment and pretending that I've discovered an absolute. I'm sure, nevertheless, that there is a solid core of racism as a group attitude among the British which resists other people out of a sense of cultural superiority or aloofness. If I hoped for some internal change for the better, it would be foolish, naive. In our travels in the so-called western democracies, I have frequently struck this bedrock. And there are acts and words that express white racism that no-one can verify or prove as they are happening or being said, but which we the 'people of colour' all over the world have a finely tuned instinct to detect.

Occasionally we were asked to Great Ayton in Middlesborough, Yorkshire, to discuss Tony's problems of adjustment. When Rebecca decided to make the trip she would say when leaving, 'Bye, *bana baka* — my children - fend for yourselves,' giving me a look that suggested, 'Don't you starve my poor children, man!' We both knew there was going to be chaos in the kitchen.

Kefilwe, the oldest of the four, was only eleven and could not be expected to cook. I hate cooking. As a boy in Marabastad, I cooked for a family of nine, including our house physician, Mathebula, who looked after our health and had free food and sleeping accommodation on the back stoep. It was a simple diet — stiff porridge, meat stewed with potatoes and, on Sundays, rice, cabbage or beans mashed with potatoes. No hassles. After I left the family to work on the Reef, I made sure eating arrangements did not involve doing my own cooking. I just hated to mess with pots and pans, even for mere survival. I ate institution food.

Back in Orlando, Rebecca was most inventive with the simplest ingredients, which turned a ghetto diet into a nourishing cuisine. Nothing lavish, just simple cheap materials knocked together with some imagination and an expert hand.

I knew it was going to be rough alone with the kids. I stewed those juicy French apples, mashed them, cooked a whole pot of custard which we always bought in an English shop on the Right Bank. I let both apples and custard cool and we had a feast. For several years custard summed up for me the delights of life. Puso would grunt with great relish. The family slogan was 'Mum's gone, let's have a custard-and-apple party!'

Needless to say, Mum would return to deal with Puso's and Chabi's diarrhoea. 'Do you want to kill my children!' she would say in despair. I got to discover an antidote at the pharmacy, though. The party continued.

Although we visited England several times, moving in and out of the colony of Africans there, we were not tempted to strike roots in the Queen's country. The foul English climate, for one thing, would not suit us. For another, I was in the wrong department: English literature. How could the English be expected to welcome an African or Asian to teach them English! Maybe at the newer universities, but these were few and far between.

We were always thrown together as South Africans, particularly in London. Some had the exasperating habit of speaking the adulterated Afrikaans of the street corner, just to feel South African black. 'These nigger creatures!' my friend would say. 'The language of conquest has got them by the balls. Maybe they even dream in it!'

Thrown upon one another like that, we became sentimental about the ugly things that sought to dehumanise us back home. Then we became nasty towards one another. You didn't care for so-and-so, he was 'stuck up', 'a born loser', 'spineless', 'fucked up', 'a sell-out', 'quisling', 'parasite', 'a spiv'. You placed a quart of Scotch or brandy or vodka in front of a guest and he ploughed through it in no time, at one sitting. Neat, no mixers. Drank in order to get hopelessly drunk, less for the socialising process. We seemed to be of little use to one another when we were not at a party or dinner. That's when I got to learn that two insecure people cannot room together.

We pored over news about home in the local press and in the South African papers that reached us. We fluctuated between the low and high: excitement and hope, despair and anger, desperation and fuckitude. We chewed on the news and hung on the thin thread of long-distance commitment.

For self-protection, or because they were not the out-going type, some managed to live secluded lives. They constructed visible defences around themselves, put on a non-committal or deadpan voice on the telephone.

Then Britain introduced the Commonwealth Immigration law. It was aimed largely at stemming the tide of immigration of Africans and Asians, especially those from Kenya, India, Pakistan. If one wanted to immigrate, there was the long waiting queue to reckon with: one had to prove there was a job to go into directly on arrival in Britain.

No, there was no England for us.

Exiles, fences, gates, nationality, citizenship . . . . Though we could travel anywhere — except South Africa — with British passports, we were suddenly stateless. The whole Mphahlele caravan.

Kenya

I had undertaken to stay in Paris for only two years, after which I should return to teaching. As there was a group in Nairobi that promised to become a viable infrastructure for a creative centre, John Hunt, the executive director of the Congress for Cultural Freedom, suggested that I go out to Kenya and establish a centre like the Nigerian Mbari. The Nairobi

group was requesting it. Yes, I should like to tackle it.
But I should also like to pull out of the director's
position at the end of two years. If a Kenya
national directed it, the centre would be seen to be
a full-blooded expression of indigenous cultural
aspirations.

I went ahead of the family. Took a boat from
Marseilles that would land me at Mombasa twelve
days later: across the Mediterranean, through the
Suez Canal, under a daytime sky that seemed to
urinate fire. Our boat docked at Port Suez on the Red
Sea and we motored down to Cairo for night-club
entertainment and to sleep over. Next morning, on
our return to the boat, the sun immediately attacked
us. The arid territory we were crossing lay there, taking
it all in without flinching, without a single stir. The
sun was singing, the earth was singing. As long as you
could feel that you were part of this greater harmony,
you could then be part of the song and not a mere
listener, and you could stretch out in surrender to the
sensation all along the blood.

When we burst into the Indian Ocean, I felt as if
we had been through a pipeline.

The family took the same route. When they arrived
I had already found a house in Nairobi. Bought it
from the son of a former governor of East Africa,
who was returning to England. Again, Rebecca took
charge of the furnishing and the interior decorations.

I had arrived in August, 1963, and October was set
for Kenya's independence. Elimo Njau, the Tanzanian
painter who housed me while I was looking for a
place of my own, felt, as I did, that a creative centre
for Kenya could not have been planned for a better
time than independence. He suggested a name, which
everyone else accepted — *Chemchemi*, Swahili for

'fountain'.

In no uncertain terms I told the group that I would not stay as director for one day more than two years. I wanted badly to return to university teaching. For the two years I operated from Paris, I lectured in Sweden, Denmark, Finland, West Germany, and France; in Senegal, Sierre Leone, Ghana, Nigeria, Cameroon, and Uganda. But this was not like regular teaching. I yearned for the classroom again.

In a few months we converted a warehouse into two offices, a small auditorium for experimental theatre and intimate music performances, and an art gallery. Much the same arrangement as Ibadan's and Enugu's Mbari centres. Farfield Foundation, now defunct, channelled funds through the Congress to maintain Chemchemi and its staff.

Njau ran our art gallery on a voluntary basis. He mounted successful exhibitions of Ugandan artists Kyeyune and Msango, and of his own work. Kyeyune found studio facilities at Chemchemi, as did Hezbon Owiti, then a young apprentice. Owiti was later to produce work that had that instinctive element one observed in the Oshogbo artists under Ulli Beier's wing, like Twin Seven-Seven.

We sent Owiti to Oshogbo to expose him to the Nigerian art circles. Ulli made rather a fetish out of the art hammered out of life experience, with only minimal guidance, as against that produced by men and women who had been to the fine-arts departments in Ibadan, Zaria, Legon, and at Makerere, Kampala. And yet it would be foolish to dismiss the artists from these schools, as Ulli sometimes tended to do, especially if they were able to wean themselves from Eurocentric training and European art history, rediscovering their own metier. Men like Tanzania's Sam

Ntiro, Njau himself, Nigeria's Demas Nwoko. A goodly
number, of course, ended up as art teachers and could
never negotiate the transition from Europe to Africa.

Frank McEwan of Salisbury had a small studio in
the Sixties where Zimbabweans worked out their own
idiom. They were surrounded by the world of Mashona
soapstone art. And yet even he acknowledged the
importance of formal teaching. The problem of
salvaging the lost religious impulse which traditional
artists derived from their spirit world is immense,
when we are speaking of modern artists who are removed from that world and who have a gallery in mind,
something unknown to the old artists. The West
African art we see in museums and in art book
reproductions, Makonde art of East Africa, Central
African art – all this speaks of a universe that seems
to resist the hands of the modern artist who wants to
pluck its fruit.

My soul was in the job. I was in charge of writing
and theatre, Joe Kariuki the poet was in charge of
music. He, Njau, Jonathan Kariara, and the *Nation*
reporter Hilary Ngweno served on my committee.
Our participants were grassroots – from the townships
and locations that were a colonial heritage. These
were on the east side, white suburbia on the west side,
the city in between, but quite accessible for Chemchemi's purpose. I travelled to outside districts to run
writers' workshops in schools that invited me, and
our drama group also travelled out. It seemed the
travels of an extra-mural donkey were never going to
end for me! But it was rewarding for me, later, to see
names from those outpost workshops appear in
Busara, edited by Ngugi, and *Zuka* edited by Kariara
for O.U.P.

I had very little time and energy for writing. The

short stories I had finished in Paris lay in my box, waiting for me to hawk them. Stories like 'Greig on a Stolen Piano', 'The Barber of Bariga', 'A Ballad of Oyo', 'Mrs. Plum'. But I did finish editing *African Writing Today* for Penguin. In Paris I had also co-edited with the late Ellis Komey of Ghana *Modern African Stories* for Faber and Faber in London.

Alliance High School for girls, just outside Nairobi, asked me to write a play for its yearly drama festival, in the place of the routine Shakespeare. I adapted a short story by Grace Ogot of Kenya and called it *Oganda's Journey*. The story itself was 'The Rain Came', which I had anthologised in Faber's book of African stories. It was verse drama, using African music. It had a folktale motif. The most enchanting element in the play was the use that could be, and was made of traditional music idioms from a variety of ethnic groups in Kenya. A most refreshing performance, which exploited the girls' natural, untutored acting.

Oganda's Journey was subsequently produced by Bob Leshoai with his Tanzanian players in Dar es Salaam, and by the Spelman College drama group in Atlanta, Georgia, both performances receiving good reviews.

October, 1963: Kenya's independence. Miriam Makeba came from the U.S. to perform. She whipped out her song magic. The crowds caught it and swallowed her up, all of her. Kenyatta was riding on the crest of popular acclaim.

Kenyatta the African enigma. Years in England. Return to Kenya 1946. The peasant revolt: 1952. Mostly Kikuyu, as most of Kenya's farming land, owned by whites, was in Kikuyuland. The Emergency, 1952-1961. Kenyatta's trial. Nine years for

him, convicted on a charge of leading the 'Mau Mau'
rebellion — a 'leader unto darkness'. Kept alone in a
hut, out in the wilds, under strict security.

His denial of involvement in the 'Mau Mau' movement was later confirmed when, as President of
Kenya, Kenyatta sent a contingent of police to smoke
out of the forests a few hundred 'Mau Mau' ad-
herents. In 1961, when Kenyatta was clearly going to
lead Kenya into independence, with Oginga Odinga as
either companion or rival, the 'Mau Mau' peasants
refused to leave the forests. They didn't see the
immediate fruits of what they fought for, what men
like Dedan Kimathi had died for. Their land remained
in white hands.

The new government seemed to be forgetting them.
They had fought for the return of the land the
English settlers had taken away from them, and to
which they had given their labour. The men moving
into the new positions of power were acting as if they
were totally unaware of the background of Kenya's
independence. Many of them had been in high school
and university during the long Emergency. That part
of Kenyan history seemed to exist as a blur for them.
Or else they had been taken in by the sermons of the
missionary mentors about the unrelieved barbarism,
the irredeemable heathenism of 'Mau Mau'. So the
peasant heroes of the revolt were reduced, in the
minds of the youth, to lilliputian proportions, or to
mere names. Indeed, when I talked to the young men
(then in their thirties) about 'Mau Mau', they quickly
changed the subject. They were clearly ashamed of
the movement. Mighty peculiar, I thought, considering
that even much older men like Koinange, then a
cabinet minister in the President's office, had been
involved in the removal of thousands of children from

state-aided mission schools to newly-established independent schools. Truly an event of historical
moment, whatever the handicaps, like overcrowding
and the grossly inadequate supply of teachers.

Independence for a small elite, penury for the
masses. Mzee Kenyatta, the African enigma, rich, un-
assailable, grinding underfoot the dissident fringe,
brandishing his fly-swish beside Mama Ngina, whose
statuesque and artless public posture belied her own
abundant bank balance and estates.

Rebecca was given a job as a social worker in the
U.N. Freedom From Hunger Campaign, taking charge
of its educational programme.

Nairobi is like an ostrich egg in the middle of
Serengeti. A busy little hive, all the movement gravi-
tating towards The Thorntree, in front of the New
Stanley Hotel. Other and newer hotels loom large on
the east side. The Thorntree restaurant was always
open, like a pot of honey. The tourists pressed their
way in and out gingerly: the Americans, with their
celluloid-peaked caps on their heads, bulging with
cameras and credit cards, flaunting their great-nation
presence; the Japanese, bulging with even more
cameras, with new industrial energy, with Yamaha get-
up-and-go; West Germans in short pants, bulging with
self-containment that is never going to spill its guts
for everyone else to see; the English bulging with a
proprietary air — Wilson Estates (Pty) Ltd. — as they
contemplate these day-old puppies who didn't know
how to govern other nations but came to reap the
fruits of what we English slaved to create in this
country. We were here first, you know; of course the
old boy's getting on in years, I dread the day he dies
— tribal wars all over again — What! Nonsense —
nobody's ever going to force us out ... what would

they do without all the foreign business? Asians —
yes, poor devils — the old man's got it in for them.
Always in trouble, aren't they? Kipling knew them to
a T. I think they've got their heads in the clouds — er
— mystics you might say — what! If you ask me the
government's got to do something about all these
refugees — Sudan, Burundi, Rwanda, Uganda, South
Africa, Rhodesia — the lot — how are they going to
make a living in this place? The teachers are already
taking the places our Kenyans should be occupying in
the schools . . . I was talking to Charles Njonjo the
other day — frightfully intelligent man, isn't he,
straight from Emzee's liberal stable you might say.
Thoroughly unspoiled — well, as I was saying, Charles
is thinking of making a law that will clear the streets
of vagrants — poor devils, why don't they take to
farming instead of flocking to Nairobi to loaf and
burgle! I'm going to have a last beer, what about you?
Super . . . I tell you I just dread the day the old boy
kicks off. What? Of course the Kikuyus will remain
on top. Frightfully intelligent, they've got drive and a
business sense. Friend of mine — fellow at the Israeli
Embassy — he says to me, you know Randolph, I'm
convinced there must be a missing link somewhere
between us Jews and the Kikuyus. We're so alike in
temperament, uncanny isn't it! Some historians must
find the link one day . . . . What, the Luo and Wa-
kamba? They're an easy-going lot — at least the Luo
have produced an intelligentsia. Just you watch, the
old boy's going to get a Kikuyu vice-chancellor for
the university and that's sure to neutralise the Luo intellectuals inside there — oh he's cute . . . . What?
American capital? Piffle, man — we were here first . . . .
Here please waiter — this way!

Eighteen months . . . . I was looking forward to

university teaching, but thoroughly enjoying Chemchemi work. It was a centre the young generation loved and made their own. But Nairobi emptied out at night, until you could almost hear its hollow sound. Only genteel night clubs, catering to the elite, glowed discreetly in the city centre — though others, on the fringe of the city, were noisy, vibrant and uninhibited. So Chemchemi activities ran during the afternoon. It suited most of our members.

I wrote an article about East African writers for a daily paper. I was accused by one of the members of my already moribund committee of having omitted a name — Rebecca Njau — from my account, while at the same time a few demeaning intentions were imputed to my article. I knew only one published story of hers, and a bad play which our Chemchemi Players had acted. One of those plays that need a table and chairs throughout! I knew publishers had been trying, so far in vain, to massage her muse to bring forth a novel.

Furious exchanges followed between me and my detractor. A plot was afoot in other quarters to discredit my work. I got wind of it. My detractor and the *Nation* reporter had long pulled out of the committee, without even saying so. Our gallery supervisor resigned. I was left with Joe Kariuki and Hezbon Owiti, the gallery attendant, now an accomplished painter.

Why all the disaffection? I asked the committee members individually, as they would never come to meetings. After all, I had only half a year to go. I firmly believed that the Congress and its sponsoring foundation could enjoy credibility only if they supported an institution managed by the people of the country in which it operated. Why, why the veiled

vendetta by the very people who had invited me? I
lost my secretary, who was Njau's sister-in-law. She
resigned.

The ministry of Foreign Affairs in Jerusalem couldn't
have guessed what it was doing for me when, through
the good offices of a white associate of Chemchemi,
it invited me to visit Israel for three months, all
expenses paid. It struck me that I could go and observe
the indigenous theatre of the Israelis. I was glad to be
able to get away from the bickering. The theatre was
fascinating. Tel Aviv was my base, from which I
visited Haifa, Jerusalem, the Kibbutzim, Beersheba
and so on.

But what Israel was to do to the Palestinians
appalled me. It poisoned the memory of those three
months.

The rot had set in, it was never going to stop. I had
it noised about that we wanted a director for Chemchemi to succeed me. We advertised formally. The
applicants were poor material. Those who stood a
chance, especially the Ugandan artists, did not apply.
Dog in the manger? Maybe. The Congress took the
stand that if there were no nationals in Kenya qualified
or willing to run Chemchemi, the institution had
better be liquidated.

At the end of two years I said goodbye to the
building that we had reshaped to the style of our
activities. I had experienced the unsettling feeling
that assails you, almost accusingly in such a situation
— the feeling that you have been building the bridge
on the River Kwai.

Rebecca thought that Chemchemi had come to
Nairobi before it was ready. Ali Mazrui, the Kenyan
scholar, thought the same. I had allowed myself to be
deceived by the surface quality of Nairobi: taken the

surface activity to be an expression of a soul in conscious search for itself. This was not an African town, and I should have understood that, even as I listened to the enthusiastic voices that invited me to Kenya. African cities like Kampala, Lagos, Ibadan, Accra, African townships like those of South Africa — *African* in the human sense rather than in the sense of the white man's 'central business district' — these are fertile ground for creative centres, when the economics are right or near right.

Kampala had Rajat Neogy's *Transition* and the old university of Makerere, while the University College of Nairobi was still lumbering under the weight of its colonial technical-college past. Ironically, had *Transition*, also sponsored by the Congress since 1962, been based anywhere else but Kampala, we would have set up the creative centre there. It was the idea of the local writers and artists, our hosts, that we aim at dispersion rather than concentration of creative energy. I know that had we found Ngugi in Nairobi, he would most likely have saved the day. But alas, we would not have survived Obote in Uganda!

Apropos of which, I have never been able to appreciate why people in government in Africa are so suspicious of academics, intellectuals, including writers, and their journals. Whenever we had an opening of an exhibition or music or drama performance at Chemchemi, the politicians in government and the civil servants never patronised us. But they went to the gala openings at the Donovan Maule, the National Theatre, and the New Stanley Hotel gallery, in black suits and shoes — all rigged up for the cheese and wine atmosphere, screw the performance and the art show.

* * *

A gong went. Someone blew the whistle. And the drums passed on the message. The Central Information Agency of America had been at it again. The Congress for Cultural Freedom, since renamed International Association for Cultural Freedom, was one of the beneficiaries of CIA largesse, through the Farfield Foundation. So was the American Society of African Culture (AMSAC), run by African-Americans; so was *Encounter* magazine in London, which had been launched by the Congress. Then there was *Transition* in Kampala. This affected the Mbari centres in Ibadan and Enugu, and Chemchemi till its demise. As well as several other philanthropic organisations. AMSAC disbanded suddenly. Rajat continued to publish *Transition*. The president of the Congress resigned, feeling bad about the fact that he had known where the money was coming from but had not thought it made any material difference as the Congress was never constrained to serve the interests of the CIA.

Why? Why? was the question. What was in it for the CIA, when it could never, even if it wanted to, dictate the activities its money made possible? Why? We had used the money to good ends, and there was no building with a plaque dedicated to the memory of the CIA.

I wrote a letter to *Transition* in reply to our accusers. I knew of no institution that we had established, I stated, nor any individual person sponsored by the CIA, who had been told what project to undertake. The Mbari centres, the documentation centres in other parts of Africa, and Dennis Duerden's Transcription Centre in London which distributed taped interviews on the arts in Africa, continued to flourish on their own. Chemchemi's closure was caused by factors other than the CIA's funding.

I said furthermore that we of the Third World were working at grassroots level, which allowed no room for such distracting heavy stuff as the CIA was known to take on. But we were also poor, and African governments had their own priorities for funding, which did not include cultural activity. CIA money had ferried us over rough waters. I didn't see anything to weep over. Rich countries must pay up. Several of our accusers should also remember, I concluded, the conferences they had attended abroad and locally, where they were accommodated in posh hotels, and dined and wined on money which, for all they knew, might have come from a contaminated source.

I could not help thinking back on the period 1949-1956 when I was in charge of theatre in the Syndicate of African Artists, founded in Johannesburg by my friend Khabi Mngoma, Wilkie Kambule and myself. Khabi was later to become founder and professor and head of the department of Music, University of Zululand, and Wilkie principal of Orlando High School, subsequently a lecturer in mathematics at the University of the Witwatersrand. Khabi was in charge of the music division in the syndicate, Wilkie treasurer. The same players who had been in my group at Orlando High continued as the Syndicate Players after finishing secondary school.

I made adaptations of folktales, of Dickens's *A Tale of Two Cities*, Greek tragedies like the story of Agamemnon, *The Merchant of Venice, Julius Caesar,* and so on. Generally, we put on plays that would appeal to African audiences and which had enough substance in them to engage the imagination as well as entertain. They also had to be plays that would not require elaborate sets. Everywhere we performed, Johannesburg, East and West Rand, Pretoria, we raided wooded areas to pluck branches for·the backdrop on the stage. It never failed to captivate our audiences. We wove African music and dance into our folktales: none of the double-breasted female dances that are today being thrown into any silly old story by white promoters who then sell the 'Bantu' stuff overseas.

Each performance included plays, solo singing by Khabi (lyric tenor) accompanied by Jacob Moeketsi at the piano, and Harold Kumalo (tenor) accompanied by Khabi alternating with Jacob. The Syndicate also promoted song recitals by Grace Mngoma (contralto) and others.

Why this flashback? It is meant to illustrate the economics involved in the performing arts. We had to present plays and music concerts on Sunday afternoons, as evenings were a dangerous time for our audiences to venture out of their ghetto homes. Our admission fees were never more than one shilling. Often performances were free. We charged higher fees when we presented white musicians who volunteered to entertain us in our ghettos.

Khabi had a small manual printing machine with which he tried to eke out a livelihood. He made the handbills and programmes for us. That was fat luck.

The meagre gate takings barely enabled the Syndicate to hire a truck to take our players and musicians to various townships and buy them lunch. We received no subsidy from anyone, and not for want of trying. Industry did not care for African performing arts then. It was a strain, but we derived ample spiritual satisfaction. We were working in a culture of poverty. Cultural poverty was not our problem. We were always scrounging for time, for more decent halls, for materials. Our people have the creative urge, but the means to promote this are the size of chicken pickings.

Grassroots. Creative energy without money to buy paper, paints or brushes or canvas, or silkscreen, or hire a carpenter to make props, or advertise yourself; without a decent place to work in. The heartaches. You're always thrown upon your inner resources. You have to make the honey in your own hive, because the world outside will not give you free materials for the enterprise. Your players and musicians live insecure lives, even though you the *animateur* may be relatively comfortable, being a professional person. They come and go, and no rehearsal is the same as the previous one, because the cast keeps changing.

I promised myself never again to get involved in this harrowing, soul-draining, energy-consuming kind of cultural activity. I would have to stop being apologetic when I approached the haves for money to promote work of national or community importance; I'd have to take the money as long as I wasn't compromising the community and my own integrity; I'd have to take what money was being offered but promise nothing . . . .

I was given a job for an academic year in the English Department of the then University College of Nairobi. The department head was the amiable and highly cultured George Wing. The principal told me that they could not give me a contract of more than two years. This would guarantee any one of the many Kenyans training abroad a job on his return. He himself was an expatriate from Sierre Leone.

I could not take the risk. Herbert Shore, professor of drama at the University of Denver, U.S., then in Tanzania, negotiated a teaching fellowship for me in his home university's English Department. We had corresponded with each other when I was in Paris.

III

Denver, Colorado 1966-1974

It worked. May 1966: the Mphahlele caravan packed pots and pans and things for shipping. Denver, here we come! Tony went to the American-run boarding school in Dar es Salaam. The agreement was that if he showed sustained interest in school and his work improved, we would send for him to join us in the U.S. He knew we meant it, seriously.

We rented a house, fixed schooling for the kids, prepared for the plunge. I was granted a tuition waiver by the university for the course work I had to do before I could be admitted for the Ph.D dissertation. I was paid for the courses I myself taught — African Literature and Freshman Composition.

From this mile-high city — about as high as Johannesburg — the Rocky Mountains loomed large, forty-eight kilometres to the west. The Colorado plains suited my temperament admirably. It was a hectic two years in Denver. The course work covered the whole of English literature from Anglo-Saxon to modern literature. It included American literature from the earliest writers to the present. After eighteen months I was ready to do the comprehensive oral exam — the 'Comps'. I had already begun my novel,

The Wanderers, in lieu of a dissertation as I was in the Creative Writing Programme of the English Department. I spent the last six months finishing it. I passed the exam in French as my foreign language with ease. Afrikaans was accepted as a second foreign language. I 'defended' the novel successfully. Rebecca completed an advanced course in Community Organisation in the School of Social Work at the University, on the strength of her very good, accredited three-year diploma in social work from the Jan Hofmeyr School, Johannesburg. In August I was awarded the Ph.D. I was also elected to the Phi Beta Kappa for academic excellence.

Zambian Excursion 1968

We had been given the Exchange Visa to study in the U.S. Regulations had it that we would have to leave, or else petition the U.S. Congress to pass a law allowing us to remain. Although Professor Gerald Chapman, head of the English Department, was willing to back such a petition, Rebecca was hell-bent on returning to Africa. By the time we had to leave, I had corresponded with the University of Zambia for a post as Senior Lecturer in its English Department. I was accepted.

I kept asking Rebecca, 'Are you ready for another African country — *are you ready?*' After Kenya I was reluctant. Indeed I had written to the registrar in Zambia to ask what protection the University would give us if the Zambian government decided to terminate our residence. He never replied. But we had to go all the same. I was offered a five-year contract.

'Are you ready?' I kept asking Rebecca.

'How ready *can* one be?' was her reply.

In August, 1968, we arrived in Lusaka. Zambia? Ask me about another country, will you? Say, the Territory of Afas and Isas.

No, but frankly, Bra Zeke, what made you quit Zambia after only twenty-one months? I mean, folks are going to say you're a rolling stone that gathers no whatchamacallit, you know.

What folks?

I don't know. Just folks, man, Bra Zeke. The fellows. I mean *batho ha heso* — the home boys.

After a long pause I tell Steve. You want to know about Zambia. How much can one know a country. All I know is that I have to write off my period there. Utter waste.

I hear you.

It's like this. The Doctor Abrahams affair. The man being chased like a fugitive from justice. Rhodesian taxis and farmers having to leave, because Zambians must own taxis and farms. I mean, those Choma farmers are Africans, and they are not mere gardeners mucking about with small plots.

I hear you.

I say to the university, I say, supposing an Immigration officer does not like me as in the case of Abrahams, and says *out* — what protection will you give me as a person who has a five-year contract with you? No reply.

After four months, our garden help — a guy from Malawi — makes off with my new Peugeot 404. He's filled it up with all the children's clothing, sewing machine, my cousin's Akai tape deck. He's been in our bedroom and taken the car keys out of the pocket of my trousers hanging on the wardrobe door. We're fast asleep. Sonofabitch even locks us in the bedroom.

Had got into the house through a window which he must have prised loose during the day. Two days after I reported the theft, word comes from the police at Mzimba, Northern Malawi. They'd stopped the fellow heading to Nkata Bay on Lake Malawi — his home. They'd suspected the car to be stolen — an ugly bash on one side, foreign number plates, you know. The thieves had also taken out my booze and had a ball on the way. Ran into a bridge, the amateurs.

I fly to Mzimba to identify the car. I find all the goods, still intact. You see, the guy was carrying cargo home, from white man's town, like in the old days — show off to the village — see me, I wasn't fucking around in the south — look at the loot I worked for . . . . These bloody village amateurs. I respect a thief who can get away with the loot and cover up his tracks. A South African wouldn't have been caught with the goods on his hands. These goddam villagers who come to town and think they can pull off stuff that townspeople do.

I hear you. Why not get rid of the loot on the way and still have it arrive at Nkata Bay?

Beats me. But don't you see — they're just rustics trying big-time stuff. They think they're carrying a buck from the hunt. They've got to carry it on their shoulders, all in one piece. The man must be seen to bring cargo home. Anyhow, when they are stopped by the police, his accomplice makes a run for it. 'Thanks for the ride!' he shouted to the driver. The guy got the slam — six years — for bringing goods into the country illegally. The old caretaker of the rest-house where I spent the night said to me, 'Dat man, he Thonga from Nkata Bay. Thonga — dey tief.'

I had a village mechanic clean the carburettor. I drove all night on dirt roads through that crocodile

country with the window on my side open because it
had been damaged during the accident.

Ag jy lieg man, Bra Zeke.

True's God. I drove those 540 miles through the
night. Hell, the bush seemed to be coming at me
all the time, only to collide with the shafts from the
headlamps and then go fleeting past me on either side;
the inky black night held, tight, allowing me just the
tunnel along which I was travelling. And I was chewing
dust, on, on, chewing the earth.

But Bra Zeke, burglaries go on all the time. What
was so great about this one? I mean, there's your new
middle class in good houses, even the back yards are
grand, and servants and jobless rustics filling up the
town — what do you expect?

Oh, by the way, when the goods were laid out on
the floor at Mzimba police station, so I could identify
them, a bicycle chain also showed up. It was doubled
and tied to a thick stick. They were going to work me
over with it if I had woken up and tried to interfere
with them. Moral lesson: never leave your bedroom
during a burglary unless you have a gun.

Wow!

But no, the burglary was only for starters — an
introduction to Zambia. It was the Dr. Abrahams
incident, of course, that did it. The government
simply gave him notice to quit in 48 hours. No reasons.
A fellow who had served a large, poor community in
Lilanda and Matero for four years, often without
charging the patients. He bolts for the Tanzanian
border because experience tells him if he has not
succeeded in wrapping up his practice and leaving in
48 hours, it's the cooler for him — to wait there until
some European country adopts him. The Tanzanians
hand him back to the Zambian police. It's the slammer

anyhow. Then Sweden offers him asylum. Then some of our South African teachers are also sent out of the country.

South African whites living off the fat of the land in the Copperbelt . . . coming and going as they please . . . . Bernard Magubane, socialist at the university, Livie Mqotsi in a secondary school — both receive notices from Immigration to leave the country. Because they have no valid travel documents.

I submit a memorandum in which I detail these events. Again, what protection do we have from the university, I ask. If they value Dr. Magubane's services, why does the university's highest official not try to intervene? No reply.

Livie Mqotsi had no one to appeal to. Ironically, his notice was handed to him while he was hosting a wake and making funeral arrangements for Dr. Joseph Mokoena, a dear friend who was killed in a car accident in Lusaka. The cold finality of Joe's exit, this other of Livie's on top of it!

Still no reply to my memorandum. President Kenneth Kaunda invited me to what he called a 'working lunch' at State House. He'd heard from the Minister of Education that I was thinking of leaving. Why? he wanted to know. So I tell him the whole story. Doesn't know a thing Immigration's doing, the President admits. But he'll check it out. You know, he says — always polite, suave but with all the visible qualities of the competent resolute leader who has made it all the way from the days of anti-Federation activism — you know, he says, we last met at the Accra Conference in 1958 — remember the commission we both served on — and now even before we renew acquaintance you're on the move. I let K.K. know that I predicted the future — now our present — that I was sure when

we met in Accra he was going to be Number One man
in Zambian politics, way above Harry Nkumbula, that
I wrote a report on these lines for a South African
journal. He asks me to let him see the article. And he
felt good, *looked* good. Please, K.K. says, let me look
into this Immigration thing and don't resign until you
hear from me.

I wait for the President's word. Nothing from State
House. No word from the university council. So I
decide the other shoe's got to drop — it's long been
pinching me. Besides, I have no moral obligation any
more to keep quiet or delay action.

The *Times of Zambia* published my memorandum.
I resigned as Senior Lecturer of English, breaking my
contract after only six months. But I stood to gain if
I served another eighteen months — gratuity, tax
refund and so on.

Know what those Immigration jokers said to
Magubane? He could leave his wife if he wanted to,
because she was pregnant. He packed up his whole
family. Livie followed, then the Mphahlele caravan.

The two years of absence from the U.S. required
by the Exchange Visa were almost over, as it happened. I suggested things to the University of Denver.
The head of the English Department offered me an
Associate Professorship. Perfect timing. Denver
it was to be. This time we would have to re-enter
on immigrant visas for permanent residence.

I made one decision that survived my vanity: I was
never again going to fight other people's cultural
battles. Even if I was to be invited or requested, I
would define the limits in a way that allowed me a
relatively unobtrusive role, under someone else's
direction, full stop. Only in South Africa, I resolved,
would I take things in hand where there was an

opportunity for initiative that needed taking. Even
then my activities would be determined by this knowledge of myself: I'm a doer among other doers, not an
administrator. Give me the job, and if I'm convinced
the moral price is right, and I'm given room to create,
I'll move in with you.

I kept up my resolution among the African-Americans in the United States.

Casualties

There, Steve, that's my tale of many cities. We had
permanent residence in the United States. You know,
I still think we who had academic jobs over there
were lucky we had something to sell. To immigrate
into that country you've *got* to have something to
sell, not just your presence. It's cut-throat. It was hell
for those actors who stayed after the musical *Sponono*
quit the States, and for those who dropped out of
school who had been brought out by the African-
American Institute as refugees.

My own orbit, Bra Zeke, is lined with casualties.
Ugly ones, beautiful ones. Look at me — but it's not
me we're talking about.

No-no-no — go on.

Well, a bunch of us came out the usual route. Then
something rotten set in. It stank throughout in our
organisations in Dar. Like a stalk-borer, like some
caterpillar feeding fat on the roots of your plants.
Our leaders began to expel one another. Some of us
headed for Ethiopia leaderless. A bunch of us went
north-west across Zambia. Bwana Safari — we called
him that — yes — he set himself up as a judge. Refugee
camp was like boot camp — kind you see in the

movies. Petty little men giving orders like *askaris*
who've just graduated from spears and truncheons,
just full of themselves. Messy business, man.

Some tribalists from the Cape didn't make life
easier either. There was talk those days of a mini-
coup that would give them power over every one,
including Bwana Safari. Internal politics of movements
in exile — they stink. So we scattered. *Kak en betaal*
— it was that. Safari was then able to sit safe and
secure on his stool.

How did he get to be called Bwana Safari anyway?

You see, he had this old-fashioned high-school
rabble style. You see in the press one morning that
we are going to march into the Republic and take over.
Like Africans on a lion hunt — stamping and singing
and cheering as they close in on the beast. To confuse
it you know, demoralise it. And you know the reper-
cussions down south. They don't play around, those
fellows, man. Then he'd tell the world we had cells in
the Republic, waiting for the sound of a kudu horn
from across the border we call *Lepapata* — you know
mos. Stupid boyish stuff like that — *baba bangmaak*.
So we called him Bwana Safari.

We couldn't stop in Zambia. The emergent Africans
wanted to jail us and we had to beg to be allowed to
pass on. We hit Katanga Province south of Zaire.
Worked our way up. The emergent Africans there
locked us up for being without travel papers. We're
not high-class refugees . . . . They spoke French, so
our words floated down on the Congo.

Malaria got me in the cells. One night I made a
desperate bid to escape. Through a window that had
no bars. In my underwear — no joking. For days and
nights I seemed to be dragging my soul behind me.
Hit Kinshasa at dusk one day, and don't ask me what

day. Made my way to the Nigerian embassy once I'd managed to piece together scraps of information about the directions.

Still in underpants?

Should've told you that by this time I had been provided with a wrapper, so I was fine — almost cool. Don't know how many times I washed my pants. Kept feeling all the time some bilharzia bug was out to get me — same feeling you get when you hear footsteps behind you in a dark street in Alexandra.

Why particularly Nigeria?

Do I know? — just instinct maybe. That and maybe also because I had read all those articles you used to write about Nigeria. I felt all along they know about us. Well, an official bought me a suit, took me into his house, fed and watered me. Said I could stay until I felt strong enough. Some light at least that came into the dark tunnel I was going through. Saved me from possible deportation, that big-hearted man did.

The Zaire jungle, Bra Zeke! Nights I sat awake. Even when I should have felt safe in a village house. The sky, the stars — the immensity of the whole thing — it simply terrified me. I had never watched the sky with such attention before. Away from the villages — remember how Conrad lingers on the fact of solitude — stays on it — shit man, Bra Zeke, seems like I felt the heart of it beat against my own: *gugu, gugu*.

Follow the river, my father always said. And he knew what he was talking about. Swallowed miles and miles of dust, that old man, from Northern Transvaal across the Drakensberg and hit the subtropical heat zone. From Natal to the Reef. Said he had the right to live anywhere — foolish old man. But everywhere he went he ran into fences. Foolish old man. That Congo solitude — you dangle on it like — like you were a tiny bird kicking and fighting to free itself from a string hitched to a star.

Nights I dreamed of Conrad's Kurtz, that crazy bastard. King Leopold's slaves and their skeletons; stacks of ivory I was trying to put on the backs of a herd of zebras as if they were a pack of donkeys, while a bunch of raggedy-assed whites were laughing from the other side of the Congo. Could hear their laughter clear across the water. I remember, in the dream, I was wondering if they were waiting for a French boat to come downstream . . . .

Though I had been initiated into fear when I served that stretch of three years on the Island. There you could only die, at worst, protected by four walls, by your fellow-prisoners, by those to whom you are important enough to keep in custody. Death can be flattering there. And then it's final. In that jungle you daydream about being torn to shreds by a monstrous solitude, by an insane freedom – simply picking you up, tossing you up on the tree-tops to pick you up again before you break your neck, to toss you into the river and fish you out again. You know how we fear to die just anywhere, specially when you're all alone – no voices, nothing – far away from your ancestors – *'n moer se skrik, ek sê vir jou.* The fear bored into me deep down like a giant corkscrew. Could feel it scrape inside my crotch and gnaw at my balls. Like you can hear those Soweto rats rustling and chewing on wood and cloth. And you lie there on the floor listening to their mischief and you know there's fuckall you can do about it.

I thought of Hammarskjöld, Tshombe, Lumumba, O'Brien, Kasavubu, Mobutu, remembering it was only three years ago that they paced this country and flew over it, caught up in a savage drama. Maybe I'm just a plain romantic. Are they really significant — I mean those guys — when history itself is simply a long, long story about man seeking freedom from one kind of tyranny and another? What do you think?

As one romantic to another, Steve — in my optimistic moments I tell myself that they are significant landmarks of history, in my pessimistic moments I see no politicians in power learning from history. They all come and pee on the floor of the house of history — just foul it up. When they remember history, it's only the people and events that glorify other men in power who come in for celebrations — those of whom the politicians can say, 'We've proved them right and we stand vindicated by them.'

Well, my friends joined me in Kinshasa — oh, about two months later. We were tossed from one official to another, one embassy to another. As long as that happened we weren't easy prey and the government couldn't throw us out. The unpredictable coons! They do it, you know. Especially when no organisation in exile can vouch for you. Seems like we were international files carted from one office to another, each with a reference number. At long last, a black American brother made things possible. Scholarships to study in the U.S.! A shipwrecked crew hanging on their bucking life-boats suddenly saw a boat coming — that's how it was for me .... I used to dream up that fancy imagery on the Island. Funny, when life's been emptied of all possibilities of victory you go to literature to look for them.

Casualties? Sure, we had several. But we all did our first degrees, that first batch. Which meant also the end of our student visas. Time to return, our sponsors said. Where to? They didn't know. Immigration put the heat on. We stalled. Some of us found a way out

— or was it an opportunity presenting itself? They married their Afro-American fiancées. Their citizenship was a protection. But Immigration never really had the heart to send people out, except for the grossest misdemeanours.

In Africa we'd have been carried by truck across some border or other and pitched into a neighbouring country, I can tell you that. A few of the marriages survived the broad daylight of truth, others busted. Mine has lasted. Terrific woman — no brag. Southern girl too. These northern ones are so uptight it's not funny anymore — uptight, on the defensive, always suspicious the male wants to exploit them.

My next dread was this — the marriage breaking up. Women have never had it so good in this country. It's a good thing, but some women can abuse their rights. To see some of our fellows trying to wriggle out of the noose after a separation is to taste another kind of fear. Divorce and death mean money and property in the U.S. Alimony, like coffins and flowers and hearses and stuff like that, are things no African should ever fool around with. They roast you man, you see yourself being turned this way and that — slowly on the barbecue grid, hearing yourself sizzle. I'm telling you like I hear the other guys tell it, I mean those who're crying.

I mean, take Fini for instance. Poor fellow was driven out of his house in the Bronx. Fini's wife decides the romance with Africa is over and he's no fun anymore. Maybe he really did stop being the lovable African. After helping him through his Ph.D. she thinks he's grown too big for his underpants. Woman from Detroit. See what I mean? I keep saying to the boys stay clear of the northerners. Too much into this male-female one-upmanship — fighting, clawing out the male's eyes practically, and Africa trying all the time to flaunt his head-of-the-family thing. I'll say this, though — I've met several black men who simply want to be mothered all the time, too. Always trying to return to the womb or the breast. Just plain spoiled no-count niggers, man. And now they've got a thing against Africans — I mean the blacks. Because they think their women prefer *us* to themselves. Who knows? May be true. I think some black women still hanker after an old-fashioned man whose weight they can feel and who makes them know at once where the authority lies. That's us, man! But they sleep with one eye open as we say, so the male doesn't exploit them. Weight watchers both ways.

I left upstate New York to live in Atlanta, Georgia. That's where I met my wife. T.B. struck and I found myself in a Boston sanatorium. You know, none of those fellows who used to be all over me in New York ever came to see me in the sanatorium. Except one. That's when I decided I was going to look after my own welfare. We'd been out of politics ever since we left Dar es Salaam. I'd been feeling stinking guilty since then. Now I hadn't the faintest desire to return. All these clowns who play politics in exile are a total mess. That was it, I was going to see to myself.

We married in Atlanta. I can never forget the African attitude in the mother when she said, 'Listen here, son, if the day should come when you feel you don't want my daughter any longer, don't kick her around, you hear? Just bring her back to us.'

I took Koni to upstate New York. The first two months we were sleeping on the second floor of a funeral parlour. A place the proprietor let us use without charge — must have reckoned it was spooky

enough. Sure the nights were spooky. I held two jobs
and managed to do the M.A. and Ph.D. at Syracuse.
And here we are. Casualties? Alcohol, grass, economics
— the country's strewn with them. Puerto Rico's fine.
We manage to bluff our way through with our Spanish.
Guess we'll be stopping here quite a while.

Summertime in London. A city pretending to be
tropical. Sunshades; scanty garments; hotpants;
humanity guzzling tons of ice-cream; piping cold
drinks into millions of bladders. This was the season
when, after seven years of exile, G.B. sent for his wife
Kenotshi. Came up from Jo'burg, with her grown-up
sons — three of them, the eldest already a man of
twenty-three.

G.B. played the alto sax. Hoped he could improve
his music reading. His sax was just fine for us in those
municipal halls where you could be playing by ear
and no one would be any wiser for it. Sound and
rhythm are all. What a musician lacked we compensat-
ed for with body movement on the floor. Just fine. In
London, G.B., like the Manhattan Brothers, had no
props. None whatsoever. His sound was foreign to the
natives. Took his life in his own hands. Struck out
for the professional route. G.B. a music maker,
Kenotshi a seamstress in a factory in the East End.
Fine.

Three years later:

'I wonder why you brought us here knowing you're
going to knock about London like this. Just selling
your tongue from one end of the city to the other. I
don't see you for nights. The night you come home
we quarrel. In front of Pirinki, too, and him hardly
fourteen. And Bra Zeke's in the next room. Can't
you even pretend to him you're okay?'

'Hei, Piri, give your papa a bottle of beer in the fridge there, my boy. Bra Zeke's with home folk here.'

'I asked you a question, Gusi.'

'Did you?'

'You heard me.'

'What did you say, woman?'

'You told me you'd left the club where you were playing. That was five months ago.'

'Yes, and so?'

'Where do you go and why can't you look for work like other men?'

'Are you saying I'm not a man? Hei Pirinki! Where's that boy?'

'Leave him alone, he's doing his homework in the bedroom.'

'Since when do I have to fetch my own beer?'

'I asked you a question. I'm not making much, there's rent, there's electricity, water, how can I manage alone?'

'Don't rub in the meaning of your name — *Kenotshi.*'

'You don't need to make fun of me, Gusi.'

'Sometimes I wonder if we shouldn't say it differently — *Ke notshi*. Every word you speak these days is like a bee-sting. It stays long in my flesh, and Makanda's ancestors alone know why my blood doesn't seem to affect you.'

'It does, you know. It makes my head spin like those factory wheels. But you're not going to drive me to the asylum — *No!*'

'Some folks say to the grave and you say asylum. Are you all right?'

'That's what I've been asking *you* all these months. Something's eating you. The sun shines into your arse because you sleep all morning.'

'I'm a musician — I can't help it if I can't find a gig.'

'You're not the only one. Thousands of others find other jobs. You're not just a South African, you're a plain black man too. Can you get it into your head?'

'You think I feel no pain?'

'What pain? What's so special about *your* pain? What about *mine*?'

'You won't understand. Sit down, Kenotshi. Everything I try in this music business simply collapses. My whole world is crumbling. I know we're a heavy load on you — me not working and all. It's not on purpose — I swear — don't ever think for one moment that I want to be cruel to you — *never* think that. I'll get it all right, don't worry. I'll work it all out. I'll find a job and still look for a gig. No, you'll never understand.'

'Ah, only too well. I'd feel pain too if I lolled around all day and then went out with the bats.'

'Watch it, Kenotshi, watch those barbed-wire words.'

'Oh why did you bring us here? — I want to know. We were all right back home even — well, it was rough, but we had people around us. I feel closed in here — this London — ugh!'

'Maybe you should go back.'

'And be a laughing stock among the people! Where did she think she was going to — I can hear them say. Some people just like going overseas, overseas, overseas — they like butter when there's plenty of jam. That's what they'll say. I'll stay here and see my two children through decent schools.'

'You exaggerate, Kenotshi. No one ever laughs at any one back home — I mean for failing. Ever see losers at the horse-races laugh at another loser? That's what we are back home — losers.'

'Oh, so now I'm a failure — is *your* horse winning

here?'

'Oh how you wear me out, woman!'

'You haven't had enough of me yet, Gusi. You haven't . . . .'

'Oh stop that crying. It upsets me — you know that.'

'Have you got another woman, Gusi? Tell me, *have* you? Why don't you answer me, *have* you?'

'We've been through all this — lots of times. Has a bull got an udder?'

'You shall not send me to the madhouse.'

'There you go again. Anyway, I meant to tell you tonight. I got a scholarship to study music in Boston.'

'Just what you always wanted to do — leave us here and never return to us, isn't it so?'

'Don't be crazy Kenotshi. It's only for a year.'

'Go, go, leave us — I know you're leaving us . . . I know — '

'Come on —'

'Gusi, something terrible is going to happen to this family. I feel it in my bones, I dream about it. Something terrible, I tell you. You'll see.'

'You're healthy — you'll come through. Me, I've got this pain in my chest — right here.'

'Why not go to a doctor? They'll treat you free of charge.'

'You just don't understand, do you?'

'Just too well. Back home in Western Township you were always running around with women — telling me the newspaper kept you working long hours — me sitting at home raising the children. You see Pirinki? He never knew his father — to say nothing of the older two.'

'Don't say things like that. It hurts me.'

'Damn well it should. And me? Do you know the hurt in a wife and mother who only knows her man in bed? And then you had to leave with the show, and stay on here to rot after it was finished.'

'I sent you money, didn't I?'

'For how long? If Father Simpson had not found money for us, we wouldn't even have travelled.'

'*Ag*, no use — no use — she'll never understand.'

'Maybe you don't know, me I know what you've been doing with other women here. Long before we came to you. People talk, you know. Is this the kind of life you were bringing us to? Gusi, I want to go back home, you hear? Give us money to go back. Please, please for God's sake. I beg you.'

'Here's a woman! You don't want to go back, then you want to. Besides, where's the money?'

'All right, I'll save up for it. Maybe you don't realise you're finished. Finished as a player. Finished, old man Gusi — me, I'm amazed at 42 you think you can still learn more music. Finished, hear me tell you. You were always a ghetto player, and this here is a white man's world — wake up, man!'

'No, I'm not! You'd like that, wouldn't you? Wait till I go to Boston and you'll hear of me out there — it'll be gig after gig. The pain inside me — it'll be a forgotten thing, I tell you. But what's the use, you don't understand the pain that's tearing me up inside. Doctors — ha! Quacks and quacks and quacks — all the instruments in the world will never get to this pain. Test after test after test and then they come up with crap like we don't know what it is but we think *miaow-miaow-miaow*. But you go back in that hole where you want to return. Not me. And I'm not going to allow you to take these children back to that dump. If you want to rot away there you should at least realise they have already tasted something of freedom.'

'Freedom to starve, freedom to blow their brains up with drugs, freedom to live in high-rent tenements like these?'

'Freedom is freedom, woman — freedom to take control of your own life — that's what I'm talking about. Ah, you wear me out. I'm going to bed.'

A telephone call coincided with the midnight chime of our clock. I picked up the receiver. G.B. had collapsed in Atlanta, Georgia. He was visiting from Boston. A few compatriots were going to carry his corpse to Boston so that the woman he was living with could bury him. He had finished two years of music school.

The octopus of American economics had enmeshed him; strangled him in no time. Tried to clear a high wall in flight from the pain that had been eating into his vitals since the live-or-die barefoot days of his ghetto upbringing. The wear and tear finally arrested the upward heave in mid-air. The fatal fall had to follow. Kenotshi never came to know it. She was in a mental asylum at the time on the outskirts of London. Three months after her husband's death, she followed him.

Ten years she waited. And waited. Serotana had jumped the fence as they say — left the country as a refugee. We called him that on account of his hunched shoulders.

Those were the days when the Man was on the loose, pacing up and down the land with giant strides. He was here, there, everywhere. Trials, Sharpeville, trials. How could one forget the tempestuous Sixties? Those he did not trample down he threw into his bag. Those were the days when the clouds of dust hung

red in the sky. Constantly. Made you think of the
dragons of folklore, blowing up dust with the wind
from his cavernous nostrils, whipping up more dust
with his feet and tail, leaving havoc behind him,
scattering villagers all over. You didn't know where
he was coming from, but he was coming all the same.
Those were the days of whirlwinds, of fear of loneliness, of longing. The dust settled in your gullet and
there seemed to be no relief ever.

Serotana was gone. Dineo waited.

London took him. Like any other African tossed
by history on to the lap of old Mother Empire. He
became just one of the thousands of West Indians and
Africans who had to survive the sting of Enoch Powell's
racist venom. He tried to find work as a journalist.
But the natives kept that house for their own kind. In
order to survive, Serotana went into full-time politics.
Exile politics.

'I wonder if the British have ever experienced exile,'
he kept asking himself . . . . 'No, they wouldn't know
such a thing.'

'I want to come and join you,' Dineo kept writing.
Year in and year out. 'This is unbearable . . . . How
long have I to keep fighting men off? . . . O let me
come! . . . I've had it up to my ears in this factory job
and crowded trains . . . . Now Mother is six feet down
I've nothing to stay here for . . . .'

Ten years. Then Serotana sent her an air ticket.

A two-roomed flat in Camden Town was the best
they could afford. Dineo dug her feet in. Thrifty,
practical. She displayed the tough mettle South
African black women are noted for.

She trained as a nurse. When she qualified she
found a job in a hospital. She saved up to buy a house.
When she did find it seven years later, Serotana

decided to bum. Bummed and drank himself into a
constant stupor.

'You never complain — why?'

'My whole life's been a complaint, Serotana, how
much more do you want to hear? If you complained
about a diet you've grown up on — what's the sense
in that?'

'You trying to shame me, working like this and
buying a house — what do you take me for? A donkey
standing in the rain and doing nothing to find cover?'

'Do you *want* to be a donkey? It's easy to grow his
kind of ears and bray, you know — the way you keep
drinking. *You* tell *me* — aren't you going to move
your bones and get out of the rain?'

'For what?'

'For what are you wasting yourself? And then you
want me to complain — to sour your life, so you have
more reason to accuse yourself and drink more? Besides, I'm too busy to sit and mope.'

'Now you're sounding like a lamb going to have its
throat cut.'

'Keep standing in the rain, old man. I've got to save
my strength and live — that's what. Now we're on the
subject — I don't want these South African louts
trooping into the house every time you have to have a
drinking concert. I've told you before.'

'It surprised me when you didn't complain. *Now*
you're acting like a real woman.'

'Ha-ha-ha-hiiiiii! You left me for so long back there
— wasn't it your purpose to toughen me? Now I'm
tough you don't like it so.'

'Don't talk foolishness, Dineo. I was too busy with
politics and there's no money in it, you know that.'

'What changed all that when you sent for me?'

'I quit the movement, you *know* that.'

'Surely not to look for work and support a loving wife.'

'You're asking for it, so you better shut up.'

'Who started the subject?'

'I've warned you.'

'Good night, my lord and master. But I should remind you — if any of that bunch shows up here to booze you up, I'm going to throw boiling water on them, you'll see — *ba tla bona bomma' bona* — 'strue — they'll start seeing their mothers fly over them like angels.'

'Leave my friends alone, you hear!'

'I'm not going to fight you, Serotana. Maybe what's left of you is craving for a fight. I won't give you that satisfaction — I've to protect my sanity and my health. So live the life you want — but I'm not going to finance it. I cried too much for too long, I've no tears any more. I wanted a child so badly. You kept saying you didn't want a child to grow up a refugee. Now I don't want it any more. Do you ever stop to remember there's a woman in this house? Wait a minute, let me empty my chest. No complaining, no. You black men spend so much time dreaming about the old days you left behind that you can't do what's got to be done here and now. That's what chokes me so about your friends. You sit here and count the political peanuts you picked up in your big rallies which you took for victories. You keep raking up dead fires and hurting yourselves to make believe you're still suffering — when you know damn well you're free to loaf or work.'

'Am I going to shut up your mouth?'

'Just you dare come near me. All right. Now you're on your feet get on with it and let me see. No? Thought as much. You've never done it before and it's too late to learn now. I've finished. Be warned about those bums. Tell them this is not a community centre or a soup kitchen.'

On various occasions Serotana had been in hospital to be dried out. But he was back on the bottle again.

'We're going back home, Dineo. At most I'll serve a jail sentence for having left without a passport, and I'll live again.'

'I'm not a goods train, Serotana — you hear me! — grinding the same track mindlessly up and down, down and up, south north, north south, because its tracks are the only world it knows. So me, I stay here for better or for worse — in fact it has proved to be for the better so far. I stay here, me, the daughter of Mabiletsa who's sleeping at Croesus.'

American Style

We had left Kefilwe and Motswiri behind in Denver when we went to Zambia. As we were not sure how things would work out, we did not want to withdraw them from the American system of education. When we returned to Denver, they rejoined the family.

The American teenage bug had got to them. The bug that told them that at eighteen they should cut loose from their family: set up on their own or with their peers. So Motswiri (18) and Kefilwe (21) came and went and came and went, dropping out of college and returning — American style.

Tony got married in Zambia — to a black American. They had a son. She left him behind, went back to her folks in the Bronx. She was keen to help him lose his wanderlust, which displayed itself in a failure or unwillingness to get his teeth into something concrete as a career, and thus channel his undoubted intelligence and sensitivity. He was painting, but would not submit to the training he sorely needed — something we wanted badly to assist him in.

We paid his fare to Denver. His wife and child joined him. It didn't work. He left for the east coast, his family back to the Bronx. Rebecca and I always asked ourselves if he was a victim of exile, or whether there was something innate about his refusal to submit to discipline — authoritarian or self-generated. Something that was there all along. Who knows with these things? There is an inner mystery about growth in the personality that resists analysis and isolation — the kind scientists impose on a virus.

During the third year back in Denver Rebecca was accepted into the Master's programme in the School of Social Work at the University of Denver. It was a two-year programme, and she thoroughly enjoyed it.

In a predominantly white city like Denver, blacks generally, but especially Africans, tend to be looked at as a curiosity. And yet it is not unusual in the mid-west and the Rocky Mountain west — away from the large black ghettos — to find African-Americans behaving like whites towards Africans.

'This black kid comes to me,' Chabi reports at home. 'He says: "You come from that place where they eat giant lizards, eh?" '

'What's wrong with those black kids?' says Chabi. 'This one says to me, he says: "Think you're cool living with 'em honkies in Bonnie Brae, right?" '

A day after I had made a TV appearance, a black girl in Puso's class teased him in the presence of other classmates: 'I saw your dad on TV last night, Puso.' she turned to the audience. 'I see Puso's dad take out a whopper of a bead from Puso's head — a real whopper to show the viewers. Why don't you do somethin' 'bout your naps, Africa? Shoot!' 'I'm Africa, I've got naps,' Puso replied, 'what more can a man ask for?'

My choice of courses to teach was pretty eclectic. I taught African, Caribbean and Afro-American literatures; the English Romantics and the Eighteenth-Century background; criticism of the novel; British and American writing of the Thirties; creative writing: fiction. The number of themes on which to base courses from these broad categories excited my sense of adventure.

As long as I was immersed in my work, as long as I gloried in the intellectually stimulating life on American campuses, the condition of exile did not weigh on me.

I visited several universities in the United States and Canada in the nine years I was at Denver and Philadelphia. About thirty — one-night, two-day, week-long lectures on some topic in African or Afro-American literature. The extra-mural donkey all over again!

The Living Dead

But one felt diminished every time another exile or refugee was diminished. Oftentimes it was diminution by death.

Like Selby Mvusi, whose remains were shipped from Kenya to his home province, Eastern Cape. He died in a car crash in Thika, in full view of the town's flame trees. He had been hounded out of Ghana when that country's immigration authorities were being instigated to run out South Africans by the white South African editor of an Accra newspaper. Mvusi went to Uganda after he had barely escaped being shipped on a PANAM plane to South Africa by order of some Ghanaian official. It is always said that Kwame Nkrumah knew nothing about this expulsion, one of several. The captain of the plane decided in Zaire that he couldn't carry out the order. He allowed Mvusi to go anywhere else he chose . . . . With a Boston University degree in fine arts, he found a job at the University of Nairobi when we were also in Kenya.

Inscrutable Mvusi . . . . Something was troubling him, chewing up his vitals. We never got to know what it was. He had created some impressive art in black and white when he was still in South Africa. After art school his creativity dried up. He was frequently negative towards other artists, including Sekoto. No African artist was any good. He would sit in the living room, with his long legs stretched out full length. He had long and large hands which would have been a bossboy's pride on a white man's farm. I imagined how those hands would simply twine around a sheaf of ripe lucerne and sever it with a sickle at one go: *twine, rip, twine, rip!* He had very little love for people. What *is* it that has knotted up inside the man? I kept asking myself. Or has exile got to him? Now he is gone . . . .

Like Archibald Jordan, doctor of philosophy in African languages. Novelist. we met for the first time at the first Congress of Africanists, December 1962. The two of us led the South Africanists' committee. Cancer ran him to earth when he was professor of African languages at the University of California, Los Angeles. He is resting in Madison, Wisconsin, where his widow lives.

Like Todd Matshikiza. His mound stands in a

Lusaka graveyard. Short little man. Unpredictable temper. A coil of barbed wire beneath the cultured, jovial, even-tempered exterior. Don't take it ill, Toddy-boy. I'm telling my fellow-mortals — aren't we all inscrutable mortals, even the most predictable fool? Remember that musical we staged at Adams College? You played the piano. The very day of the performance you said, *I'm not going to play anymore.* I sent the late Walter Gumbi to intercede, beg you not to pull out. Without you we'd have no music, no play. About noon you say *okay.* We go into a dress rehearsal.

You created 'Matshikeeze' for us in *Drum*, and then it died when you highballed to London and then on to Lusaka. Almost regained it in *Chocolates for My Wife* — but I guess that's what exile does to one's style. Remember also how you wept when you told us Art Tatum was dead? How you wept when you told us comedian Victor Mkize had died in a car crash on the way from Durban? That was Matshikeeze through and through. The few times I've seen Esmé whom you left behind — calm and pretty as always, the very picture of composure — have made me remember how she fought hard for years to stop the leak in your busted dam. Seems like it had begun to crack even before you started work on *King Kong* and she couldn't prevent the crack from widening once you'd gone with the show to London. I also hoped I could arrest the flow, Todd, when I obtained a grant from Congress to help you study orchestration and keep you in food and shelter, but . . . .

Remember, Toddy, the dinner we had at your house? You had invited a bunch of us from *Drum* and *Post* and our wives. I remember Esmé sitting under a lampshade after she and Rebecca had washed up. They sat next to each other. The line between light and shade made an arc below Esmé's nose so that her eyes were inside the shadow. Her face was just breathtaking, like that. So calm, so coy-looking, yet so present, so full of compassion. You know, that kind of compassion on a woman's face that seems inexhaustible, all-encompassing.

I was thinking this when a voice from outside (I mean outside my tiny, contemplative corner) said, above the babble, 'You're just a hobo, George Gaboo, just a hobo.' It was Henry Nxumalo.

'At least I beg on the Jo'burg City Hall steps, Henry, but you beg at Joubert Park among the drooling Whites — where you're not allowed to sit.'

I was yanked out of my corner, only *then*, by Henry's 'I won't take that crap from you Councillor-whatever-your-name-is!' This was accompanied by the clatter of side tables as Henry stood up. Soon there was a scuffle. He hammered George on the shoulder with his fist. Two other boys and I leapt towards the pair to separate them. Henry's arm shot out like a piston towards me, and the blow sent me reeling back. Man alive! If there hadn't been the wall behind me to check my backward momentum . . . well, you can imagine! Amazing how much horsepower a Henryful of liquor — no small quantity — can pump into a man's muscle.

On my return from the wall I tripped over a fallen side table. Silly, because those days I had no taste for liquor and so was shamefully sober. One of the legs of the table broke. Councillor George Gaboo saved himself by walking out of the house the moment he wrenched himself free from Henry's hold.

I turned to you and said half in jest, half serious, 'I believe you'll want me to pay for the table now, Todd?' You raised your shoulders, turned your head left and right in the obsessive mannerism you had, as if you were constantly easing the hold of your collar round your neck. Then you looked me straight in the eye and blurted, 'Fuck you, you hear me, fuck you, I say! What d'you take me for — a fuckin' third hobo?' You then said to Henry curtly, 'Hey man, go home.'

Henry took a deep breath and asked us to take him home. The first and last time I ever heard him make such a request.

And Can Themba. He lies in Swaziland. Canadocea — what a name for an unclassical fellow like you. When I say this to you in that Fordsburg shebeen, you turn round and say, how come a barefoot boy wallowing in the dust of Marabastad with two large holes in the seat of his pants found himself saddled with a Hebrew name like Ezekiel? I say maybe my illiterate father Moses thought Hebrews were sweet. But no — I remember now — Ezekiel was my granny's father's name – granny on my mother's side. You then say, I forgive you, son. And you look at Casey and you say, now look at this mosquito — why would son-of-Motsisi be called Casey? I bet you his father originally said he should be Malachi or Shadrack or even Hitler. And this mosquito was clever enough to duck them all. You see, son, we were colonised, and the white man's name spells power. Trouble with you, Can, I say, is that you're too intelligent to have been at Fort Hare. What have you got against the Fort? you ask. Nothing, 'cept that all Fort Hare guys think the same way. And then you accuse me of being envious 'cause I could never get there.

You pulled the strands together in *Drum*, Can. And your diction was high voltage. You gave your verbs colour and power — you let them yield all the energy you could extract from them. One lousy thing was that you couldn't sing — you always sang or whistled out of tune, off key — remember? You were down on religious sentiment, on the sanctity of man's life. The ultimate cynic. What was it you feared — your own intellectual brilliance? Apolitical too, remember? You'd hear Mozart at Bloke's place, and you'd say, who's weird music is that? And Mozart is sentiment. Why? Let it be, let it be. You had a will to die, as a compiler of your writings was later to say. Actually called the volume *The Will To Die* — I'll have you know.

You know, Can, when I came back I so wanted to see Casey. I had written to him twice from somewhere during my wanderings. He never replied. Back here I was in the north and couldn't make contact. Then he goes and dies. And I say to Rebecca, there goes another of the *Drum* majors. But at least he lies on ancestral ground. Cold comfort? You'll never know he's also gone, Can. *You* knew what the spiritual wasteland is, in spite of yourself, you the equation that could never be solved; you who were incapable of even hating.

Like Gwigwi Mrwebi. Township jazz, sax. *Drum* circulation boss. Lies somewhere in the United States. You used to say to me, *Kyk hierso, nefie,* you'd say, *jy's a teacher nie a reporter nie.* Fuckoff and go back to school, man. I'd reply, what can I do man, *wat kan 'n mens doen in hierdie omstandighede?* Listen to him, outjies, you'd say, just listen to him. That's no damn shebeen language. *Omstandighede* — hell, *sê conditions,* man. What's wrong with *conditions?* And then you burped, Gwigwi. A large royal burp. Remember you used to say to me, *nefie,* I just take soda water and my tummy sits easy on my belt. Chases your gas out of the whatchamacallit like nobody's business. So far away, Gwigs — so damn far away.

And Alfred Hutchinson, prose writer. The road to Ghana, after baling out of the Treason trial of 1956-1960. London, Sussex. Now your body lies in Northern Nigeria. You loved me so, Hutch, as I loved you. Gentle, vulnerably sensitive and yet private. Your short stories still possess that haunting ring, like your play, *The Rainkillers*. The melody of a soul in torment. *Something* tormented you, Hutch, though you could never let on that it did. The unhappy ending of your marriage, and Africa took you back to her bosom. Remember the Donaldson Orlando Community Centre, when you taught in our private school? We never said much, until we met in London. A product of Fort Hare and yet not of it. What ails thee, knight at arms, alone and palely loitering? Such desolate loneliness as I always read in your expressive face, Hutch, and which I could find no answer to, till it sent a spear through me. At last I decided, not without anger and hopelessness, to give up searching. You were not part of the herd. But I've no instinct for that myself. Only, with the kind of partner I have, maybe I can afford not to be part of the herd. Northern Nigeria — Hutch — is such an outpost. How I wish impotently that I had been there so that we could help each other over the long interminable exile that grinds some of us under. And your letters about your marital troubles pierced through me, and I wished I could jet it to Surrey . . . . Oh Hutch!

Like Arthur Nortje, now lying in Oxford, England. I never knew you, Arthur. But I know now from your *Dead Roots* how lonely you must have been. Loneliness hounded you and grounded you. You *would* go and do something like that — die and leave us on our own — with no more from your pen to renew us. We cannot afford to lose any more poets. How close to my bone when you say 'the isolation of exile is a gutted warehouse at the back of pleasure streets . . . the solitude that mutilates . . . .' Those long silences, the tenacious hopes, the polluted mind, the pain that constrained you to sing . . . . Ah, Arthur . . . was it a will to die — that stuff you were taking in the solitude of your Oxford rooms?

And Nathaniel Nakasa, journalist. You were just a cub when you joined us on *Drum*. Like Lewis Nkosi. But you stayed on the job. Until you became a reporter to reckon with on a white paper. Then the exit. The ugly experiences with immigration authorities in East Africa. New York. A black South African reporter in New York! Then we heard of your assignment to do something on the South for *Time*. Something went wrong with the job? Then the final violent exit when you took the jump many floors down to the Greater Silence. What hurt you, Nat? What it was that you succumbed to, when you had survived all this I've come back to, will never be known. Your boyish face as I last saw it in 1957 remains indelible in my mind.

Like M. Mangoaela, lying in Washington D.C. Killed by asthma and hypertension. You had it rough at Howard University, didn't you — with that yearly contract as lecturer in African languages? Washington was the worst place for asthma — you must have known that. When I asked you to come and take my position in African literature in Denver which is a mile high, you were fearful that you would not fit in — because you had never studied African literature in English and French, you would have a lot of reading to get through . . . . I tried to press you, but you knew best your own capacities. I keep feeling Denver would have given you a new lease of life, even though you had only the Master's. Couldn't blame you, though — as one gets older, one's desire for adventure grows pale.

The political movements also sustained losses. Men I had met countless times at the crossroads of exile. Like J.B. Marks, Moses Kotane, Robert Resha, Duma Nokwe. Then there were David Sibeko, M.P. Naicker, Eduardo Mondlana of Mozambique, Herbert Chitepo of ZANU. More recently, George Peake, and Tennyson Makiwane who was murdered in the Transkei.

I was touched when news came of the deaths of these men. But why was I not affected in the same way as I was by the departure of these men I have been talking to? Maybe it is the degree of intimacy with the writers that deepens the sense of loss. The politicians were public men in quite a different way from the writers, and intimacy with the former is subject to fiercer storms and winds. In addition to which I was not really a political activist, and still am not. The greater part of my active life has been with writers, artists, teachers. Then there is another kind of grief that moves us. This is when someone has been assassinated whose cause we also share. But this is an occasion that stuns us even before we can acknowledge grief. Martin Luther King, Malcolm X, Onkgopotse Tiro, Chitepo, Mondlana, Anwar Sadat, Sibeko.

Against the casualties are those exiles who are still vigorously alive and have commendable courage to show for it: Mazisi Kunene, teaching African languages at the University of California, Los Angeles; Dennis Brutus, who until recently taught at Northwestern University, Evanston, Illinois; Keorapetse Kgositsile, teaching at the University of Dar es Salaam; Daniel Kunene, teaching at the University of Wisconsin; Arthur Maimane, journalist in London; Bloke Modisane, about whom I know nothing more than his long

stay in Italy after England; Mongane Serote, in Botswana, with a most adventurous poetic style and a
startling directness of impact. No frills, no convolut-
ions but always refreshing, who has now published a
novel — *To Every Birth Its Blood;* Isaac Makhudu
Rammopo, teaching at the Teachers College, Zatia
(Nigeria), an old childhood friend, who is talking
seriously of returning home.

I cannot help but linger a while on the last two
exiles I want to mention. Alex la Guma, London, and
Lewis Nkosi, head of English, University of Zambia.
Alex was at the vortex of the turbulence during the
Fifties and into the early Sixties as a member of the
Executive in the Congress Alliance. The Defiance
Campaign of 1952, the Coloured People's Congress,
the Treason Trial of 1956-1960, acquittal, house arrest,
exile. Throughout he had been writing articles and
short stories for *New Age* and *Fighting Talk.* After his
prize-winning *A Walk in the Night,* Alex wrote more
short stories and brought them out in one volume
together with the *Walk.* Abroad he continued to
produce novels.

I met him a few times in London and at an African
writer's conference in Stockholm in 1967. A self-
avowed marxist, Alex documents his setting (District
Six in the earlier fiction) minutely, so that it takes on
a life of its own as a character. Human character must
itself be seen to be intimately involved with setting.

There's nothing in Alex of the radical posturing we
have come to associate with marxists who enter every
debate with the rhetoric that is a routine attack on
capitalism — a way of self-introduction. Alex is cool,
and his face radiates a warmth that can't escape you.

Lewis has written short fiction, a play, and he has
steadily been turning out criticism. He was on *Golden*

City Post when I was on *Drum*, having arrived practically green from Durban. He looked frail, half-starved, as if any moment you could fly him as a kite. I used to see him with fat books under his arm which he must have been studying privately. Even began to talk like a man who has made a startling discovery. And yet he still has a sense of fun. Not in the least the studious-fastidious anti-social type. The exile. The London *Observer*, free-lancing. Then the academic — a Master's and a Doctorate.

In Paris I had edited the *South African Bulletin,* which the Congress had asked me to initiate. A fortnightly news digest and editorial column. I had ample freedom to express my views editorially without claiming that they were shared by the Congress. When I left Paris I asked Lewis to take over the editorship. He made a magnificent job of it.

His critical writing has grown from strength to strength in perceptiveness, depth and self-assurance. His latest essays — *Task and Mask* — show a firmer grasp of literary events than the rather tentative *Home and Exile.* Needs to be compassionate, less pedantic in tone, and less absolutist. But this comes with age and maturity.

Since 1966 these living writers in exile have been banned from the South African public under the Internal Security Act. This law provides a listing of authors whose works may neither be circulated nor quoted in South Africa.

For my part, I have described how the books that could not be circulated while I was 'listed' have been released. *Down Second Avenue* and *Voices in the Whirlwind*, for example, are now available. Those that were banned under the Publications Act remain prohibited: *The African Image* (revised edition) and

The Wanderers, which I had reworked from the Ph.D.
book for publication by Macmillan of New York. The
new manuscript was also entered in a contest organised
by the journal *African Arts,* University of California.
It won first prize as the best African novel for 1968-9.

East African Publishing House in Nairobi had published my short stories — the South African ones and
those written in exile — under the title *In Corner B
and Other Stories* (1967). This volume and *African
Writing Today* which I had compiled for Penguin
were also axed under the Publications Act.

Abroad, some of us felt cheated out of something
— an audience — and had to be content to write for
that vaguely defined 'world intelligence'. We would
never know the reactions of those whose concerns we
shared in South Africa, and who made the material for
our writing. We might be applauded or discredited by
critics whose criteria we didn't care for. We were
indeed like disembodied voices crying out for a
dimension that will give them meaning.

Even as I mumble thus to myself, I am aware that
writers don't make revolutions, they wield no power
that immediately counts in the struggle for political
and economic power. Creators of serious imaginative
literature are engaged in a middle-class occupation,
and can only be read by those among the educated
who move beyond the drug-store thriller. It does not
matter if we write about the concerns of the common
man sometimes or always. We are not read by *him.*
The politicians and financiers run our world, not
people who play with images and symbols. Politicians
and financiers run the Third World even though they
may not live there. Yet we keep writing, because we
are obeying a compulsion. I might go insane if I did
not write. It is a therapy for ourselves, and it is no use

deceiving ourselves that the world will be saved by poetry or the arts in general. But we must produce literature because it is a cultural act, a cultural imperative. I can only see its cumulative impact in the context of a national culture, a culture that has a definite geographic place.

If a writer wants to promote a political revolution he must go out among the crowds as a *man*, go into action. If he must write, he has to use the prose of everyday life. That speaks a direct language. He must know that his imaginative literature is, in public terms, at best an investment in the cultural well-being of his people that will mature, if it ever does, in the distant future.

Imaginative literature should revitalise or keep alive a language and experience, and it should increase our capacity to feel. These are perennial revolutionary imperatives. Literature should not have to wait for the day of conscription or the draft.

I look at the Rockies, thirty miles to the west of me. I don't like mountains. The mountains of my youth still haunt my dreams and I remember the dark nights when I often had to sleep in them. Whenever I draw near the foot of the Rockies, they loom before me, unfriendly, like giant apes marooned on a patch of Time. And I cannot join the crowds that seem to experience an orgasm in their contact with the mountains. I cannot be ecstatic about snow either.

The tyranny of place .... When I arrived in Denver, Colorado, in 1970, I bought a house, whose owner decided to leave a piano in the basement because it would cost sixty dollars to have it carried out. He flatly refused to acknowledge the responsibility to have it removed. I started to hack it down with an axe. I threw the iron frame down on the concrete floor and the damn thing shattered. Some friends and others who heard of it were horrified, because the instrument was still in good working condition. That was a moment of glory for me. I did not see why I should inherit someone else's junk. You love your own junk because it has a smell that expresses *you*. I needed more room for my four children: if they want to learn to play the piano, they can work and buy their own when the time is ripe. I resented being drawn into a piano-ornamented culture.

This mood of rejection, of revolt against the brittle elegance of suburbia, its rectangular, well-ordered, antiseptic manners carried over to another object — the crabapple tree. This highly fertile thing grew in front of my yard. We spent the first summer sweeping away fruit that had fallen and was decaying in the water on the sidewalk. By the next summer I had got someone to dig out the damn thing. Again some of my tree-stricken friends expressed horror. Kill such a lovely tree, ecology and all! You could have made jam with all that fruit; you should see the blossoms in the spring . . . . So they said. But my next-door and opposite neighbours were happy, annoyed as most suburbia is by highly fertile things and beings. Having been raised in the country where you have all the wild nature you want, and more, and in an urban slum where we swept the yard every day, I can't get excited over the tending of a lawn. I'm still working on an idea: that of digging out the confounded stuff in front and terracing that part of the yard with stones. Then I can hose it and sweep it in the good old style.

I seem to be doing everything to court and diminish alternately the tyranny of place. A tyranny that gives me the base to write, the very reason to write. And yet only seldom does an exile get to live on his own terms. I don't know. You look at the Rockies. They seem to say to you, you've been moving fifteen years. Here's where you stop. Try climbing over and you stop dead at the Pacific. You're not Cortez, you know . . . . If I can't return to Africa, I must still have place. I must know who I'm speaking to. Not place in the theatre of the mind. But a place that contains real life. There's the rub. I must stay with the South African reality. A reality so deeply rooted in thirty-seven years of my life that I can never lose it. That is its tyranny and its value as the root of my kind of commitment to human justice in a place called South Africa.

Exile. From innocence to experience to the acceptance and resentment of placelessness, of the memory of the cries and sirens. The voice of caution against the urge to throw yourself into other people's cultural battles and causes, in search of a commitment, merely on the strength of one's colour . . . . The ironies and paradoxes of the black world. Oh the games we play with one another, we blacks. Pan-African slogans notwithstanding! Fiction resists ideology even while it can be informed by it. Hence my fixation on peace, on another dimension, or level, or order of commitment.

It's a long black song. They sang it centuries ago, our ancestors. And here we are out in the cold: exiles. We are the never-ending story that began that long time ago. We are the extension of their woe. Of their blues. Sophie Tucker, I hear your blues:

> *You said you love me but you treat me wrong.*
> *I ain't never loved nobody and I never will,*

hope I never will.

But that's not the theme I'm talking about. Yes, we
sing your blues too, there on high savannah in the
Transvaal. The story of the forsaken wife, lover,
brother . . . . But tonight it's not that theme that's
rankling in my head and sucking slowly on the marrow
of my spine. It's not that the man done treat you
wrong here in this south.

Always someone had to be taken far away from his
home, and his woman waited and waited. There was
Makhanda, called 'the left-handed', on Robben Island.
His women, his children, waited.

There was the man of Gaza kingdom in Mozambique the Portuguese took to the Canary Islands. He
died there. His women, his children, waited.

The European and Arab slave-hunters chased after
Africans, black also hunted black. The slave trade
propped Asante Kingdom in West Africa.

The unbroken songs of sorrow . . . . I hear them in
your blues, Nina Simone. You tell me you want a
little more sugar in your sugarbowl. Let me hear some
more:

> *I want a little sweetness down in my soul*
> *come on, save my soul*
> *I could stand some loving*
> *I feel so sad.*

And the women and children waited, waited, for
those who might never return, for those who might
bring back only broken minds, broken bodies. So it
must have been for Makhanda when the British sent
him to the Island. Tried to swim for it, but . . . .

You say, Nina, you say:

> *Ain't no use listening*
> *Old Man Sorrow's coming to*
> *keep me company*
> *whispering beside me*
> *when I say my prayers,*
> *Old Man Sorrow mounting*
> *all the way with me*
> *telling me I'm old now*
> *since I lose my man.*

I hear you and words sink deep and chill my marrow because the record of history unfolds interminably. Replays to me the bitter conflict.

I hear women cry for men and sons taken away in droves to the mines. A rockfall down the mine. Mine collapses. A flooded pit. Eroded lungs. Anything. I don't know why I keep on listening to the sting of your words.

> *Mister Backlash, Mister Backlash*
> *just what do you think I am?*
> *I'm going to leave you with*
> *the Backlash blues . . . .*

Still the blues come rushing at me. You're on, Dinah Washington, you're on. I hear you. And I know you were hurt bad, black woman. You burnt yourself up. Slowly. Till the fire settled down to a smoulder. The next thing you were out and gone. That stuff you pumped into your body: how could you have outlived it? But tonight it's not that that's on my mind. It's:

> *tears can never mend a broken heart*
> *I'm closing the door of memories.*

And I refuse to close the door. Because the storm out there keeps raging. And it's howling and banging about like some beast in torment. I cannot but remember. Your blues lyrics take me along with you when you sing:

> *on the lonesome hill*
> *I look down with tears in my eyes*
> *on the house we used to live . . . .*

Your song grinds blues home into my wounds, Dinah. Takes me back to *my* south. It's always someone who's taken away from those he loves. They wait. For all the fire of bluestone in my wounds I keep listening. It's a fire that ennobles sorrow. So let me keep listening:

> *Nobody knows the way I feel this mornin'*
> *If only I had my way . . . .*

But I couldn't ever wish for the graveyard, Dinah. No, couldn't pawn myself. Don't wish to be a sinker on a fishing line, like your song says. But I could scream and cry (like you):

> *This mornin'*
> *I'm leaving here on a southbound train*
> *this mornin'*

They wait for men who never come. And the woman must cry like you, Dinah:

> *Blues ain't nothing*
> *but a woman crying for her man.*

He is gone to the mines. He has jumped the fence. Tunnelled through the womb of a continent across the Limpopo, then the Zambezi. Holds on to the cold respectability of professional politics. Because he was never accorded it before. He has always been in funct- ional resistance politics — out of a desperate necessity. Or he settles for the dubious security of the profession- al refugee. Or for the other dubious respectability of academic life. Always the outsider.

Back home his woman waits. You said it, Dinah:

> *When she wants lovin'*
> *everyone can understand*
> *Blues ain't nothing but a good woman*
> > *feelin' bad*
> *disgusted and feelin' sad*
> *Blues ain't nothin' but a common lowdown*
> > *disease.*

You keep pushing, Dinah, don't you. Relentlessly. Your song bores into me like a corkscrew. Because I can hear this woman echo it:

> *The brook runs into the river*
> *the river runs into the sea*
> *If I don't run into my baby*
> *the train's goin' to run over me*
> *If I could holler like a mountain jack*
> *I'd go up on the mountain*
> *and call my baby back.*

Must the woman orchestrate your cry, Billie Holliday,

now a long time gone but still grinding the blues for us? Can she say to her man,

> *Love some other spring,*
> *sun shines around me . . .*
> *Let's forget the old dust*
> *and love some other spring . . . .*

No. Deep down in her heart it's cold. Her story has been told millions of times. It's the long black song.

Immigrants

Americans like to say that they are an immigrant nation. Except for the Indians, who were found there, and the blacks, who were shanghaied. They like to open up their insides and display them on television, in the press, so that they show every little disorder, the muck in every little pocket of the anatomy. Generally, they talk just too much. Tune into any telephone-talk programme on the radio and this confessional diarrhoea cannot but alienate you, if you're not American. And then you remember how many lonely people there are. People who haven't the slightest capacity to create their own avenues of amusement. And then you think you understand a little about the compulsive talking on the radio programme.

Our children, not counting Tony who was in Africa much of the time until 1972, adjusted effortlessly. We never insisted on their speaking Sesotho with us. We spoke English and Sesotho between ourselves. We reckoned that a child conquers his environment through language. And the best medium was that which dominated their learning environment at school and in the street.

At home a child only hears an adult vernacular, or at best the language of other children if he has brothers and sisters. Some immigrants persistently spoke their home language to their children in the hope that even if the child did not find the language of practical use in dealing with the larger environment, his mind would record the sounds. Came the day of a return home, the language would spring cheerfully to life like some resilient Arctic plant in the spring. I have observed the expression of harrassment and bewilderment and insecurity in the faces of such children.

So we decided that if our children wanted to return home, they could learn or relearn our mother-tongue and any other African language of their choice. If they decided to remain abroad, English as an international language would be an asset. Besides, Africans readily learn the language of their milieu, the language they need for upward or horizontal mobility.

But the cost — ah the cost — of the adventure! You learn not only a language but also the culture it carries. The peer group soon rushes in like bedbugs upon the unprotected outsider, the human flesh lying naked on a bed. From then on it was a desperate silent war between us and the children's peer group. Each of us wanted to stake a claim on the children.

The American culture, to whatever extent we can call it 'American', was sucking them in, limb by limb, voraciously. There are levels at which it is extremely accessible, even pleasurably so. Not because it had anything to gain by adding five young Mphahleles to its numbers. But simply because its mouth is forever open. To use another analogy, American liberty, however relative, forges its own chains of enslavement. After all it is a living organism. But this organism continually splits into smaller organisms, into micro sub-cultures: the rich, the poor, some of whom make up the contingent that receives foodstamps and welfare; Catholics, Protestants, the youth, the drug community, bohemian types, the white Mafia, the black Mafia. Then there are groups that are committed to a cause, e.g. blacks, Puerto Ricans, Chicanos, Indians, the gays, women, Republicans who will lay down their lives and cheat and lie in support of big business, including corporations, Democrats who support big business without shouting about it and are anti some-thing that is superficially regarded as 'conservative'. Racial groups referred to as 'minorities' often find themselves pre-empted in the nation's consciousness by women and homosexual groups. Then there are the black Muslims and their factions, the anti-Castro Cubans of Florida. There are the twilight creatures like derelicts, drunks, drug addicts. And so on, a list that could extend into sub-divisions.

This can be so painfully bewildering for immigrant families. One is constantly fighting to instil a basic sense of common decency in one's children, in the absence of a communal structure that could foster and promote a distinctive pattern. This is one para-mount thing African-Americans enjoy and which neutralises or diminishes the pain of white racism and political impotence at the top levels of national administration. The Jewish community, especially the contingent of two million in New York city, seems to have had the advantage of being able to negotiate the transition from an insecure immigrant status to that of economic privilege and therefore political power. They were born with the right colour, after all.

Consider speech habits. Much of America, including the northern African-Americans, have lost the dignity and gentility of language on which young-elder, child-parent relationships hinge. A father or mother calls a child and the reply is 'What?' varying in tone from apparent impatience to genuine desire to know what the parent wants. No equivalent of 'what' in African languages that I know of would sound polite. So our children have grown up to say, 'Yes, Mama,' or 'Yes, Ntate.'

Their male and female friends phone and say, 'Is Puso there?' or 'Is Chabi there?' — without any word of greeting or request to speak to the boys. We gave up trying to correct them, but our boys understood where the rudeness lay.

What we refused to abdicate was the right to expect the boys' visitors to be polite and not just ring the doorbell and ask straightaway, without greeting, 'Is Puso here?' Even the simple 'Hi!' or 'How you doin'?' we wanted to refine. 'You're going to have to greet properly in this house,' Rebecca would say, 'this is not a restaurant.'

I consistently refused to chauffeur my boys to their dates. Africans never enter courting relationships their children are involved in, until they have developed to an unmistakable seriousness. We are generally not curious to know our boys' girlfriends. If I drove them to their dates, how could I cope with the natural caprice of youngsters, the fickleness, the adventurous nature of love affairs? American parents, on the contrary, like to get involved in their children's amusements, in their dates. They love to be consciously 'doing things with them'. They like to wallow in the molasses of their children's love woes, fancies and ecstasies. We could not with any feeling of certainty condemn these concerns as wrong. They were simply alien to us.

Our eldest three children, who are on their own now, have lived their cycle of rejection and reconciliation, departure and return, in their relationships with us. Nothing essentially different from what has been going on in Africa this half of the century. But the cultural base was lacking in the United States. In Africa you don't have far to run if you try to flee family controls. Soon you run into a whole formidable network of cultural sanctions from one community to another. And you get to know that silent conspiracy that howls its censure in your ears. In the U.S. it was relatively easy for one to disappear into the larger milieu where communal censure is almost unheard of. Because the milieu is fragmented.

But there comes a moment every immigrant youth — European, African, Oriental, Oceanic, Puerto Rican, Chicano — comes to acknowledge along with the realisation that they are still outsiders: it is that the parents are still where they always were culturally and provide a climate of love, stability, protection. They will always be there, like a boulder.

Eighteen is a crucial age for the American. At eighteen a person can do a number of things without parental permission. Military service starts at eighteen.

In some states, if a person leaves home at eighteen, no court of law can order him to return. Parents who want to continue to exercise loving authority over him or her, especially in order to see son or daughter safely through school or college, must simply seek another approach.

We saw black boys persuaded by their white peers to take off. Especially when they wanted a black boy who could fulfil their own sense of power and supremacy over blacks. The perverse irony is that the day the black youth wakes up he finds that his peers have moved back into white conventional life, moved into good jobs. He may even have to seek employment through them! He has come full circle. He learns once again the meaning of blackness and whiteness. The bitter lessons of inequality that he is still impotent to reverse.

The traditional African attitude, too, is that the eighteen-year-old is a man or woman, capable of self-care. But the wrench is seldom as violent as in the United States. The African male has by then been learning to be responsible — right from the age of ten. As culture was a way of growing up in traditional societies, the person was taught from stage to stage to accept and learn what was expected of him or her at any particular age. The eighteen-year-old already knew that he must soon provide shelter for his future family, even before he married.

One of the most psychologically traumatic breaks with tradition among urban Africans in our country is the fact that they are compelled to live with their parents for too long — often till they are 25-30 — because of lack of apartment buildings where eighteen-year-olds may choose to go. Not only are homes over-crowded, but also young people begin independent living too late, if ever. Marital relations often suffer badly because of this.

Even apart from the possibilities at eighteen in America, there is a continuous in-and-out mobility between school or college and work. A highly industrial country makes this possible. One can hardly imagine, in Africa, a boy leaving school because he wants 'to straighten myself out first' or 'to get my shit together', or 'to think things through' — with the intention of returning to finish his studies later.

I admire such a system very much and wish it

could happen in Africa. All too often we expect our children to take the straight traditional route from high school to post-secondary schooling, without considering that either we or they may be taking too much for granted. We are wont to assume that they must prepare themselves for a good paying job, not to create jobs for themselves, be their own masters.

The way of all African education is to prepare for servanthood. Only incidentally or by accident of birth can you find yourself in the position of employer or rise to that status. For a student to do the other-than-conventional, there is often this need to stop in one's tracks, return into society to work and think, and move back into regular studies.

But I'm a dreamer. African economics are rough, the labour market is rough, the majority of us are Third World consumers, even the blacks in an industrialised South Africa. So we push the children into and through the dipping tank, tell them to keep moving because there are younger brothers and sisters waiting in line for the same 'golden opportunity', as prize-giving-day presenters, foundation-stone setters and ribbon-snappers are fond of calling the disinfectant. They must keep moving until they reach a level from which they can compete adequately for respectable employment.

This is the cultural equipment we took into the American setting. At first we resented watching our children act out the American ritual, but we came to understand, to accept here and reject there. As we did not want to live indefinitely in the U.S. the tug-of-war had to continue . . . .

IV

Philadelphia 1974-1977

We arrived in Philadelphia, in May 1974. I was going to start work at the University of Pennsylvania in September as a tenured professor of English. We had bought a house in Wayne, some 24 kilometres from Philadelphia on the Western Mainline. It was a pleasant satellite town, part of Greater Philadelphia, predominantly Italian. There was a negligible number of blacks here, as most blacks lived nearer the city or in it. Much as I would have preferred to live in one of the black suburbs, I had taken what was going during a rushed five-day visit.

We sent my sister in Soweto, Tabitha, a ticket to fly and visit us. We hadn't seen each other since 1957. She came to us haggard and weary. It hadn't been easy bringing up seven children single-handed after she and her husband got divorced back in 1955. Tabitha returned to South Africa after three good months looking healthy, her full-blooded colour restored. She had celebrated her fiftieth birthday with us in November.

Penn has a most impressive campus, among the most expensive in the country. The Afro-American novelist, John Wideman, had invited me there to teach African literature and creative writing; he himself was on his way out to the University of Wyoming, Colorado. The faculty included a batch of distinguished writers and scholars.

Motswiri was on his own in Denver, Kefilwe in Washington D.C. working while she studied at the American University. Tony was somewhere on the east coast. So we had only Chabi and Puso.

My entry into the English department coincided with that of Houston Baker, Jr., the youngest scholar I had ever met with a full professorship. One of the most brilliant black literary critics, too. He soon became director of Afro-American Studies. I was in for a stimulating time.

Rebecca, who had graduated M.A. in Social Work on the eve of our leaving Denver, found a job with the Philadelphia Psychiatric Hospital — a project concerned with the parenthood of women who are emotionally disturbed.

She drove the family car to Philadelphia and I commuted by train, an easy twenty-five-minute journey.

I'm at 30th Street Station, Philadelphia, on a warm August afternoon, waiting for my train to Wayne. A white woman comes up the stairs, obviously drunk. A black woman is close on her heels, also unsteady on her legs. The latter goes to a phone booth. I stand staring out at the high-rise buildings across the Schuylkill expressway.

The light is taking on a soft twilight texture when everything seems to wait for who knows what. White woman's voice drags me out of my reverie: 'I admire you people for your patience — you seem so stoical and resigned, not like us — look at that gentleman pacing up and down because the train's late.'

Patient — maybe — but stoical? I say to myself. She's got to be one of those fallen angels who are more than just literate. 'What's there to do but wait?' I reply, refusing to engage her in an argument over who 'you people' are and how can she make such an outrageous non-statement! Besides, a woman looks obscene, especially one of the master race, wobbling like this in a public place. You don't take much notice when it's a man.

'Where do you come from?'

'I'm African.'

'Oh, I thought you were Indian from India. Your shirt — is it African?' I could hear the next question forming in her mind, 'What part of Africa?'

At which point black woman joins us. Had they come from the same fountain? I wondered. I decided it was unlikely.

'South Africa — Johannesburg.'

'I'm Belgian — how stupid we were to lose that country. All that wealth.'

'You lost the Congo, not South Africa,' I say firmly, as if the Belgians are right now trying to lose South Africa, and it's doomed to be lost. I continue, 'And you had bought it from your King Leopold the Second, who had stolen it from the Africans and had millions worked to death on his rubber plantations. Do you know him?'

I'm feeling mean and wishing this August twilight hadn't thrown this baggage on to me. And yet I don't do either of the two things I could easily do — walk away, or keep quiet. Maybe I do want a little diversion to kill time, and there are worse things than inanities on station platforms.

'Never heard of him,' Belgium says.

'That figures. You sit in your comfortable European

houses while your kings and missionaries and mining
moguls mess around in Africa and you don't even try
to know their names, wow!' I'm working up an appetite
to lecture her, but my tobacco won't catch fire.

'You had no business being there in the first place,
honey,' black woman says. 'Tell us about wealth —
shoot!'

'I think you're wrong,' Belgium remarks.

'Oh, come off it. My grandparents were slaves —
and that's not so long ago.' She turns to me directly:
'Not all of them are the same though. I work for a
southern family in Ardmore. I clean their house and
stuff and they treat me decent, you understand?'

'Excuse me!' Belgium shouts. When we look at her,
now a few feet away, her wobble is exaggerated, and
her legs are trying to cling to the platform, astride,
like a cow ready to pee with a generous swoosh. Before I'm aware what's happening (I think generally
the only sound that startles me, actually gives me a
start, is a gunshot or anything like it — a tyre burst,
for instance) — before I'm aware what's taking place,
Belgium keels over backwards, her legs still astride,
like a doll that's been pushed over and can do nothing
about the position of its limbs. Her head hits the
floor with a loud thud. Instinctively black woman
and I go over to raise Belgium by the arms, and lead
her to a bench to sit with other people.

For their part, they just continue to look ahead of
them, at the nothingness across the tracks. They seem
too bored even to turn their eyes towards Belgium as
she throws her bottom down. They want to pretend
nothing has happened.

When I relate the incident to Rebecca in the evening
she says, 'Oh, how could you do that!' with a look on
her face that adds, *how could you deign to handle*

such trash!

'Just one of those instinctive reactions,' I reply.

She makes a sound of disgust, which makes *me* wonder now why I placed myself in a position where I would need to react instinctively. But that's me. You instinctively give a woman a ride in your car and then run into murderous suspicions you could never have predicted . . . . You lend money on an impulse after hearing a hard-luck story, and the skunk never comes back . . . . That's me.

And yet I'm a slow thinker and puzzle long about people's behaviour before I arrive at a judgement. I find myself in a situation I hadn't bargained for, one that compromises me or simply reveals my asinine attitude: for instance the belief, however momentary, that something is not yet there if I don't see it or feel it.

Rebecca, on the contrary, is capable of snap decisions. She draws clear lines that will determine her initial attitude to people. Belgium is just trash to her and has to be left alone. A drunk is a drunk, a thief is a thief. I consider what effect stern measures may have on our children, for instance. One of their friends may be a bad sort. Mother decides that he must be kept out of the house. Not because he may be white, which he happens to be in many cases. But because he is a bad sort, shows no respect when he is visiting, does not greet. While I'm still speculating on the whys and wherefores of a child's behaviour, Rebecca has long anticipated his or her next move, assessed whatever influence an outsider is exerting on a child, and gone out to head off a catastrophe. And goddammit, she is often right! Or should I say she has often acted in time to reveal *something*. The sceptic in me will constrain her to wait until we have told the children to talk to their friend about his or her conduct: they also visit his or her home and are well received.

Rebecca takes more pains, though, to sort out her clients. Here she goes to the other extreme. She tends to absorb a client's troubles until her own life is soured day after day, unable to shake off the mood. For this reason she found herself more and more unsuited to the U.S., where the social worker is mostly a relief officer who must not allow herself to be scratched by every nettle she holds in her hand or every bush she walks through in the landscape of poverty, anxiety neurosis, drug addiction, and multiple family problems. More and more she began to feel that in Africa such involvement might be more constructive, that she needed to identify with a culture in which compassion registered. She is aware, on the other hand, that her approach to human problems is severely ethical or indeed moralistic: she feels passionately *what one's behaviour should be*. Because of this, she is always going to have to rethink her set of ethics in relation to the social problems of other people whose ethics are totally different from hers (and mine), which derive from African humanism.

The sceptic married to the absolutist; introvert matched with the extrovert; the dreamer married to the pragmatist, the action person. It has worked. For two years of courtship and thirty-seven of married life.

Dogs and cats, cats and dogs. Dog diarrhoea messes up pavements in Philadelphia as it does in Paris and New York. Dogs foul up the parks and university lawns as well, outrageously indulged by their owners. Gravestones for pets, some with animal stone figures perched on top, inscriptions and all. The dog food industry has grown so huge that it boggles the mind.

'Champ's very moody since Bob died . . . .'

'Give Smokey his diet pills, Ruth . . . .'

'And don't forget that he loves Oxheart . . . .'

'Our Marie is so depressed since Champ died . . . .'

'Now you sit right there, Toby, you naughty boy. Mummy will feed you in a minute . . . .'

'Please don't sit on that chair, our cat Suzie won't like it . . . .'

'Time to go out — come, Schnozzle . . . .'

'And I call him but he keeps running across the street after the ball . . . . It's just disgraceful for people to drive at such speed in a suburban street . . . . And now my little Rover's dead . . . . What shall I do without him — the house is so empty . . . . Oh, Molly, what shall I *do* . . . . I look at the chair where he always sat and it's like he's going to come in any time and jump into it . . . . I'm just not myself . . . . This apartment will never be the same again . . . .'

'When's the burial?'

'Tomorrow. Was at the dog morgue this morning. His crushed little body . . . . It's hideous, all these trashy drivers deserve to be shot . . . .'

'Fix me another Martini there, please Jess, like a good girl.'

'Don't you think you've had enough for the evening? Is there going to be a gin-and-vodka drought tomorrow?'

'You're saying it again. I drink too much. I'm not an alcoholic, you know. Am I now, Misty? Talk to me, you wise-looking animal lying down there with your chin on your legs like you dig everything that's on my mind — thank you honey. Now you listen to me y'ole big dummy — I mean *you* ole dog — you're a

dumb four-legged creature. I could just crush your
dumb skull and that'll be *it* with you. Maybe you also
believe I must go to AA, eh? I'll bash your brains out
if that's what you think. I feed you, bed you, wash
you, brush you — buy you the best canned food there
is — right there on TV — you've seen it displayed and
you've barked — and you lie there like the master of
the house himself and still you think dirty about
me . . . .'

'You're sick, talking to a dog like that, what's he
ever done?'

'Keep out of this dialogue, Jess. Don't stand between my anger and the beast, to paraphrase Shakespeare — was it King Lear? — the old coot just never
knew how to be angry — just drove him plain nuts.'

'I'm going to bed, King Lear — King Lear my foot!'

'Go and leave me to my so-lil-o-quy with this dumb
Misty, before he dies.'

'You're not going to do anything foolish, Jonathan.
The last time you mistreated him and the Society
warned you. Why do you keep him anyway, if you
don't want him?'

'Ah, but I *want* him, you see, I want him here to
talk to — seeing as how my — my darling wife has
turned into a silent grouchy fusspot.'

'Have it your way, but if I hear any sound from
him I shouldn't be hearing, I'm calling the police, you
hear me!'

'Don't mind her, Misty. You just listen to me,
dummy.'

'Grrr-grrrr.'

'Okay, okay — just trying to be friendly.'

Kroshka? It's Russian for tit-bit. His size tells you that.

Indeed, Kroshka is a bit of a dog. But so much of a

middle-class creature, like the rest of American dog-and-cat society. He has the exasperating habit of licking your leg if you have no socks on. Under the table during a meal. I complain a few times that he's threatening to get into the leg of my trousers. My hosts let him do a number of small but irritating things. During liqueur and coffee the host throws a squeaking toy to him. All the time he's playing with the toy, tossing it about and enjoying the noises from it, conversation has turned to him, as it is bound to do.

Do what you damn well like, Kroshka, play with your master, show off before other members of the race, nestle warmly in their flattery, just anything you like, but don't mess with me, boy! I don't like pets, I *hate* them when they lick at me, so don't come between me and serenity, love and peace. Just back off, precious Kroshka. I hate dogs and I hate people who fuss over the likes of you and don't care if some of their guests may not care for your race. They tell me you're well-travelled too — been to Russia and everything — but just keep away from this African . . . .

That's the lecture I give when Rebecca and I are back home, which I wouldn't dare deliver to my hosts. And I have never been invited to a dog-addicted house whose hosts were not themselves lovable.

'Why this address after the dinner?' Rebecca asks. 'You talk almost as if Kroshka was my dog!'

'Why do I subject myself to such evenings? — eh — tell me.'

'What's up — you guys were served minced meat and spaghetti again?' Puso asks coming downstairs.

'Food was good,' Rebecca says, 'but your father was offered a doggybag, can you believe it!'

Puso almost flips over laughing, until he chokes.

* * *

Before Melissa left Connecticut for Maine, she sent off Bangkok, her beloved Siamese, by plane. She said goodbye to her folks, then got on the road to hitch-hike.

'I just can't wait to see the look on Bangkok's face when I find him down there,' she had kept saying to her folks, 'I just can't imagine it!'

Melissa never returned to Connecticut, never reached Maine. After several month's search, her skeleton was discovered and identified in a forest in the middle of nowhere. Her skull showed evidence of a brutal assault.

Race. Colour. The most emotive words in the dictionary of human relationships. All my life I have had to grapple with their meanings, with the energy they generate.

Pretoria, my first home, was a cruel town to grow up in when I was a boy in the Thirties. Our parents, who knew what they were talking about, were constantly warning us to keep out of the white man's path. You stepped off the pavement when a group of them came on abreast. In the shops white folks became sharply aware of your presence. They did not like it. You could never be invisible.

You developed the instinct to smell out places where you were not allowed to be. You were poor and they were rich. Your folks did their washing, worked in their kitchens, and the prosperity of suburbia dazzled you as you cycled or walked to fetch and deliver laundry. Whenever I biked in the suburbs of Philadelphia my mind never failed to travel back to the mornings and afternoons wheeling through Sunnyside, Hatfield, Arcadia, Brynterion. Rows and rows of jacarandas, brooding silences, where even the winters

seemed fashioned to keep whites comfortable . . . .
And always I said to myself, 'It didn't have to be so
rough . . . didn't have to be . . . .'

Only when I was in high school in Johannesburg
did the cobwebs of naïveté seem to clear from my
eyes. Suddenly you realised the Master Plan they had
devised. But you had to survive. Reaching the 'top',
preparing for a career, had become the sole obsession.
As if you were yourself preparing to fit into the grand
design. It was a fatalistic operation. You didn't reason
why the reason was, or had to be, what it was.

There was more fear than hate in us during the
Thirties and Forties. Because you were always the
one to give an account of yourself: your pass, your
need of a job, your residence, your awareness of
authority's huge wings beating about your ears . . . .
Even got to the point where you envied him his power,
almost admired him. For a while these emotions pre-
empted hate.

The day the other man hurts you, humiliates you,
assaults you — that, I think, is the day you begin to
be aware of hate. As long as the pressure holds from
the other side, hate is sparked again and again. There
is always the time, the place, there are always circumstances that bring it to life. And then of course the
agent, which becomes the object. And yet fear will
still lurk somewhere. Often you hate simply because
you are afraid and tell yourself you shouldn't be so
full of fear.

I have never, in all sincerity, been able to say that I
hate white people. It would not be saying anything
meaningful or concrete. Because I have also known,
after all, compassion, human decency, in particular
white individuals. And yet, alas, we live in an age
when group attitudes have broken up our lives, so

that we pretend we mean what we say, in order to whip up violent feeling, to win a following, to be politically 'correct'. And we plunder the painful facts of history in our public rhetoric, our sense of humiliation or power, to win votes and esteem. Almost as if we were happy to belong to a history of three centuries of conflict. Rightly or wrongly, anger becomes a compulsive way of asserting our ethnic or racial or political identity.

I have felt what I took to be hate so deep in me that my blood stream felt literally poisoned. If it was really hate, and you multiplied it by so many black souls, I think we would be telling a different story about South African race relations today. I think a frightful catastrophe would long have broken upon us all. On reflection today, I think it was a protracted state of anger and indignation marked by high points of hate directed at white individuals or institutions for what they had done at a particular time and place.

Powerlessness reduced to a stagnant dull ache. How then, did I not equally feel a long continuous period of euphoria in which time, place, event and the actor of compassion and decency merged? I do not know. Maybe it was because such occasions were isolated; maybe because while human beings need compassion, it loses much of its warmth during the distance it has to travel from a position of power and privilege (white) to that of an inferior status (black). I also think that *something* happens to the correlation between stimulus and response in the felt traffic of race relations spanning three centuries, even if defined only by work situations and by a counter or window frame between the server and the served. This something confounds any attempt to arrive at an equation that may inform us how much hostility and how much compassion are in operation or possible.

How long, how long will it be before we live our true selves, black and white?

There was a time when, after the war, I believed passionately in a non-racial society. Or more precisely, believed it possible in the near future. We preached it in the 1950s. But the concept was resisted furiously from the other side. They jailed its proponents and scattered others into exile, banned others until they were six feet down. Our humanism cost us that much.

The alternative would be to consolidate our humanism so that it informs our black institutions short of promoting 'independent homelands'. *Could* we do this without running the risk of being called anti-white? Shall we ever run our institutions — educational, creative, recreational — without fear of surveillance and even brazen white control? Already the concept of Black Consciousness has suffered a backlash, and is now a synonym (to white authority) of subversion, racism.

May 31, 1975: Khabi Mngoma visited us in Wayne during a tour he was making of the east coast. Eighteen years — that's how long it had been. We drank hard and jogged hard. We spent hours during the two days' visit paging through the past years. We had stopped writing to each other after the Nigeria days: one of those lapses in communication that occurs between beloved friends for which reasons are impossible to find, or just not worth the trouble of figuring out. The one friend with whom I continued to correspond throughout the years of absence was Norah Taylor. Norah, who had introduced me to theatre in the 1940s. Norah who had given me individual lessons in her studio in Rissik Street, Johannesburg. Norah who had monitored my theatre productions when I was at Orlando High School and after, and encouraged our Syndicate of African Artists (run by Khabi, myself and Wilkie). Norah who had continually helped my family financially after I had been fired from teaching by the Transvaal Education Department. Norah who continued to help with speech and drama in African schools and teacher-training colleges . . . Norah who had nursed a sick husband for twelve years until he died, during which time she was cooped up in their house, cut off from the world . . . .

Khabi told us about the mighty choir and orchestra he had built up, and the exciting things they had been doing for African entertainment since we had been gone. In the meantime he had studied and attained a string of licentiates in music through the University of South Africa and Trinity College. He was thus amply qualified to set up a department of music at the University of Zululand, a job he had been invited to take on in the year of his visit.

I reminded him how wrong I had been − grossly wrong − when I wrote in *Down Second Avenue* that, because of his failure to find sponsorship for music studies in England, he would most likely end up singing an item or two at an occasional party or some such function. Of course I was then projecting into his condition the despair and bitterness I myself was loaded with when I left the country. But when one ends up being *happy* that one has turned out to be wrong, it blunts the edge of self-reproach.

I think Khabi realised somewhere along the line that he was stirring the embers of a desire in me, stoking it with more wood, fanning it. The desire to return. 'Come back, please come back,' he kept saying. The memory of his visit kept the desire alive and burning fiercely. He was *doing* things, and he had *community* — we didn't need a rationale . . . .

Philadelphia, December 17, 1975: every so often you
hit a certain age when you pause on the road of this
life to take stock. I remember doing it when I hit 21.
A muddle-headed pause it was, I'll tell you. Like when
you drive into a parking spot off the road, marked
out for a scenic view. Another pause at 30, then 42,
now 55. Odd intervals, I'd say. Because really I've
come to measure my life in decades. *Me* and *myself*.
Although I can't say for sure at any time which of the
two is observer-commentator, and which the driver. I
live in a glass-house, the one I ran into eighteen years
ago. It's roomy but borrowed. I can live in it as long
as I pay the rent and as long as I don't start kicking
things about, scratching or staining the walls, I'm told.
I can see the change of seasons, light tints, patterns of
shade clearly when the rain is gone. In a way I could
never have done in the painful south. I go down into
the cellar often, to sharpen the arsenal of my brain,
oil and grease it, generally train the panzer division
of my mind.

I'm not here because I was invisible. Sometimes
it's cold in here, sometimes warm, and sometimes full
of light, sometimes shadows come down upon me.
There are no ultra-bright light bulbs, not one, not one
thousand three hundred and sixty-nine of the expensive filament type. I have ghetto blues too, and so I
know what I've not done to be so black and blue. I'm
not invisible, I say, have never been. How could I be?
For every one of *them* there are four of *me* in that
southern corner of Africa. That's why I ran. Always I
hear a river. So often it has become part of *me* and
myself. For hours I can stop and listen to it, feel it
rub against the sides of this glass hole, sometimes right

under my basement. Sets wild things quivering and
grating like pebbles back of my skull, sending clues to
my ego centre about the togetherness of happenings
even while I hear a war-cry; voices from the whirlwind
prophesying chaos and doom I think not even that
dome-crazy Kubla Khan would have dreamed of in
the splendour of his sacred river . . . .

Not yet time for him to stand and stare out of the
window, stare at nothing special, just stare, fingers
interlocked behind him or twitching with arthritic
messages, or arms folded at the chest. Just staring,
rain or shine. Not yet time for him to scratch his
armpit self-indulgently, mop wet eyes with back or
heel of hand. Not yet time to act grandfather: that
can wait, he says, until he's a drooling old fart too old
to care when children climb on his lap or tug at his
sleeve. Brought up five of his own children and says
ho lekane ho lekane — enough is enough! That was
steep and rough enough in the ghetto shanty for him
not to want to mess with the dumb things now,
whoever their parents might be. Never had a babysitter
for mine, he says. Says why should these young folks
have babies and not want to look after them without
conning grandpas and grandmas with chocolate candy
or tobacco to baby-sit? If I had to do it all over again
I'd still have five from the age we were. We'd still
look after them. I'd still come to this point where a
day with small kids — well that's the day I resign.
Now look at the mess around us — look, these people
hang on to their children with hoops of steel, man,
won't let them go live their own lives until there's a
crisis. See them go, and then pa and ma after them
again with hoops of steel. Parents want to drive them
around to keep their dates, lend them cars for their
dates no matter how erratic each new friendship: see

them almost kill their children with protection and entertainment; see them project their own neurotic anxieties into their kids and dogs and cats; see the children try to run from them as they grow up and ma and pa still after them with hoops of steel. What a mess. Hear the kids talk to their parents or about them and the parents follow the book that tells them to give children free scope and speech. See them resent parenthood, drag it into the mud I say, and pa and ma out again after them with hoops of steel. Funny how a culture helps people contain its own mess, its own miscarriages and abortions and monstrosities. Same as with us. We do it with theatre, ritual, poetry. Don't know how *they* do it, those. Give me small kids in small doses, mix the dose with Scotch every time. 'I thought Africans loved children?' I dare him. He replies, 'Of course, but we don't devour them and the day we also allow them to devour us — that'll be the day the grief of the gods'll strangle Time, mutilate it, leave us wandering mindlessly without day, without night.'

I could, if I chose, renew my lease indefinitely in this glasshouse, quite forget, write off my past, take my chances on new territory. I shall not. Because I'm a helpless captive of place and to come to terms with the tyranny of place is to have something to live for that saves me from stagnation, anonymity. It's not fame you want, it's having your shadow noticed, it's the comfort that you can show control over your life, that you can function. Comforting also to feel you can coil around the ego centre, feel the juices flow within and when time is ripe, uncoil, stretch out and feel the spiral motion of body and mind interwoven with other lives at a specific time and place. The place is not here alas, so the moment must wait

its renewal time. Something else: I could seek to enlist
for the black American cause. I'm still a captive of
the place I've fled. And as my mother used to say of
hasty marriages: how can anyone see a mare gallop
past with a saddle on and no rider, not knowing
where she came from, where she was going, and just
get on top of her? And to fight a cause you've got to
feel its history and its future in your blood and bones.
And the common pangs and joys, the crossroads and
forkways of blackness? Yes. Time enough to learn
and feel them. That is all, that is all that's possible.

Not yet time for him to fart like a horse or dangle
on an elongated burp without a care about who's
around. Nor time yet for him to gargle with words
and syllables and sighs and saliva and spit them out
together. Nor yet time to slip over on to his side
before he carries his partner to the hilltop, or before
she ferries him across the river, flip over and wheeze,
the heart panting like it's just turned back on the
edge of a precipice, now scared of what could have
happened, partner looking at the ceiling and thinking
madly, 'Superannuated cock!' or else 'Well, we're not
getting any younger dear, don't fret on it . . . .' No,
not yet time: he can hold his own still at the peak of
manhood. He's past the age for any new regrets to
bother him. They can wait. The old ones have
mellowed. They don't affront him, stick their tongues
out at him, or stab him between the ribs with needles.
They plod like oxen inside him resigned, enduring,
sure of surviving many more ploughing seasons or of
getting their freight to its destination, noble in their
patience. New regrets can kick about, buck like an
untamed donkey, head down, ears pointing back at a
mean angle, tail swishing and fanning off one anal
explosion after another. He has learned to wait, dead

certain he'll wear off the young bucking regrets.

Teaching, writing, writing, teaching, the same interminable cycle in the long, long quest for a metaphor, for the right word, lucid, fresh like water straight out of rock, or like city lights on a clear night that I have viewed from the foothills of the Rockies, reassuring, promising, seeming to breathe like the life that is stirring down there. If only, if only — ah these days the *if-onlys* seem to come from unexpected corners, in numbers, in broken ranks like bedbugs — if only I could teach in my own native land or continent! Here among strangers the young grind the aged under with steamrollers, here where to be forty is an affront to youth, I can't help but say under my breath as I stand before undergraduates: you're going to listen to me, you dumb clattering tin-cans and cymbals, you bouncing bundles of tender cartilage, because you want to gather grades like ripe mangoes strewn on the ground, because you love the system you despise, because you're on your way up the middle-class totem pole you spit upon, because you crave the respectability you pretend to scorn, because to shake off Papa's subsidy you've got to earn your independence, because among your stampeding herd are those who'll take to other hills, other pastures, other streams, for their own survival . . . . I know left to yourselves you'd kill me, kill all the fifty-year-olds because they stand for the stability you still have to earn . . . but you're going to listen, aren't you? Yes? I thought so . . . . The gods help us: how can a man teach among people whose cultural goals he cannot share? How long can one subsist only on the mental stimulation one has found?

A little while longer, you keep saying to numb the pain: just a while longer, the lease must hold, stretch it out a little longer just to function like they'd never let you do in the painful south. So inch along, there's ample margin for your classroom style to stretch, expand its muscle. The solid core of students — ten or eight or six — will still be there to join you at the crossroads where minds must meet and rub and mate. For I'll concede this much as one of many, many dissenters — there's something rotten in the state of middle-class values: certain notions of success, the way parents want to devour their offspring, the where-did-we-go-wrong refrain of guilt, the phoney sanctity of marriage and notions of man-wife fidelity and Christian morality. I choke with anger at the elders who declare wars recklessly for no love of the country that is threatened, and push youngbloods to the battle-front, outlaw them if they don't comply. And then my river whispers *it's none of your business here, none, you hear!* Anger splutters and settles down to a smoulder which is called indignation. The glass around me registers again on my senses, reminds me that I have been looking at the landscape outside so hard the glass dissolved, merged into the light out there.

And so the passion will seize him again and again and the teacher's love of adventure will renew itself again and again and the lease will hold unless — unless — who knows? He'll tell you at this point it's no longer from here on up but from here onward and abroad because he's not burnt up, not bored, not jaded. A sentimentalist to the core, doesn't mind if he's thought to be making a fool of himself in broad daylight.

Yes, maybe we really only respond to happenings, to the moment, to the times, to place, to human traits — to particulars, and the devil take the hindmost. You see families scattered by decree, or people starving in the midst of abundance, and you think the world can never be too compassionate. You hear a loved one has been tortured by the secret police, they tell you he's now a broken man and you think no apocalypse could atone enough, even if a court found four million South Africans guilty of genocide and other crimes against those who stand against tyranny, banished or jailed some, sent others to gallows, sterilised all adult males and females.

So much to learn to endure or just to know at fifty-five, so much to reaffirm, so much to taunt the adventurer. Old hates and loves and prejudices have multiplied their roots, sent them deeper down for more food, for more voracious appetites because your enemy and your friends are not around to absorb the ache and fury of desire. Hates and loves have now grown fatter leaves and covered them with hair so they can resist drought for long, long years.

Time today to take stock of the ego centre, wait and listen to the river washing its shores, to the echoes of the hunters across the Limpopo and the Zambezi, listen to the ancient debate over which things must come first, things the ego centre will recreate as ever it perceives them. Things I'd only guessed at stare me now in the face and seem to say to me: *you cannot do us* or *we can be done* or *narrow focus, man, conserve your energy, don't spread yourself so thin, no one has guaranteed you twenty more years.* You have no audience that's relevant in the long run, yet the ego centre will not set you free from the sweet and burning urge to play at images and symbols. Something tells you also at this point that to make a novel sometimes you've got·to shut the door to the ego centre so you can listen better to the people's drama and music. But comes a time when you don't care to shut the door anymore when it's been flung open so many, many times in the painful south. Comes a time when you want the heat to stay on in the ego centre so you can hear the voices, feel the pull and push so you don't forget, not ever, who you are, whence you came. The voices and the push and pull drown the people's music and drama or speak out of turn. It's no longer a matter of *negative capability*. It's knowing when to shut the door, how far to open it, how real are the song and drama, how to meet the tyranny of time and place and memory that keep bearing down on you so you feel the pulse of every minute of your growth and decline and wear and tear, so you hear your soul and body clock ticking, so you leave your fingerprints on everything you touch in fact and fiction, so there's little else to do but define and redefine yourself, stay on the post and monitor the spiralling of your life as it moves from ego centre to whatever it aims to reach, until it seems you'll yet preside at your own funeral just in order to feel it does not matter any more that you plundered the drama of your life by the decades contained in page upon page rolling relentlessly, urgently, from Ego Centre Press: to feel the only thing that matters is you did what you had to do so that even if you ended on a semicolon or hyphen, this moment, now clinched, has saved you from yesterday's cliffhanger, indeed cheated you out of forthcoming episodes. Of course you could, as you preside, spy on the ancestors' rehearsal of your welcome.

Meantime no silencer, no cancellation, can make amends. Ego centre must hold, though the doors to it might flap and slam in the storm all our waking hours, the centre must hold even though not to cancel

memory — to keep on plundering it to recreate something beautiful and all-embracing out of personal
sorrow is pain enough. Rather use it as the poet does
and move to other modes of prose pressurising it with
poetic energy, move towards a metaphor that will be
an open book for those who care to read us . . . .
Oh, by the way, while I think of it hand me that rag
so I can wipe the mist from the glass — you know
what a long, long siege the drizzle of the Delaware
Valley days can keep us in . . . but rather this than
mind-boggling snow — one of Creation's white catastrophes.

You came to the painful realisation that you were
irrelevant to American education and cultural goals.
You had burned your fingers several times before
during your exile trying to help other people fight
their own battles. You could only think and talk on
the side of other blacks. Maybe even write about it.

Journalistically you can establish the connections
between the black peoples of the world. You can
capture the general mood, the yearnings of militants
to assert a Pan-African identity. You can do it to
some extent in poetry. Only to the extent that poetry
gets things together, that it operates through a unity
of sensibilities, of concerns, of feeling, and the poet
can overlook diversities if he wants to produce only
public poetry. But even in poetry you can find that
you have been speaking to two audiences each from a
different black area and projecting a set of revolutionary assumptions that do not in fact apply equally to
both. If a black prophet arose (and often the black
poet wants to speak with prophetic earnest) and predicted the same future, the same route to that future,
for all the black people of the world, we would
certainly think he was a freak. One must sacrifice

authenticity somewhere — place — in order to let one's poetry speak for peoples across cultural boundaries. And yet poetry can unify so many disparate elements.

In fiction, as in drama, you work with diversities, conflict, and you need an intimate familiarity with the world you depict. You need a locale, its smell, its taste, its texture. You can arrive at an ideological position in the end which has implications for the whole of the black world. But in the process of composition, you are tied to the place that contains the experience, however fictional it may be. Some people say they can write novels in which place does not matter, in which place and time do not need physical and temporal qualities. They can create a theatre in the mind. This kind of experiment goes against everything I hold sacred in the composition of fiction. The tyranny of place is something I submit to. In the final count, it is tyranny I would rather try to understand and deal with, so that I know how to reconcile its imperatives with the condition of exile, of placelessness.

Since 1972, when we were in Denver, the desire had been taking hold, and the roots did not lack water. If it had to be Africa again, it must be South Africa. Anything else would be mere adventure, which we had no taste for any longer. We wanted community, we wanted a cultural milieu in which our work could be relevant. International living had equipped us with experience of immense value. But intellectual stimulation was not enough. American culture was too fragmented for us to be able to define the goals of our own careers in relation to it.

As we were considered to have become British

nationals (no matter how the United Kingdom itself viewed nationality that was not based on the birth of one's father in England) we had to approach the South African government through a single person in authority. Dr. C.N. Phatudi, Chief Minister of Lebowa, agreed to make representations on our behalf.

For the next five years the bureaucratic caterpillar ground slowly. As some of my books were being banned, it halted several times along the way. Also, drivers were changing fast. Each new driver in 'Bantu Affairs', then 'Plural Affairs', then 'Development and Co-operation', stopped a long time in his seat looking at the landscape through his binoculars to ascertain where he was supposed to be going, why? Where had the vehicle started out from in the first place? Why . . . . Dispatches were sent out, and I wrote back. Dispatches ceased, and I took it some new driver had lost his bearings through what must have grown to be an enormous territory contained in the Mphahlele dossier. No doubt, Security was also making a number of reconnaissance flights. As if our wish to return might just be part of a grand design of apocalyptic dimensions.

Telephone calls were coming through in Philadelphia from some mysterious persons who wanted to know how they could penetrate South Africa, some voice purporting to represent the New Black Youth Revolutionary Council . . . . Some voice saying it wanted information on how to speed up and intensify the trade boycott . . . . On and on and on. At one time, when I was thoroughly bored, I replied, 'Isn't there a whole dump of revolutionary shit in America that requires your energies to clear?' Was Security busy?

We waited. Which wasn't anything new. Until we were both thirty-seven — when we left the country —

we had known the pain of waiting — for the unknown.
And anyhow our jobs were secure, and I have always
prided myself on possessing an asinine persistence.

   Puso and Chabi were restless. But we told them
they had a choice: to try South Africa or stay, as long
as they did not abandon schooling. There would
always be a chance of returning to the U.S. Chabi
decided to return to Denver where his brother was.
After much apparent debate in his head, Puso decided
to come with us. Kefilwe and Motswiri had their own
commitments.

V

Reconnaissance... and Back to Base

May 1976. The unbelievable had happened. The Black Studies Institute in Johannesburg invited me to read a paper at its inaugural conference and actually succeeded in its request for a visa to be granted to me. Nineteen years, and now I was able to re-enter South Africa! I had even decided I was not going to try to apply, but Rebecca urged me to do so. The visa came.

For days and nights after this I kept asking myself, what awaits me out there? How will they receive me — my people? The first wave of the schoolchildren's revolt that had broken out on June 16, 1976 in Soweto had subsided, after more than 300 children and youths had been gunned down. How much police surveillance would I be subjected to? The last question did not bother me, not at that time: if you're black in a situation of sustained racial conflict, police surveillance becomes a way of life. I thought that even nineteen years couldn't have uprooted the police terror I had known for twenty-five years of my life. I should still be conditioned enough not to bother.

Finally, there I was at Jan Smuts Airport. July 3, 1976. My passage through the Immigration gate was smooth. But at the sight of a young policeman in uniform my heart missed a few beats. Old memories . . . old encounters . . . old fears . . . I was back, *that* was clear.

I was emerging on to the concourse when I was startled by a tremendous shout. And they were on top of me — some one hundred Africans, screaming and jostling to embrace me, kiss me. Relatives and friends and pressmen from my two home cities — Johannesburg and Pretoria. I was bounced hither and thither and would most probably not have noticed if an arm or leg were torn off of me, or my neck was being wrung. Such was the overwhelming ecstasy of that reunion. The police had to come and disperse the crowd as it had by now taken over the concourse.

My friends from old times — Khabi, W.B. Ngakane, Zeph Mothopeng (with whom I had been fired from teaching), Nimrod Mkele (whose brainchild Black Studies was), Teddy, soon took me in hand. I knew well what must be uppermost in their minds — the same, still sharp grief the killings had left in all of us who can still be outraged. Among them were the stalwarts who had survived Robben Island and other prison islands on the mainland, house arrests, ten-year banning orders. The scars on my friends' faces were clear all right.

On arrival I gloried in the human warmth I was wrapped in. A sensation akin to what you might feel if you had been driving through hundreds of kilometres of pitch darkness and then you rode into the dawn and your body began to tingle in the warmth of the rising sun.

Next day as I was taken round in Soweto, that haunting refrain from Sterling Brown's 'Old Lem' kept tapping on the door of my mind: *They don't*

*come by ones, they don't come by twos, but they
come by tens.* A trail of grim happenings lay before
us: charred government buildings, liquor stores,
government beer halls, a bank building, overturned
vans: all signs of the mid-June events.

How can I say it all? I was on killing-ground yet
there was jubilation as more friends and relatives
came to see me at my sister's, as I visited and met
more people from whom I had been cut off since that
sixth day of September, 1957. Even then, the ones
who always come by tens with arms of steel were
still sniffing around, keeping watch at every school to
prevent possible arson.

What a homecoming . . . .

The kids resented Afrikaans being imposed on
them as a medium of instruction. An added problem
in the learning process already made excruciating by
tuition fees, money for books, overcrowded classes
averaging eighty per classroom from primary to secondary school, unhealthy living conditions, low wages,
overcrowded houses where it is impossible for kids to
do their homework, lack of school and community
libraries, and so on. So Afrikaans merged into the
larger symbol of authoritarian rule that blacks resent
and chafe against.

In 1935 when the Johannesburg City Council put up
houses in Orlando East, several with two rooms, the
largest having three, including a kitchenette-cum-
dining-cum-sitting room, these structures were said to
be temporary. This was the beginning of the greater
Orlando. Then, years later, as an extension of Orlando,
four-roomed brick houses were put up. Now you
could get two bedrooms, a kitchen and a dining-living
room sufficient for a sofa and four dining chairs
around a tiny dining table. The bucket lavatories, as

in the older Orlando, were out in the backyard.
Although today the sewerage is water-borne, the outside toilets are still there. Most families wash out of
moveable basins in the bedroom — which means
sponging. You found no ceiling, and you had one fixed
by a local artisan, out of hessian sacking. You paid
for it, painted it white so as to decrease the sagging,
stained the grey floor, plastered the walls inside,
landscaped the tiny yard yourself.

This was where I went to live in 1946 and where
our first three children were born and raised. Compared with the boxes that have been constructed in
the last two decades and already look slummy, these
Orlando West houses of the Forties were the strongest
structures ever to be put up for Africans by a municipality or state between here and the Equator. They
still stand firm, neat, and cosy if small.The project
was never to be repeated.

More and more people were being removed from
areas considered too near the city, where they owned
houses on mortgages that bled them to death. In the
south-west, the municipal councils simply added more
houses, but with poorer materials. Matters grew worse
when the central government took over housing for
blacks (including Africans, 'Coloureds' and Asians).
Sanitation deteriorated and there was overcrowding.
Lavatories leaked and dripped and wept and hissed
for months without local-government attention.
Soweto had become monstrously slummier after we
left the country . . . .

When you occupy a township house, after all the
graft and perquisites you've had to pay, which no one
can nail on any official in particular, and which must
therefore be talked about in whispers, you have to
bash down walls, punch new doors, replace the syn-

thetic tin doors back and front, change the rooms about so that the kitchen is at the back, spread outward as far as the small yard will permit, pull water into the house, take one end of the house nearer the toilet. This can only be done if a loan is available to you. This is the metaphor that explains black life. You're always being pushed into the system of an architect you don't know, on whom you have as much influence as you do on the elements. The same with education, taxation, rural settlements, industry and so on.

No bathroom, no sinks, no drainage. In my sister's house where I stayed for a few days in the typical Soweto dwelling produced over the past twenty years or so, I washed out of a basin that stood in the bedroom on a movable iron frame. A bedroom filled out only by a bed and a movable cabinet closet. The water came from a pot on the coal stove. Shave first, devising a way of removing shaving cream that clings to the razor at intervals, having no tap to flush it out. Throw out the water; wash face and sponge top part of the body and arms, throw out water, sponge the lower part of the body and possibly wash lower limbs, throw out water. Wet hair and comb . . . .

The house has four rooms. My sister gave me hers and slept in the living-dining room; second bedroom is occupied by two daughters, each with two children, and her own three sons, aged ten, twelve and fifteen. They eat on the kitchen floor, others on the living-room floor. Multiply her coal stove by at least 500,000 and ponder the pall of smoke that greets every morning, every night. It seeps through doors and windows, starts clawing at your throat and piercing your lungs, telling you another Soweto day has begun.

Night reading is impossible, the newspaper or anything else, unless you are accustomed to paraffin lamps and candles. If you have grown out of these as I have in the years of exile, it is a futile attempt. Because my sister's house is so full, I went to stay with a cousin, in one of those few experimental houses owned by the occupant — in Dube, which they stopped developing almost as soon as they had started to open it up for selling on a 30-year lease. A crude little structure, but there is a bathroom with a toilet inside, and a guest room, as there are only three persons in the family. My cousin can hardly be called middle-class, but he is a little better off than my sister — so false the economic standards are which maintain the white middle-class at a level at least five time higher than that which the African professional might relatively consider his own. My cousin is proud of his little house, even though the living-dining room can barely squeeze in a sofa in addition to four small chairs, table and stereo box.

There are no apartment houses for Africans in South Africa. Single male hostels for migrant labourers, yes — dormitory style. The result is what you see at my sister's. Divorce, separation of any kind, invariably means that the women and the children must return to the parents, unless the man loses the case. Maybe the government does not consider that Africans also experience deprivations of this kind. The widow or divorcee or deserted or aged woman is perpetually plagued by offical questions as to her ability to pay the rent. There is a concerted effort to make her feel insecure, so that she may, in sheer desperation, move out to the rural areas.

Sons can only apply for a house if they are married or about to marry. The waiting lists are interminable. Authorities simply close their ears to the constant appeals from the people for more and better services. More and more Africans are enlarging and improving the houses, indicating a superior sense of utility and aesthetics.

Back in the United States we watched with mild amusement the middle-class guilt feeling that continually pushes some whites and blacks out into the ghettos, looking for vibrant life, for feeling, for gut agitation, for a cause. Like whites who slash and patch trousers, stink up the university campuses and speakeasies with stale sweat, until they feel alive again. People who have never had to live with rats and cockroaches who are looking for muck and pain.

I had come back to township living after tasting the sheer physical comfort that space and toilet facilities afford, and now ghetto living stood out stark, intolerably painful. Detentions, bannings, arrests, imprisonment, death in the cells — these have taken a terrifying toll on blacks, unparalleled before Sharpeville. The children who have fled across the borders have undertaken so much at a tender age, have hit the long, tortuous, uncertain, often soul-mutilating road of exile. My personal experience, like that of hundreds of my fellow-exiles, has been that once the sense of adventure began to wear off, nostalgia and the distance from meaningful involvement, from relevance, began to gnaw at one's vitals.

As I go from one township to another, it comes home to me again how trapped we are in municipal housing projects; life turning around in circles, unable to link up with the larger, more hopeful, more purposeful life outside. Trapped. That's what ghettos are for. You are constantly trying to extend yourself, but always you are just, and only just, above the muck and smell of it.

All these and other age-old irks have gathered up
the bacteria that have been working their own mischief in the underdog's esteem for himself. And the
boil must burst. It continues to fester; it will burst
again. And again, until . . . . For all the rhetoric the
political chiefs in exile have sustained, on international
time and money, for all their posturing, for all their
rival claims that they directly engineered the revolt of
the youth in this country; for all the claims authorities
made about new and old communist plots, the one
stark truth remained: that these youngsters were
made by the conditions I have sketched out. They
have no way of knowing the political leaders who
went into exile or were jailed for life, as their organisations abroad have been banned since 1963. Several of
the children were either babies or not born yet. Besides, which organisation of the stature the exiles boast
about would start something in which kids had to
confront guns with rocks? The students did it all on
their own, driven by the demons of hurt and humiliation, by their own esteem for themselves.

Self-esteem? You cannot talk about self-esteem
without thinking about education. White people have
sought to block or disrupt traditional continuity in
bl ck life, while doing everything in their power to
institutionalise continuity of their own making. Their
expensive monuments — statues and buildings, town
and street names, public holidays like December 16,
October 12, when their heroes must be remembered,
their cultural organisations, the content of their
education — all these entrench the white man's self-
esteem. Our heroes have been discredited, no 'national'
holiday is intended to enhance the black man's respect
for his own history.

'Bantu education', introduced in 1953, disrupted

a tradition which the African would, if allowed to plan his own education and define his culture for himself, have revised and refined in a way that would give him self-esteem. And yet 'Bantu education' was being peddled by the white politicians as just the kind of system that would help us restore our tribal cultures. They knew that nationalism had cut across our ethnic boundaries. This had to be destroyed and with it the unity it had forged among the African peoples. The apostles of 'Bantu education' evidently saw black nationalism in South Africa as an extension of the larger movement for nation-building in post-colonial Africa. Missionary education allowed for freedom of intellectual mobility, though this was censored by such religious authority as we had absorbed into our consciousness. It also made us ashamed of our indigenous culture. The missionaries could only conceive of the kind of education they themselves had received in Europe — Protestant or Catholic. But for us in South Africa it was a Christian education for a conquered people, and was not aimed at cultivating an independent mind. Its saving grace was that one could, as an adult, disengage oneself from it, re-educate oneself and develop a constructively critical attitude. The missionaries provided the basic skills for acquiring knowledge, good libraries, and a learning environment. We had to be careful, on pain of expulsion, not to allow politics to go beyond the level of school debates. No independent interpretations of history, geography, the Bible, were allowed or encouraged in the classroom.

Either way, before or after 'Bantu education', what we were learning at school had very little to do with our daily torments, our living conditions. Most often it was an escape from our miseries. Try to chain the

mind and deny it a good education and it will revolt.
Try chaining it with stronger bonds and it will turn
against the master with a pitchfork. It happened in
1976.

Because of our preoccupation with the things that
help us survive our condition, with the sheer
mechanics of living, African parents have tended to
regard school as a shelter for their children while the
older people are at work during the day. They have
never, as a pressure group, asked what their children
are being taught or sold short by the teacher, himself
a victim of the system. The year of the revolt explod-
ed in the faces of parents and teachers. Not in so many
words, the children were trying to tell everybody
that they were being denied a proper education; that
what they were getting was not helping them to cope
with their miserable environment, to comprehend
it so that they might better be able to deal with it.

Tuesday, July 6. It had been a time of riotous
partying and reunions in Soweto over four days.
Today, Seshego, Pietersburg. Khabi drove me there.

Coming through the highveld and then the bushveld I kept saying aloud, *This is my kind of
country . . . not the tall mountains, not the lush
vegetation . . . give me the expanse of bushveld where
I can see the blue horizon out there.* Colorado, where
I lived for six years, is prairie country. But it could
never be the same as this. The Rockies get in the way
somewhat: they were all right at that distance. I don't
like mountains stooping over me.

But something strange happened to me once, driving
with the family from Denver to California. We took
the south-western route through Durango, crossing
Zion National Park in South Utah. For some forty-
five minutes we meandered through a narrow maze,

in and out between tall gigantic rocks. Just naked rock structures that have no vegetation on them. Each time we took a curve one high rock after another shot up in front of us, towering over us as if some hand were moving them this way and that, and as if it were going to obstruct our progress and close in on us . . . . If Nature was out to frighten us, Rebecca and me, it certainly succeeded. Sheer perpendicular terror leapt out of those rock structures. When we spilled out into the plains, I was trembling. We took the northern route back to Denver — through Sacramento, California, and Salt Lake City. When we hit the Rockies again, I could have stopped the car to hug them. They looked warm, draped as they were with lush green, in contrast to those rocks in Zion National Park, one of Jehovah's catastrophes.

Tonight we are talking with a bunch of lecturers at the University of the North in Sovenga, in the house of my friend Moshe Nkondo. It's a gay evening. It gives me immense joy to be talking to these young men. They fire me with more and still more enthusiasm, hope, fortitude, zest for adventure. But they also tell me things that fill me with trepidation, foreboding . . . . It's all about culture, the politics at the North, the final return. I particularly wanted to test their reaction to the possibility of my joining them. I was glad to know that I would be welcome among them. But of course I also knew that I was talking to people who were bound hand and foot by severe controls, whose movements were being watched, who had a separate academic staff association from that of the white staff, whose organisation was banned from campus by the university administration while the white staff enjoyed campus facilities. Some of the Africans had been terrorised into silence, but those

who felt free to talk to me and Khabi seemed full of
hope. Several students had been expelled after the
series of campus upheavals — demonstrations that had
been going on since the late Sixties.

Here is an institution that purports to be for Africans, and yet does not reflect an African character,
has a rector who is a mere signature, a megaphone for
orders that are issued by whites who are above him.
The government imposes its own system of university
administration. There is hardly any meaningful contact between the university and the African communities in the same district. The people regard it as they
would a white elephant, distant, inaccessible, alien to
their culture and aspirations. Still, I decide I must
apply for the vacant chair of English.

Wednesday, July 7. We have come to visit Dr. C.N.
Phatudi, Chief Minister of Lebowa. He and his Minister of Internal Affairs take us around. In his aristocratic
fashion, he gestures this way and that and makes us
feel at ease, as long as we bear in mind where we are.
Then protocol breaks down, and we are invited to
lunch with the two at Hotel Seshego.

Even in those few days I had been back in the
country, I had had a glimpse that confirmed my view
of the situation from outside: here, as in the urban
areas, the people's survivalist strategies were straining
towards something nobler than mere survival. We are
all trapped as a conquered people. I could not presume
to judge the territorial leaders from the relatively safe
position of exile, whatever my negative views about
separate development imposed from the assemblies
of power.

A telephone message comes through to Seshego,
while we are still in the Chief Minister's office: Aunt
Dora, my aunt of *Down Second Avenue*, died last

night in Atteridgeville, Pretoria, aged seventy. She was sickly for a long time. The last of my mother's family to go, she dominated the household on Second Avenue, Marabastad, and I grew up under her. Strong, often recklessly so, the veritable product of black ghetto life. She could have been midwife to a lioness, as we say in Sesotho. Her death is the end of a long episode in a story spanning a hundred years since her late father was born. Aunt Dora died a ravaged, withered and mindless woman.

I am driven to Maupaneng village in Mphahlele district, sixty kilometres south-east of Pietersburg. That is where I spent seven years of my childhood as a herdboy. I have never returned to it since that winter's night, during the Depression, when my mother came to pull us out — my brother, sister and me. I could never return, even for a visit. It was associated with the memories of a domestic break-up, too painful for me to retell. Before I left Philadelphia, I set my mind on revisiting Maupaneng. It was to be part of a pilgrimage.

The mountains and the valleys that have continued to enter my dreams all these forty-five years, like a ghost that refuses to be laid, taunt me to get out of the car and walk. But we have little time. I'm trying to take in these three weeks in voracious gulps. The river that used to swell fiercely and drive fear into us; the mountains that used to hug to themselves the palpable dark of the moonless nights teeming with glow-worms and fill our dreams with witches' goings-on, the villages that clung to the foothills: all these shrank into a manageable world of my adult mind, real or imagined. Maupaneng now has only six houses, and erosion has walked across it with giant hooves, leaving marks of devastation all along the valley. Rain

has been bashing down the banks of the river, so that
the remaining houses and the ruins seem to be fighting
a rearguard action against the mountain. But the
thatched houses still bear colourful patterns on the
outside, made with earth paints by the women,
evidence of the vibrant life that used to fill this valley.
Hlakaro River ('Leshoana' in *Down Second Avenue*)
is dry, choking with rock and silt, and we actually
drive over it! What humiliation for it! The house where
we lived with a stern grandma and aunt and uncle still
stands. My grandma died in the early Seventies. To
the news of her death, like that of my father's in 1948,
I responded with a curt but neutral *ao,* which in
Sesotho suggests *Is that so . . . .* They and my aunt
were a stone-hearted trio, with the exterior of spiked
cactus. My aged aunt keeps the house. The fireplace,
kept circular by a bicycle rim, is still there. The stone
they used to grind sorghum on, with the grinder on it,
sits near the fireplace. I cannot imagine that, small
as it is, the floor used to accommodate five persons
sleeping on grass mats. The house in which Mother
and Father slept whenever they visited at Christmas
time, and which was used by my uncle, also now
dead, still stands. The mimosa tree is gone. My aunt
now uses a coal stove which one of her nephews lent
her, and wood as fuel. There is still a mud-wall
enclosure, which made it possible for us to sleep
outside on summer nights to escape the grey bugs
that always descended on us from the grass thatching.
On rainy nights they feasted on us. And we never
fought back: didn't know how to.

The goat kraal has been empty these many years.
The cattle kraal has disappeared.

My aunt receives me with something like timid joy,
but I sense an age-withered stone underneath her

broad smile . . . .

We go to the Methodist church — across the river — that we used to be herded into by God-fearing folks. It still stands on the edge of the river opposite Maupaneng. I remember the revival services when preachers shouted themselves hoarse. I remember the old women who sat on the floor at the back, not on benches, so that they didn't have to kneel during a prayer. Not far away is a clearing with pools of tree shade, where interdenominational services were often held on occasions of drought or some other natural disaster. The clearing is smaller, because the river has chewed up much of it and inundated it by turns.

Next, to the school I first attended — the first community school ever to be set up in the Transvaal, established by Chief Mphahlele. It was not attached to any church. The road to it from Maupaneng is still as sandy as I remember it from those days. The main building has survived since 1921 — the date on the foundation stone — and is still in use. It was in this little hall, on this wooden floor, that my odyssey began in 1924. I have come back, my elders, you who went down under but whose shuffling, whose whispers I can hear on the ground, in the air. Take me back . . . . Around the school grounds, where also stands a forty-year-old secondary school, is the bushveld. Still largely unpeopled as it was in those days, it stretches away, interrupted only by the blue hills.

Back in Soweto I ask Khabi to stop in front of my former house in Orlando West, opposite Uncle Tom's Hall, which was not there in my time. Just to see what it looks like. The owner has changed the yard landscape I laid out and terraced, and now even has a driveway for his car. A dull pain presses against me inside as I recall the happy years — such as we could salvage from ghetto conditions — we lived in the house. When I suspect that I'm almost enjoying the pain, I say to Khabi we should leave . . . .

What a homecoming.

At last, after all the tension generated by security police, we started the conference of the Institute of Black Studies. It was banned from Dube, part of Soweto, so we shifted the venue to Wilgespruit Farm in Roodepoort, an inter-racial conference centre. Notwithstanding, the hall was packed. Security police also attended, now a feature at meetings as inevitable as an open mouth. It became quite evident how hungry our people are for ideas. Moshe Nkondo read a paper on South African black fiction; Fatima Meer, from Durban, on apartheid; Herbert Vilakazi, from the United States, on the sociology of apartheid; Dr. Mamphele Ramphele on Black Consciousness; Njabulo Ndebele from Lesotho on literature in indigenous languages; Jakes Gerwel from Cape Town on South African literature, and others. My paper was 'Exiles, Prodigals, Homecoming and African Literature.'

Soon after the conference Mrs. Meer was banned; so was Dr. Ramphele, who was also banished to Tzaneen in the northern Transvaal. With big names like Dr. Nthato Motlana and Nimrod Mkele, who conceived the institute, the occasion augured well for a body that would establish and consolidate a machinery for the communication of ideas among our people. But always the presence of security police was like a dark cloud hovering over us.

My first job after Adams College in Natal was in this valley where Ezenzeleni Blind Institute and Kutlwanong Deaf and Dumb School stood. I worked as a clerk for the late Dr. Arthur Blaxall and later as his shorthand-typist. I also taught typing to the blind, carried the baskets and mattresses they made to customers in Johannesburg's suburbs and firms, and brought back those that needed repairing. I was twenty-one that year, 1941. The war was raging in Europe and North Africa. I felt unprepared to teach conventional school and wanted to matriculate first, by private study.

Looking at the hills around, locating the house that used to be Arthur Blaxall's, the buildings that the schools occupied, I remembered how I used to scale the boulders around for exercise, how I hiked along the ridge as far as Sophiatown. The schools for the handicapped have long since been removed to the rural areas as they were regarded by the authorities as a 'black spot', defacing a white area. White suburbia has taken over, except for the farm down in the valley, Wilgespruit, which is an ecumenical centre.

I remember also what bad and now discarded verse I used to write·here. At one level I was just a bundle of confusion. At another, the verse was a sad commentary on the way we had been taught poetry in high school and teachers' training college — the way that leaves you with the impression that pastoral surroundings must inspire the writing of poetry, and that poetry must express 'nice' sentiments.

We are all full of hope that the foundation has been laid for the Institute of Black Studies. But when power flexes its muscles and puffs these days, the creative imagination is threatened. Yet it must endure. There can be nothing sinister in the spread of wholesome ideas if they are allowed a free platform, free debate, free scope for their realisation, if they ride on the broad daylight of a people's faith in themselves.

Back in Soweto I continue to meet people. They tell me that, sad as the events were, the kids who demonstrated against Afrikaans and were cut down should be a constant reminder to Pretoria, that as long as policy is rammed down the throats of vote-less millions, as long as people are forced to live below the standards of human decency and dignity, material-ly and spiritually, you don't need agitation from out-side. The eruption of anger becomes spontaneous. I am reminded myself that children have no way of knowing that parents do everything to protect them from the hurts only they (parents) know; the hurts from which the children's grandparents tried to protect the mothers and fathers of today, and so on through the records of black-white encounter. And yet, as someone else said to me, it is always a new generation that must push beyond the frontiers where its fore-bears stopped. The rejection of the values of yesterday is something parents must learn to accommodate.

My friends tell me further that, since I left the country, blacks talk back to the white man. They don't make it easy for the white man to shove them off the pavement or highway.

I meet people who bear the scars of Robben Island and of other kinds of mainland prisons. Like Zeph Mothopeng. Like Barney Ngakana, who was banned for two five-year terms; women like Lilian Ngoyi and Albertina Sisulu who have seen one banning order after another for the last eighteen years. Around these and other stalwart survivors are the shattered lives, the broken families, the motherless or fatherless children roaming about without purpose, sinewy remnants of those who shared the travails of detention and the long stretch. Scars that scream out: *Who will atone? Who will atone?*

Another feature Soweto has taken on since I left is the large number of people I meet who visibly bear the marks of excessive drinking. Unhealthy, flabby faces here; a stooping, shuffling gait, drooping midline and shoulders there; the missing teeth — all very depressing. The lotus eaters . . . . Sensibility blunted so that you can suspend pain for a while, in the never-never land where it is always twilight . . . . And you know, as you look at these people, that there are compound problems weighing heavily on them that have so much to do with the deadend trail of black living.

It was James Baldwin, the African-American novelist, who said that those who debase others are also debasing themselves. This comes to me when I see Alexandra Township's compound, its hostels for single persons. They look like dormitories into which a battered regiment might have retreated to wait for better weather, greater courage. The detention cell, intended to hold people apprehended in the compound, has plastered walls inside. The dormitories are not plastered. And inside Alexandra there are deep furrows, alive with muck and maggots floating on the water, that run a metre away from the front doors down several streets.

We buried Aunt Dora in Atteridgeville. I had intended to visit her on my return from the north, but her death forestalled me, ending an episode in my own life. She was a small, wasted figure in her coffin. The ashes of a fire that once burnt bright on Second Avenue amid the rubble and muck and stench of Marabastad. I was back in the rhetoric of death and life during the nights of the wake. Words, words, words, poetry as ritual, ritual as poetry, death as the poetry of life and vice versa. That is how the African can soak himself in grief, until he can endure the sense of loss and its pain and not break.

I visit at the same time the graves of Mother and my brother, who lie in the same cemetery. But words outside ritual can dissipate the wonder of death . . . .

The next day I went to the site of old Marabastad. At one end I found the market and the Indian shopping plaza. First Avenue still exists as a pathway. Second Avenue and others can easily be made out because the Asiatic Bazaar, where the avenues continued, still exists. The Bazaar, where we used to raid backyards for discarded tomatoes and overripe bananas. Fung Prak's, the Chinese malt mill opposite our house, is gone. I stood where our house was, dominated by a God-fearing grandmother and a fearless chucker-out of an aunt. I scooped up some earth and rubbed it between my fingers.

I meet Danie in Atteridgeville. The noisy boy of Second Avenue days was always singing Paul Robeson's songs, especially the ones from the movie *Sanders of the River,* as he came up from lower down, or was walking home. Moloi, the boy with the lovely tenor next-door, died early in the Seventies. My memories of Second Avenue, indeed of Marabastad, are inevitably wrapped up in my constant thoughts of Moloi, Rebone, Oripa of First Avenue, Makhudu of Newclare who often came to play with us, and Danie. But Moloi's death, like Oripa's, hit me especially hard, because Moloi is the ragtime and blues that keep vocalising unsolicited in my mind.

I was invited to a luncheon to meet a group of Afrikaner journalists. I had never before had a discussion with an Afrikaner, except with those who had taught me Afrikaans in high school and at Adams College. We have always been apart, so I've never felt any inclination to speak to one as you would speak to an equal. Were you eager to talk to them? a friend

wanted to know. I was curious, I tell him. To sum up
the conversation: I asked which was the most forward-
looking of their papers. *Beeld*, all agreed, although
Rapport had the largest circulation.

How far does the paper go? For the moment, not
very far. But there is a build-up of liberal opinion in
Beeld and this should increase the still-small constituency of Afrikaner opinion that wants reforms.
What kind of reforms? Everthing short of a mixed
parliament. Afrikaners won't go for that. Because
Afrikaners think of themselves as a nation, so all the
other ethnic groups, too, should regard themselves as
nations, and *feel* separate.

Has anybody ever considered enquiring and listening
to what Africans have to say on the matter of separate
nations? It is in the nature of power, says a man, for
the strong not to feel the need to speak to the underdog. But now they feel the need. Besides, says a lady,
there were not always outstanding educated Africans
to talk to. But, I respond, since 1910 articulate and
vocal African politicians have pleaded and insisted on
peace and unity, especially unity among all black
groups, and on multi-racial parliamentary representat-
ion. This history has been documented. How is it the
Afrikaner knows so much more about what we want
than we ourselves? Deadlock.

What a sad country.

I found Nadine Gordimer still hacking a way
through the system, a boulder too much for her,
organising literary contests to help boost African
writing; continuing to speak up against censorship in
South Africa. In her house I worked out part of my
apprenticeship in short-story writing in the Fifties.
She read manuscripts and came back with stimulating,
illuminating criticism. Listen to her talk and you

observe the gulf between her kind who are liberated but don't carry political weight, and about ninety-five percent of the white population — people scared of the black man's shadow, scared to be liberated lest they despise themselves for it, or lest the new person in them should make intellectual and emotional demands they could not handle.

What a sad country — a nation refusing to become a nation . . . .

Dr. Phatudi, the Chief Minister of Lebowa, promised to keep pushing the matter of our return.

Back to Base

I was back in Philadelphia on July 27, 1976, after the three stimulating weeks. In September I received a brief and cold reply to my application for the vacant professorship of English at the University of the North. I had submitted this during my visit. Professor Boshoff, the then rector, had written. The Chief Minister investigated. He had been under the impression, said the rector, that Professor Mphahlele would not be allowed to return to South Africa! On what basis? the enquirer wanted to know. No reply. Then the Commissioner-General, through whom every territorial authority has to communicate with the central government — a fake-consular role — decided to leave this world. The Chief Minister had to start from the beginning with his new overlord.

While I was writing one letter after another, and government machinery was grinding slowly, Rebecca and I had a lot of time to turn the question over and over — when to return?

Social work and education, for Rebecca and myself

respectively, can be fully rewarding if they are part of a cultural matrix, and promote the extension of culture, the growth of a people. Because education *is* culture, and because social work, beyond mere relief and sugar lumps for the aged, deals in personalities and groups of personalities, who in turn shape culture and are shaped by it. This could only be realised in a cultural context that we could grasp.

The politics? What was the worst that could happen? If our minds dwelt unduly on that, then it would be no use thinking of returning any longer. *There are people living here* — that was the immediate answer. It sufficed. We wondered what would be best for the two dependent children, Chabi (going on eighteeen) and Puso (going on seventeen)? It would be unfair to expose them to South African conditions, now that they had become cosmopolitan.

The older three had long got used to living independently in different cities. Whenever we reckoned the profit and loss entailed in exile, the line between them was never clear when it came to our children. What were losses to us, they regarded as gains, and vice versa. And in exile, formulas and conventions that work in a native culture have to be sacrificed. It was enough that they felt happy in America, whose lifestyle they had adopted without being American down to the marrow. And America, of all the countries in the world, provides the adventure young people are most attracted to. Anthony seems to have mastered the art of being an individualist; Kefilwe is calm and self-reliant, with a literary talent; Motswiri devotes himself to his art in graphics, highly sensitive and therefore vulnerable. Exiles and immigrants: America teems with them.

What if we saw the youngest through college first?

They preferred not to take that route right away. We would find ourselves returning in time for retirement. That wouldn't do. We had to establish a presence and prepare for what we could do during retirement while still physically and mentally active. Retirement and old age in the United States, especially for a black immigrant, can be excruciatingly rough; retirement and old age among your own people can be a gentle process, but you have to *earn* that phase. Suppose They deny you an opportunity to teach where you want to? Suppose They neutralise your presence? Suppose indeed They would not tolerate an African professor over a white staff who are less qualified? An institution that is a product of 'separate development'? How do you reconcile this with your rejection of the system?

Looking at the English syllabus I was sure that a good teacher — and I am vain enough to consider myself a born teacher — could inject life and new ideas into it. It is not much different from that at the University of South Africa. The low standards of high school and primary school create difficulties for the student at university. I was confident that if given the opportunity I and others could devise a way of getting freshmen students off to a better start. Standards remain low at university only when you have staff who are themselves not self-confident, not well qualified. They then assign work which makes no demands on themselves or their students. Standards also remain low if the teacher, however good, is not allowed by the head of the department to experiment, to inject a sense of adventure into the syllabus, to stimulate the students.

I would be dealing with minds that were already alert, aware of the poverty of their education. I am an idealist, an empiricist too, and I keep pushing, wanting to move mountains, hitting the wall and hurting myself in the process. But it won't let me be — this drive always to try to do better, to excel myself. The minds I would be dealing with were already unchained — by their own effort. Give people a poor education, and the mind will soon find out. Revolt is then inevitable.

No, the mind cannot be chained forever. This much They know — the strong men all over the world. Vinoba Bhave, the Indian mystic, said in the Thirties that when people in power fail to reach a captive's mind, to bend it to Their will, They try to get at it through the body. When They still fail, They mutilate the body.

And so the debate continued. We must hit the road back while the sun was still up. We sold our house while we waited for entry visas, and shipped our goods as soon as we were reassured that we could re-enter. The visas came two days before we were booked to leave. What a homecoming. They hold you on the line while they do other things.

VI

This Native Land, This Furnace

We arrived on Rebecca's birthday, August 17, 1977, five years after we had begun to return.

A number of people were at Jan Smuts to meet us, including my sister and some of her children, Khabi, the late Baldwin Mudau, and my cousins. We stopped in Atteridgeville for the night, and headed north the next day, to Mphahlele district. My cousin, Phankge, had invited us to stay with him. He had written to us in Philadelphia, 'Even if some of my children should need to go sleep with the baboons on the mountain, you must come and stay with us.' He is principal of a primary school. Puso drew crowds around himself because he could only speak English. His audience was intrigued by his accent and fluency. We had chosen the north because there wouldn't be anybody in Soweto with a big enough house to accommodate us and our bags, let alone the furniture and other things still coming by boat. Then again, I was hoping to be employed at the University of the North, where the post of English professor was still vacant. I was going to wait for it to be advertised. I wanted to allow the University no excuse that I was out of reach.

I discovered jogging routes that restored a full acquaintance with the landscape I had begun to re-discover in 1976. My cousin's house is a few metres from the primary school that launched me hesitantly on the road to — how could one have guessed at the destination then? I followed the routes I remembered as old trails I carved out with the goats and cattle forty-five years before, leading to good pasture.

I see Hlakaro now, bloated with sand and rock, as a sign that the old-old partition between the 'heathens' and the Christians no longer holds. The village that nestled on the foothills on the other side of Maupaneng has merged with the others where the churches are. The whole area is built up in modern style, except for a few clusters of rondavels with bright and decorative earth colours on the walls. Cultivated fields are few and far between, and foodstuffs are sold at absurdly high prices in the stores. Rural poverty has spread all over. The owners of the new-style dwellings will mostly be teachers, nurses, clerks, storekeepers, and workers who live in the urban areas but for whom a house is a psychological compensation for the political and economic security they lack.

Sounds of birds, the smell of foliage, the August-September dusts, and the January-February smell of wild cherries, of *morula* fruit, took me way back to the years when I had stood naked in the elements, as reckless and free and innocent as nature could be.

Then we moved to Lebowakgomo, twelve kilo-metres from Mphahlele proper. It is a new town being built by the Lebowa government and the East Rand Administration Board. East Rand workers are being told to buy houses here, rather than hope for municipal dwellings in the urban areas, and North-Sotho speakers can generally buy here too. Another conspiracy to keep more and more Africans out of urban areas. Water toilets and small bathrooms are built in. The yards are fenced, the streets are mostly tarred, and electricity is being installed.

Puso and I got down to planting a lawn. During my mountain hikes I found plants that suited my rockery admirably. Throughout the blazing hot days of November and December we surrendered to the instinctive drive that says *there shall be a garden.*

I gave Puso regular English lessons to keep him busy while we waited for a reply to his application from Lesotho High School in Maseru. By the time the reply came in February 1978 saying he should come, we had all had second thoughts about the enterprise. He was too restless and psychologically suspended between acceptance of the South African human landscape and resentment of its political climate. He would have to learn Afrikaans if he attended a South African school, and the bush town of Pietersburg had already soured his life with racism. One day he had drifted into a Wimpy Bar and sat down at a table to be served — as anyone might do in a hamburger joint in the United States. The African waitress told him politely that he was not allowed to sit down. We hadn't seen him go in. Outside he puffed and blurted, 'These turkeys!' And then we were seized by the dread that Africans in this country learn to know from the age of five — the terror that police represent. This time, on his behalf. If he was to be picked up . . . for *anything* . . . . It could shatter him, particularly if he couldn't make those telephone calls a person is allowed to make from the police station, in the U.S.

In March of 1978 Puso and we decided that he had better return to the United States. He would stay with his sister in Washington and resume his schooling there. It was done. We had to give him back to America, as it were. Either way you bleed, if you are a black person. Some bleed fast, others slowly.

When in February the University of the North said 'No', the government service of Lebowa offered me a job as inspector of schools for English teaching. Rebecca had found a job in government service as a social worker.

In the ten months I worked for the government, I had the opportunity of travelling the length and breadth of the territory visiting schools and demonstrating aspects of English teaching. I saw for myself the damage Bantu Education had wrought in our schooling system over the last twenty-five years. Some teachers could not even express themselves fluently or correctly in front of a class, and others spelled words wrongly on the blackboard. The classes were grotesquely large, often one hundred students in Standard Nine, where numbers are supposed to thin out into an apex. Because of a shortage of qualified teachers, some found themselves thrown into English where their specialisation or love did not lie.

You fended for yourself as an inspector travelling from one circuit to another. You asked for accommodation and food wherever you happened to land, because the only hotel that admits Africans is the Holiday Inn in Pietersburg. Your journeys took you to districts lying at a radius of 200 kilometres and more from Pietersburg. In the old days African inspectors bicycled and walked and hitch-hiked on wagons. Today you motor, but eat and sleep where you can. Whites can always motor back to some hotel for the night.

So the central government tells you that 'homeland' departments of education are now autonomous; so you sweat your ass off trying to devise new strategies for the teaching of English and other subjects (Maths and Science are the other two in the problematic triangle); so you visit schools and teacher-training colleges to lecture to teachers; so you submit reports on your activities and present recommendations. There is no response. Not a word from either the African assistant secretary or his white superior. You had better settle down to the painful realisation that you're never going to hear a thing from either of them.

No ideas are solicited or volunteered on educational planning, on curricula. Although the teacher has a choice in the matter of what text-books to use, he can move only within the circle determined by Pretoria. Also, he is most often ill-qualified to decide which text is best for class use. Autonomous? The examiners are still mostly white. School publishing is largely in the hands of Afrikaans companies. There is a lot of collusion between examiners, the inspectorate, the Department of Education and Training and publishing houses, so that certain books should be 'pushed' in black schools, and others played down. Pretoria says these territorial governments may take over the whole examination system if they have the personnel and the money. But of course there is no money.

Rebecca and I are driving from Sovenga, on the Tzaneen road, back to Lebowakgomo. It's about 9 p.m. and raining gently. I have my lights on full beam as it is a dark road. A pick-up overtakes us and keeps a more or less constant distance. The driver waves for me to pull up on the left and stop. It's dark, it's raining, and I do not intend to stop for white men on such a night — *any* night at all. 'Keep driving and don't stop,' Rebecca vocalises my thoughts. Clearly there is no way they can stop me, short of swerving right in front of me, and suddenly too. But they will be risking an accident, although *we* are more likely to get hurt. We overtake, and I step on the accelerator some more. They obviously don't want to leave us alone. We feel safer in a well-lit town like Pietersburg, but only relatively so. Africans are not welcome in a white man's town at night. We stop at a Portuguese café to buy bread. The pick-up pulls up in front of us.

'Why do you keep bright lights on with us in front?' Slim says, clearly not caring for an answer.

'I wanted to see better.'

'Don't you know it's against the law?' Beef says, hands in pockets.

'You mean to see better?'

'We are army security,' Beef continues, 'and I have handcuffs here.' He produces a pair that is certainly not the kind police use. 'Do you want us to take you to the police station?'

My mind darts back and forth and one flash discloses a picture of Steve Biko, chained, naked, cold, bruised, and in unspeakable pain. Terror seizes me by the throat. From sheer speculation on what *can* happen.

'We haven't done anything wrong,' says Rebecca belligerently. 'Why did you harass us on the road?'

'*Moenie daai kak taal praat met my, hoor!*' Slim says aggressively.

'I don't speak Afrikaans,' Rebecca says.

'Wait a minute,' I try to pacify Rebecca in Sesotho, '*Ke nkga lesepa fa*' — I smell some shit here. I have still enough breath in me to drive the metaphor home: '*Lesepa la bosiu he le ma mong wa lona.*' No one will ever know who did it.

'No, we don't want to go to the police station. I'm sorry if I offended you with the lights.'

'Where's your pass?'

'I'm still waiting for it from Pretoria.' I kept up the language of the master. 'I applied for it in October.'

'*Jy lieg.*' — It's a lie. 'Your car registration says LEB,' Beef observes. 'Why have you only now applied for a pass?'

'It may have got lost, I may have only just arrived back in the country, I may be an immigrant . . . .'

'Where are you going now?' Slim says, maybe too lazy to try to unravel these possibilities and the reason for my tone of voice — between argument and doubt.

'Lebowakgomo.'

'All right, open your boot.' Beef directs his torch-light into the boot and then inside the car.

'All right, go!'

I drive around the block, stop in front of another café and buy bread. When I return to the car, there is the pick-up, alongside.

'This is not the way to Lebowakgomo,' says Slim.

'No, but I'm going there.' They wait until we have pulled out.

The voice of fear that has been building up in me tells me to speed, because they may be out there in the dark, out for a night's fun. I push past 120 kilometres and stay there, until we enter Chuene's Pass. The moon is bright. Its brilliance washes the stretch of mountain called Mogodumo-tshadi (the female). Further down into the gorge is a deep-deep shade thrown by the other stretch — the Mogodumo-tona (the male), which towers over us as we pass, on the dark side of the moon as it were. At night Mogodumo looks fearful but conjures up an image of ancestral spirits whispering words of comfort, eternal safety. As I've

said, I always think of it as the mountain of the gods.
We are home and cosy. I slow down into Lebowakgomo valley. We have left the sign showing the
Pietersburg-Lebowa boundary — whatever it means —
far behind.

'Bloody fakes!' Rebecca puffs out. 'They may be
nothing like army security, and those handcuffs look
like the wire toys we used to play with as kids.'

Thinking back on that night, I wondered why
people who, like whites, have all the power they
could ever want should play at petty demonstrations
of authority. A paranoid nervousness . . . . They still
don't feel or believe They are fully in charge. It seems
the more power a man appropriates or is given, the
more often he turns it against himself, is driven to
mutilate the physical being of other people in the
process of tyrannising himself. He is the first person
to submit to the very authority that is handed down
to him. Eric Fromm must be right in his reasoning
about this.

I arrive at Groothoek Hospital, Zebediela (Lebowa)
with the middle finger of my left hand split in two
from the tip to a millimetre above the first joint. A
power lawn mower did it. Rebecca, who has driven
me, remains in the car. I wait my turn in the queue at
the window where one is given one's file, and in the
queue waiting to be attended to. The pain is almost
intolerable. I'm taken in to an African doctor. He
recommends an X-Ray. I go and wait for the radio-
grapher — about thirty minutes. I feel as if at any
moment I shall flip over, unconscious. Back in the
consulting room, the African doctor explains my case
to a white doctor, evidently his superior. The white
doctor is short and stocky, dressed the way so many

doctors are on Sundays when they are on duty in hospitals.

'That will teach you not to mow lawns on Sundays instead of going to church, ' says Dr. Shorty.

Suddenly I feel a knot of something tighten just below my navel. My lips begin to quiver, as they often do when the blood is boiling. 'Whose Sunday and whose church are you talking about? What makes you think I ever go to church? I have full control over my Sundays.'

'Oh, is that so?' Shorty says, with a tone that suggests, you didn't do so well with your lawn mower on a Sunday.

This infuriates me even more. 'Look here, white man, don't give me that muck about Sunday and church. It's the white man's Sunday and church, *yours*. *You* people brought the church to Africa and fouled up the continent. And you still want to drive us to church — what's it ever done for my people, damn it!'

'Look, don't give me grief — I was only joking.'

My voice has been rising progressively so nurses and patients gather at the open door to listen. I realise that the African doctor has slipped out quietly. Still louder: 'Shit man, go and crack your stupid jokes over somebody else's head, damn you! You whites are so arrogant.'

I stand up and leave him sitting at his desk, his head bent over it. The African doctor is waiting to stitch the finger in another room.

I go down to Venda in the north to do my research into oral poetry. September 10, 1979 is the week of the 'independence' celebrations. The stadium is full, but I observe that the people are not jubilant — they don't scream or ululate. Nothing ecstatic here. They seem to be going through a programmed expression of emotion. The people seem to drag their feet to the stadium. Wednesday afternoon is the opening of the buildings 'donated' by the central government of South Africa. The Deputy Minister in Dr. Koornhof's department is guest speaker on Wednesday afternoon. As the party moves to the new buildings — Parliament, High Court and ministerial-departmental blocks — the President-to-be is walking between two white officials. Somehow he looks like a prisoner between two plain-clothes detectives, or they like two mafia men leading a renegade or the Godfather's rival. Weird. Looks so unreal, and yet I feel the ghastly and sad reality of it — damn it! I'm wide awake and this little drama is actually happening. That's independence!

I don't go to the midnight celebrations. I had fed my curiosity enough for the day, for a hundred years. Nthambeleni Phalanndwa, poet, takes me to Rashaka-limpani Ratshitanga, poet, in Sibasa district. An earthy man who farms a small hillside plot. He is disillusion-ed with modern life as determined by western culture and technology. He has a simple home. His daughter serves us food, but she can't be more than eleven years old. This man communicates with warmth and profound conviction in his way of life. He says to us: 'Ever since I stopped going to church and turned to my ancestors, I find I can wake up in the morning without being afraid.'

I move on to other villages to record poetry.

When I joined the University of the Witwatersrand in February 1979, I was permitted to honour an invitat-ion I had accepted from Professor André de Villiers, director of the then Institute for the Study of English in Africa at Rhodes University. I was being offered a research fellowship at the Institute for two months. In lieu of research, Rhodes accepted my proposition to finish this memoir, which I had begun in Philadelphia. So March and April it was to be. This is how my journal entry reads:

There are good people here. André de Villiers is an enterprising person. Warm and gentle, a poet who comes to the reader/listener direct, with no intellectual fanfare and horseplay, no steel armour some versifiers put on when they lack an emotional centre.

The weather has been mostly foul, except for the last week or so of my stay. I can't even believe the sun has been out for the whole day today. But the flat I have rented is comfortable. Rebecca and I have never been apart for so long in all our thirty-four years of married life, except for the six months when I taught in Lesotho, 1954. Because it gets very lonely, I grow restless. I am a poor worker if there are no voices in the house, no rattling of kitchen things, when Rebecca is gone some place for more than a week. I begin fidgeting and finding excuses for not knuckling down. But I have surprised myself these seven weeks. Not having transport, I cannot make excuses for not working.

So by some will power, such as it is, I am putting a number of hours into this work, including weekends.

Grahamstown is a quaint little monument of a town. Wherever you go the town seems to be one whole network of 1820 cobwebs: eyes blinking, you are always trying to free yourself from these cobwebs. The town conducts itself as if Dick King were still riding — that *ruiter-in-die-nag* legend so well loved in the white man's interpretation of South African history.

A fishbowl, says a former Johannesburger who

teaches at Rhodes, that's what Grahamstown is. Everybody is inquisitive about the next person's personal affairs. It seems to be a catchment for people who feel old. The town is cut off from the rest of South Africa, contented with its fishbowl of oxygen.

You stand where the monument itself is, on high ground overlooking the wooded town. You look across at the African township on the opposite side. You remember how depressed you were, moving among the one-room tin shacks and brick boxes out there. But this is not an uncommon contrast in South Africa. What makes you uneasy is that this costly Settler's Monument of a building is an outrage against the poetry of architecture, just as the Settlers themselves entirely dismissed the humanism of Africa which they found here. I'm told that the monument's only saving grace is that it is being used for various concerts and get-togethers. By whom? Mostly whites, as the Africans live so far away.

The English have that deceptive, genteel and aloof manner about them that makes you think that they are accessible at any time. Watch it. Your dignity is likely to run into a wall and come away with a bleeding nose. You come by the local speakeasy or Tiny's Steak House. They look intimate and you are tempted to enter. Your instinct warns you in time: you're in South Africa, you are unlearning international habits.

In Pietersburg, your reflexes jerked back into place as soon as you entered the town. The very faces of the whites look unhappy about something, forbidding. You could never be tempted. But of course, whether tempted or forewarned, you're equally thrown on to your blackness. There is no logic in having returned to put up with a place that does not even pretend to be civilised in the way human relations are regulated and conducted. No logic. But there is something deep down there, something one cannot verbalise: it is self-justifying.

Has our idealism betrayed us? We often ask. Is our return an admission of defeat — the failure of long-distance commitment? In spite of the ease with which we have travelled in and out of the concourse of international cultures, in spite of the good jobs we have held, of the better education our children are enjoying in an open society, in spite of the freedom of mobility and association it affords, have we not been unconsciously nagged by the fact that nowhere in this white-dominated world have the black peoples any power that really matters; that where it does matter, for instance within independent African and Caribbean nations, it is diminished whenever the black world tries to sway the white world one way or another, on United Nations and other platforms? Have we not in fact been startled to realise how individual black nations can be manipulated by whites, who have superior technological and material resources?

Yes, these are weighty questions. But we could have created a little corner of our own like other relatively free blacks in the outside world, where racism takes forms that are not loaded with the pain we experience in South Africa. The matter always comes back to the personal search for relevance, to one's cultural milieu. We have come to learn the significance of the collective consciousness in the African-American's survival, rooted in the cumulative process of his culture. And we have observed how this consciousness of a culture is moving beyond mere survival. This is what we came back to — a culture that needs now to go beyond survival.

My friend André and I take a trip to Umtata, Transkei, where the university has invited me to give a lecture to students and staff. I talk to them about my travels abroad. I emphasise what Nigeria and African-Americans have given back to me: self-pride, African consciousness.

The auditorium is packed tight. Several students are standing outside, listening through the windows.

I tell them something about African humanism. I suggest how, if our education system is based on this philosophy, it will truly express our independence of mind, a decolonised mind. I sketch out a plan whereby we should get to know ourselves, our continent, through a study of African history, religion, cosmology, literature and the arts, before we move to other world areas of knowledge, through a combination of our cultural resources and others at the higher levels of education.

I try as best I can to explain that we can still find our way to the ancestors who are a vital part of our humanism, that this is a state of mind, which is why it can work in urban areas as well as in those rural areas where the traditional institutions no longer exist. Our behaviour patterns should also reflect this. But we should not regard culture as a museum artefact: it should continue to absorb and redefine the technological, economic and political systems, which we must master if we are to participate effectively in international business and politics. We have to expand our intellectual horizons by studies and research conducted outside the lecture room in addition to what the syllabus prescribes. I end on the note of rediscovery – the rediscovery of self and identity.

It is altogether an elevating experience for me to be talking to these students and their lecturers.

The next day I am asked to talk to the interracial staff association on my university experience in other parts of Africa and overseas. The central theme deals with the role of ideology in African universities, the efforts of the African intelligentsia to reconcile this with universally-acceptable standards of higher education. This also involves the reconciliation between a university's need to explore its cultural milieu, the local cultural materials, with universally-accepted standards of higher education. Part of this process can already be observed in the Honours programme of African Literature pioneered by Dr. Norman Hodge, professor and head of the English Department. This becomes an extension of the undergraduate treatment of the subject where it will ideally be on a par with British and American literatures. The only other southern institution that has shown this kind of bold and forward-looking syllabus is the National University of Lesotho. Someone in the group comments that mediocre literary criticism in Southern Africa exposes shortcomings in white as well as black school education. Credit should be given to those whites who eventually develop, through their own re-education of the self, rounded, empirical and humanistic attitudes.

When I lecture to the teachers and inspectors of education in the afternoon at the Umtata Town Hall, it is also in the presence of the Secretary for Education and his deputy. Developing my two previous lectures, I continue to drive home the point that right from primary school we need to devise projects that will send pupils into the community to discover their own folklore, local history, local heroes, geography, ethnology and so on. The knowledge of facts and the recitation of these from the teacher's notes, the terror of examinations projected into pupils by teachers and inspectors, are part of a long tradition of South African education: authoritarian, often even autocratic, as distinct from humanistic at the profoundest spiritual levels.

I thought it folly for Africans who claim to be masters of their own destiny to adopt, as Transkeians have done, the system of Cape education for whites. Systems of education are not bought over the counter; they evolve as a collective creative enterprise informed by a cultural identity. I am assured that the Cape Province system is only a temporary measure, the first step towards complete disengagement from Bantu Education.

I am asked later, by some of the university staff, what happened to the efforts of some of them to give me an appointment at their institution. All I know, I explain, is that permission was sought from and given by the Transkei's Education Department for me to be appointed. When the Council was to discuss it, an order came from the top in government circles not to proceed with the matter. The stream got swallowed by the sand right there! White-listing? Rumours? Past misdemeanours? 'Higher' orders from the Republic? There is a long knowing smile all round, accompanied by head-shakes. Then I remember Mr. Cruywagen, the then Minister of Education and Training, who promised to veto any appointment I might be given in an institution under his control . . . .

Last year, November 1978, I was invited by the National University of Lesotho, Roma, to give a public lecture. I spoke on 'Exile, the Tyranny of Place and the Literary Compromise'. The auditorium was packed, with some students spilling on to the stage. Another moving occasion. Question time. A group of refugee students from South Africa decided to bait me. I was accused, in effect, of intellectual dishonesty, of rationalising my return and aborted intention to teach in a university (The North) that had been established under a system I had attacked and was attacking. How delighted Mr. History would have been to hear these students!

In brief I explained that wherever African students are to be found, and I am allowed to teach them, I will *do* it; I had come back to claim my ancestral heritage, to assert my role as a humanist; there was nothing that said a person cannot or should not work in a system he abhors.

Nothing I said cut any ice with that bunch. Abrasive vocabulary came at me which amounted to a charge that I was a traitor to the cause in ever having returned. I knew only too well that my account of the trials, the pain of exile, was too close to the bone for those young exiles. It would have been too much for them to admit this. More words came at me from the gang, intended to lash me to a mimosa bush full of spikes. I bled a little.

The students wanted to know how I could dare say that I did not want to become a professional refugee. Were liberation movements — Mozambican, Angolan, Zimbabwean — not known to have marched back and reclaimed their countries? And how could I dare say that literature did not mount revolutions, that people did not wait for a poem or a play to be composed before they could wage a strike? I had indeed gone on to explain that if you wanted to move people to action you needed to write everyday prose for directness of impact, rather than indulge yourself with images, symbols, and metaphor. Furthermore, I had said, literature as memorable language was an on-going revolution: it renewed experience for us, revitalised language.

A pseudo-marxist voice came riding on the warm air of the auditorium. A white woman's. Now you're negating your responsibility to the masses, the voice said, with a lofty sense of self-importance. I said something which did not express a tenth of what I *really* felt for fear of offending my white hosts. What I constrained myself from saying was that I knew my constituency, to which I was answerable, because I was communicating with it. It was African, and she was not in it as she, a white person, did not share my culture, my constituency's culture . . . .

In the midst of all this, a student rose to read a tribute signed by one hundred students of English, which also pleaded with me to accept an appointment at NUL if offered one. I promised that I would not dismiss such an offer.

I thought of those rusted screws exiles often drive into one another, those labels they stick on one another . . . . But if the Supreme Soul in you is in charge, verbal bullets become mere feathers before they reach you, or a volley of rubber balloons. A nuisance, but the Supreme Soul is in charge . . . .

After a long discussion with my friend Chabani Manganyi, a professor of psychology who is writing a psycho-biography of Es'kia Mphahlele, and Norman Hodge, head of English, André and I leave Umtata for Coffee Bay, to relax; eighty kilometres from Umtata.

Umtata itself is a small nondescript town that used to be the white man's preserve before the South African government gave Transkei a longer tether to run its own affairs. The whites who remained and obtained Transkeian citizenship are of two groups:

those who genuinely feel that they have a better
chance of happiness in a 'state' run by Africans, and
those who desperately want to be free of the responsibility of having to contribute something towards
a greater unified South Africa, scared even of a
possible bloodbath, real or imagined. They feel safe,
they can still hold on to their possessions, the comforts
they were born into, the white man's heritage.

There is this fellow, G.M.C. at Coffee Bay, for
instance, who became a Transkeian citizen. He recruits
labour for one of the Transvaal mining groups. He is
nicknamed by the local Africans 'The Locust' on
account of his tall and slender figure. We watch the
scores of people who come to Coffee Bay to apply
for contracts. Out of a hundred he may take ten. The
others will keep coming once every week, and new
ones will come.

The Locust is proud of his Transkeian citizenship.
Talks passionately about it. Speaks fluent Xhosa, too.
He conducts himself in a way reminiscent of the outpost white folks we read about in Conrad and Plomer.
Only, he is enough of a realist to escape some of the
fierce features of Conradian and Plomerian characters
who act out a revolt against their own kind. In Coffee
Bay you can have it both ways — the seaside recluse
and the busy world outside. There are two hotels and
a few families live in their own houses on leased
ground, which they may not pass on to their children.

For temporary escape, André comes to Coffee Bay
occasionally for about two days. During the two days
he dives for much of the time, and spends an evening
with the locals. They like his company. He is the only
intellectual among them, and they seem to like the
idea of a professor letting it all hang out and talking
their level of stuff. Some are businessmen whose visits

are a regular feature; there are residents who do nothing, most probably living on some inherited fortune or on the expectation of plenty. Groups come here on holiday too, like three couples of advanced middle age whom we find on the day we arrive.

Evening. The three couples have been bowling during the day. Now they are playing dominoes near our table out on the terrace. It's bang! bang! bang! punctuating stretches of silence or near-silence. And *that's mine, this is yours . . . . She's nuts, if you ask me . . . bang! . . . Ah, you're losing sonnyboy . . . . Oh no, Richard, oh no! Who else is ready for another . . . Esther? . . . . Let me . . . now let's see . . . one gin and lime, two beers, brandy and ginger for myself . . . hic, oh boy . . . that game killed me . . . . I'll give you a good massage tonight, dear . . .* bang! bang!

There are four of us at our table. André is talking to Edmund and Tracy opposite him, while I'm eavesdropping on this rattle going on next to me. André's the real poet, the way he interprets this whole Coffee Bay scene.

These prosaic folks think of him as the mentally-fatigued professor who merely wants diversion. Nothing more. But his poetic perception as he gave me a run-down of the resort on our way from Umtata confirms my own view of this evening. Sheer decadence. And André, although he is well known here as he has made visits over the last five years, can detach himself from it while he is surrounded by it. For two days he can escape from the crush of academic life and planning.

'I could never stay here longer than that,' he says. 'I belong to a world of action, punctuated by moments when I must seek to think and feel more profoundly . . . .' And as he says this his soft eyes, bearded face

and low-keyed voice converge to express a gentle
intensity of feeling. There have been fleeting moments
when I have noticed on his face a profound sadness.

Enter Mitchell, riding on his mouth. Hell, I think,
the kind of fellow who can't hitch his mouth to a
post outside. He rides in on it, and he keeps riding. A
joke, followed by his own guffaw, a joke, a broadside
at André, then a loud guffaw ... bang! bang! the
Kissinger club next to us continue with their domino
game, biting off chunks of the night, chewing it,
slamming the domino bits upon it, chewing it, and
something tells me the foursome ritual is going to
survive the midnight hour. Like the eternal ocean
breakers down there in the bay, grinding through
time. Only, the breakers are mindless of day or night.
The sound of ocean breakers is always alien to my
feelings. As the Scotch gets to me, it becomes even
more peripheral.

After André has introduced us to Mitchell, the
mouthrider buys me a drink and becomes very friendly.
He and André evidently play this kind of verbal game,
although the poet, for his part, treats him with a
superior air of tolerance. Often the mouthrider takes
on the character of ocean breakers between us: *whaa,
whaa, boom, bam, plat, shshsh! whaa, whaa, plat,
boom, boom shshsh!* .... 'Thank God there's one of
me,' Mitchell says. 'The world court summoned my
mother.'

'How's that?' I ask.

'Because my mother stands accused of not having
brought me and my twin brother into the world
sooner.' A guffaw that causes even two members of
the Kissinger couples to look at us. Bang, bang, the
game's yours! *Whaa, whaa, boom, boom!* the breakers
continue down in the bay.

There's only one woman among the bar sitters. 'The local women don't join their men in these goings-on,' says André. 'The domino players are only week-enders.' When we give a young Umtata woman a lift to the Mnqanduli crossing, she tells us the thing that annoys her about Coffee Bay folks is that the men are real sexists. The women always stay home, the men go about their games.

When we disperse at the hotel everybody is face-less to me, except of course André. Decadence? This comfortable living while the hinterland is starving is a microcosm of South African white society. Transkei to Namibia. So it shall be for a long time. We are seeing a new cycle of ninteenth century colonialism beginning, with the independence of our ethnic en-claves. We want money to run the administration, to run the schools, to finance agriculture, water conservat-ion; just keep on bringing us food from mother France, mother England, mother Belgium, mother Portugal, bring us technical aid and expatriates with it, we beg you . . . bring in the cargo. Pacification of the natives, but of a different kind this time around . . . indirect rule, but the most sophisticated version; not from overseas, but from just across the border.

The next day I go out for a jog. Later I take a plunge into the sea. This mindless element that keeps coming at you, this seascape — how boring. Under-neath is a life I know I shall never see except on the movie screen, in books . . . .

We say goodbye to Coffee Bay decadence, head for Grahamstown. I am alarmed at the vast stretches of unpopulated land, except for scattered clusters of villages, from Idutwa to Nqamakhe to the Kei River. Eastern Cape Africans build on the tops of hills, something you rarely if ever see in the Transvaal, where they build on hillsides, in the foothills. These rondavel houses do not have wall enclosures like ours in the Transvaal, where *lapa*, the courtyard, signifies a family unit. Their houses are two-toned on the outside — white and evening grey, where ours are mostly decorated with various coloured patterns.

Around Mnqanduli, on the east side of the Umtata-Butterworth highway, is a stone to commemorate Dick King's ride from Port Natal to Grahamstown, which he is reported to have undertaken to inform the Eastern Cape English of the Boer siege of Port Natal in 1842. A journey he is said to have done in ten days, across Pondoland. He was guided for a long stretch by an African, Ndongeni, who ran while King rode. Ndongeni is never mentioned in any memorial stone or plaque.

André and I decide to stop on the roadside and piss on the stone . . . . Where is Ndongeni? we keep asking, as if the stone will itch from the urine and start telling. Later I wonder if Ndongeni can really be said to have been a hero in the view of Africans: he was not helping *them* after all! And yet there was later to be the *Mendi*, which sank, taking with it Africans who had gone to fight in World War I. Our people continued to commemorate the event every year, until somewhere in the Sixties. The Africans who fought on the side of the Boers against the British today count for nothing in the memory of either group. So much for memorials that look at history with a squint: pee on them.

Heroes . . . hero assassination . . . who's side are you on? Whom are you speaking for? Where are the African heroes — in the memory? Where are the institutions that could assert a collective consciousness in the African? We are teetering on the edge of somewhere between what the master mind has designed for us and the self-censored memory of our past heroes, between our resistance against the design and the need to recreate traditional myths, lest they consolidate a separateness . . . . Where is the end of all this? But I keep telling myself that we stand a better chance of strengthening ourselves if we recreate our traditional myths than if we seek integration with the whites on *any* terms but ours.

Detentions, court trials for alleged terrorism, detentions under the internal security law, for several other things. We come back to South Africa to find that these have increased in severity. Death in prison cells has become a feature of the times. Censorship of the written word — the censored imagination — has also become a thing South African society takes for granted.

We talked about censorship in the round-table discussion we had at Rhodes University on April 17, 1978 — Nadine Gordimer, André Brink and I — all three novelists, in the presence of an audience. Brink felt that it was too costly to try to contest the banning of a book and was not worth it. He believed that the writer must keep on at his or her task, because books outlive censorship in the long run. Miss Gordimer commented on the lack of public concern over banned books. I wondered if that was not because in fact too few people read our works to constitute a book-conscious public strong enough to dramatise their concern. Maybe we are not all that important as writers, especially where there are bigger issues in the land like detentions, arrests and so on, when the physical pain that accompanies these issues is so acute. And the public can always buy another book,

André put in.

I am aware that a writer must continually ask himself what his role is in relation to what his society is going through. The death of Steve Biko and the manner of his dying stunned many of us. Time and again the picture of a man manacled to a steel structure and then put into a van and driven from Port Elizabeth to Pretoria — indeed to his grave if he was not already dead — haunts me. Other events tear me up inside. But the writer seldom, to the best of my knowledge, thinks of abandoning his art because it is powerless against the forces that destroy human life. He feels diminished by every death that occurs to those who are ground under the political steamroller. And yet he feels that if writing is what he can do best, even when he is not necessarily producing the literature of direct opposition, he has to obey the inner compulsion to give words to what he feels and thinks. Beautiful because powerful words that only the imagination can shape. Because imaginative literature is a compulsive cultural act.

In December of 1978 a telegram came from Grace, Khabi's wife, to say that he was lying in hospital with critical injuries from a car crash. He was in a coma. Rebecca, Puso and I drove the ten hours from Lebowakgomo to the University of Zululand. He could not talk to us. We were to make more trips by car to Zululand to see him.

Khabi had driven into a stationary truck thinking that it was moving. He was very badly broken up, his hip was busted, his foreleg and his chest had suffered a severe impact.

On that first visit Grace gave us a small silver oak, less than a metre tall. We planted it in our front yard at Lebowakgomo. It is now a towering tree, sturdy. Whenever I look at it, four years later, I cannot but remember a man fighting for his life in a Zululand hospital, broken up considerably, in and out of a state of delirium, the body struggling to stand up to weakening kidneys, hypertension and other enemies, and his wife waiting at his bedside. He triumphed miraculously in a matter of three months, by sheer will power. To see the car he had driven — a shapeless mass of steel — you could not imagine that a living person could have been dragged out of it.

The silver oak has now become for us a symbol of that vital force by which a man's body clawed its way up out of a dark pit, from the bottom of a sheer drop, reaching for air and sun.

We have become closer than ever before since our return — Khabi and I. As I grow older I realise my circle of friends near and far has been shrinking considerably. Those that remain I cling to jealously. I feel it isn't a decreasing capacity to love. Because now my love has gained greater intensity. And I don't consider this intensity a singular virtue either. I feel enriched by love and impoverished by obsessive hate. It's as simple as that. And I realise that I do not have the capacity to hate intensely as I used to have when I was younger, much as I would really love to hate passionately, murderously, as a weapon against those I have no means of destroying. Like those who debase us because we are of a different race and colour.

After Tim Couzens, Senior Research Fellow in the Institute of African Studies, had broached the matter with Karl Tober, Professor of German Studies, then Deputy Vice-Chancellor, the latter put all the energy he could into securing an appointment for me in the

Institute. His words were, 'I see this as only the beginning of great things that you can do in this university.' Professor Van Onselen, the Institute's director, recommended me for the rank of ad hominem professor. It was awarded and I became Professor of Literature.

I have just finished the initial three-year contract as a Research Fellow, during which time I have been recording live performances of oral poetry in the northern Transvaal villages — in Venda, Tsonga, and North Sotho (Pedi). The Venda and Pedi have been translated, and the Tsonga translator is still working on his portion of the project. These are literal translations which I shall adapt into English.

Throughout my research the one thing that has shaken me up more than any other has been the appalling degree of rural poverty. The pastoral life that provided the impulse for traditional poetry as an oral performance has wasted away to a great extent. Migrant labour and the strenuous demands made by large populations on the little arable and grazing land still remaining have been draining the blood of the people. The poetry that was born out of conditions of plenty and a self-sufficient humanistic culture is still remembered, but only by the old people. And 'old' means from fifty upwards. The festivals that required and shaped the poetry have become mostly a memory. The mission station played no small part in ruthlessly discouraging traditional custom as 'heathen' and anti-Christ. Those who recited for me showed an admirably stubborn loyalty to their glorious past, and were proud to be able to perform. Those who admitted that they could not remember said it with a tone of regret, a sense of spiritual loss.

The mother of a Lutheran minister out in Sibasa,

Venda, agreed to recite for me, with the help of three other women. We had two sessions, at the beginning of which she said, 'Let us pray.' She prayed to the Christian God — that was clear even in her language. I surmised from some of the vocabulary that is close to Sesotho that the prayer was for forgiveness: they were going to do something unchristian, 'heathen' . . . the authoritarian conscience . . . .

For the rest of 1982 I shall be teaching African literature on a regular basis in the Division of Comparative Literature — a division of German Studies headed by Professor Reingard Nethersole. The Faculty Board asked Tim Couzens and I to plan for a department of African Literature. I formed a committee to assist in this venture consisting of us two and three educators outside Wits, and chaired by myself. The syllabuses were approved from committee to committee and the proposal is now in the hands of the Department of National Education for whose approval we must wait before we can begin, we hope, in 1983. Karl Tober's words . . . If the department becomes a fact, it will be the first of its kind in the whole country. First, though, as we have been advised, we have asked for a 'division of African Literature' in Comparative Literature, which is the politic thing to do before a department can stand a chance of being established.

This Sunday morning, as I am making an entry in my journal, I am listening to Beethoven's 'Pastoral' symphony on my stereo. This is Selection Park, Pimville (part of Soweto). We are renting a house belonging to Dr Tshepo Gugushe, a dentist. It was to be a three-year lease, but he had to relinquish his side-job as assistant dean of students at Glyn Thomas Residence, Baragwanath Hospital — black medical

students. After a seven months' tenancy, to end
December 31, 1979, we have given up the house. We
are now house-hunting again.

Ah yes, Beethoven's 'Pastoral'. Takes me back to
the Fifties when I first met Clara Urquhart, who later
introduced us to her friend Enrico Pratt. He painted
the pastoral scene hanging over my head at this
moment. Did it in 1953 as a symbol of a journey on a
dark road, with burnt-down trees and grass and red
earth on either side. Ahead are shades of blue, grey,
brown, to depict the break of dawn. Enrico consciously
meant this to console and inspire me, just after Zeph,
Isaac and I had been fired from teaching for preaching
against Bantu Education, and been banned from
teaching anywhere else in the country.

This rugged-looking, heavy-set Italian, who always
needed Clara to interpret into English everything he
said, was full of robust affection and generosity. He
had a thick brown-and-grey beard that seemed itself
to be the instrument producing his voice. A loveable
pair, Enrico and Clara. She has been living in London,
he in Milan. He used to play the violin for our audiences at the Bantu Men's Social Centre whenever the
Syndicate of African Artists organised Sunday afternoon concerts.

The moment we arrived in Johannesburg to work
at Wits Rebecca and I realised that we were being
recycled into the 'Bantu-designated' stream. I had
been living out of a suitcase with friends before
Rebecca joined me. When we jumped at Dr Gugushe's
offer we had declined that of Wits to occupy a three-
roomed apartment on one of its estates 25 kilometres
north of Johannesburg, beyond Alexandra. Our extra-
mural activities would be based in Soweto, 22 kilometres west, and we did not know what white hooli-

gans looking for fun might do to Africans living in
what was generally a 'white area'.

In the U.S. we lived in predominantly white suburbs
— Denver and Philadelphia — without feeling isolated
and scared of white backlash. We still kept contact
with blacks in the areas where they predominated.
Maybe we didn't feel odd because taking the United
States at large, blacks and whites are found living
together in an atmosphere that has passed the stage of
political self-assertion or block-busting. In our tightly-
segregated society the menace was still there. Wits
University could only intervene *after* the catastrophe.

Selection Park — an ironic name for a place that is
forever being invaded by a mischievous stink from the
nearby sewerage works — is an area that has been
opened up for those who want to build on the 99-year
lease. It stands on ground that for years was a garbage
dump.

We had not asked for a lease from Dr Gugushe
because the accommodation had been offered by
him, not sought by us. He was now compelled to
vacate the apartment which he was occupying rent-
free as dean of students because he was being asked to
resign. We asked him to give us time to look for
alternative shelter. He was adamant.

Because we were overtaken by the deadline, he
caused a summons to be issued to have me evicted. I
had to appear in front of a magistrate. I had no case
to plead but that I had failed to find a house to rent
anywhere in Soweto. What I had hitherto only intel-
lectualised about became a stark reality in that court.
The law has no respect for issues that have been
clinched by word of mouth, with only the human
understanding and mutual sympathy to back the
agreement. The claimant's lawyer was making the

whole case sound big and elaborate. It must have looked to the observer like a singles match in tennis rigged
up to be the event of the year, with one of the
opponents standing stock still, hitting only the ball
that comes straight at him, and no further than the
net either.

I was given until January 31 to quit and pay the
hotel expenses the claimant had to meet.

We went to Frankenwald estate after all, where we
had been offered an apartment previously. Extra-
mural activities had to stop. Rebecca was now working
in the Community Health Unit of Wits Medical
School. She was a senior social worker in a research
team that was pioneering a comprehensive health
centre in Senaoana, Soweto.

In the meantime we applied for a site in Selection
Park at the West Rand Administration Board (WRAB).
It was granted. We asked Murray-Roberts Construction
to build a house on it. They went ahead, in the belief
that the 99-year lease would be easy to obtain once
the building operations had started.

I was told by the Commissioner of Co-operation
and Development that I was not entitled to the lease.
The builders completed the house all the same. I had
lost my Johannesburg residential qualifications, WRAB
said. An application would have to be made to the
Minister of Co-operation and Development for special
dispensation. WRAB did this. The long wait.

Several visits to WRAB in New Canada. It's right
now on the Minister's desk, Mr. Marais B. kept saying.
'But who knows, he may not grant the dispensation
. . . .' His words only took on meaning when I was
told that Co-op-and-Develop had rejected the application. Wits intervened. No dice.

The Mphahlele file was growing fatter still. Charles,

my director at the Institute, quipped when I reported to him, 'All that's left, Zeke, is for the country to institute a Department of Mphahlele Affairs . . .'

There was the labour front to reckon with. We were being recycled.

I had sent to Pretoria my driver's licence (issued 1941) and the fat reference book, and applied for the new consolidated book. I did this fully realising that I had come back as a man among other people whose lives were being processed and programmed day after day, through paper-work long enough to cover the circumference of the globe several times over. The Reason Supreme for my return transcended all these mechanics. The fat book was warped already, and I had carried the two items about with me for twenty years as if they were collector's items or charms that dangle from a chain. The new book came within a matter of weeks.

But Immigration still had us down in its records as British citizens — aliens . . . . It demanded that my British passport be stamped with a permit to work in the country. I went to Pretoria for this. A British subject carrying a pass and compelled to live in a black township . . . . 'The Queen must know about this — you must protest to her,' a friend said with mock seriousness.

Together with John Samuel, director of the South African Committee for Higher Education (SACHED trust), Dr. Peter Hunter of Wits, and Fanyana Mazibuko, also of SACHED, I was delegated by the newly-formed Educational Opportunities Committee to visit the United States to explore universities and colleges likely to offer places tuition-free for black students who wanted to further their higher education. Fanyana and I applied for passports. His application was re-

jected outright. Interior wrote to me to say that as I
had British nationality, I was not entitled to a South
African passport.

I wrote back to tell the whole story. Interior had
written to the consulate in Washington D.C. to say
that I could re-enter South Africa on condition that I
went to live in Lebowa and sought employment at
the University of the North. I was refused a job at the
university, there was no suitable employment for me
in Lebowa. I had come back for good. I had a reference
book as further proof that I had no intention of
emigrating. I was thinking: you come back and pick
up the badge of oppression again in order to belong —
the irony of it! This is what I felt, but never write
poetry when you communicate with government: it's
disastrous. Stick to literal prose meaning . . . .

Interior wrote back to say that I would have to
renounce my British nationality and apply for a re-
sumption of South African citizenship.

Rebecca and I visited the British Consulate in
Johannesburg. We signed forms in which we renounced
British citizenship. 'This will be sent to London,' the
consul announced, 'but the renunciation can only
take effect when South Africa has given you back
your citizenship — and, mark you, not of a homeland or anything like that.'

Good old United Kingdom — always protective, I
think.

'Suppose the worst came to the worst,' I put in.
'Suppose South Africa sends us packing — could we
enter Britain as immigrants?'

'No, not since the Commonwealth Immigration
law. Not unless your father was born in the U.K. You
are only British by registration.'

'That I know. Every time we have visited Britain,

we have been sent to the section set aside for foreigners
— I mean at Heathrow. Of course I invariably went
first to the window for U.K. citizens, just so that I
might look at the face of the passport official sending
me to the foreigners.'

'What did you discover?'

I was sorely tempted to say 'F. . . all,' but I said
instead, 'Portrait of a civil servant as a young man
looking straight through a window frame.'

He smiled tolerantly.

'What British colonies could we go to if we could
not enter Britain as immigrants?' Whereupon I take
out my notebook in mock seriousness.

The consul goes to his filing cabinet and fishes out
a pamphlet, opens it and reads out: St Kitts, Hong
Kong, St Helena — not very far away, Falklands, and
of course we still have Gibraltar.

I write them down. Then he says, 'Of course we are
not unmerciful — we would take you eventually.'

Poetry into public service, I muse, won't go. And
yet public servants may very well be avid readers of
poetry . . . .

I sent copies of the British forms to Pretoria, and
left it to the two institutions which would eventually
steal the march on the other!

Realising that I was not prepared to travel on a
British passport, by which time I had returned it to
its rightful owner, Pretoria conceded that it would
give me a travel document (not a passport) to go to
the U.S. Having had to postpone that first trip, the
three of us went to the U.S. in March, 1980.

On December 17, 1980, my birthday, we were
summoned to receive certificates granting us back
South African citizenship. Pretoria also wrote to say
that those of our children who were born in South

Africa were henceforth South African citizens. Puso,
born in Nigeria, would become a citizen by descent.

As I had been invited by the University of Denver
to take up a visiting professorship in the English
Department in the spring quarter of 1981, I applied
for a passport. It was granted.

By this time we had taken occupation of the house
in Selection Park, on the understanding that Wits
would pay the construction company its price so that
we would become tenants. Agreements were made
between Wits and WRAB and myself that if I obtained
the 99-year lease, I should take over the house and
arrange a loan from a building society.

Rebecca had been signing in at the WRAB pass
offices every month to renew her permit to be in 'the
proclaimed area of Johannesburg' while in the employ
of Wits. Our lawyers took this matter and that of the
lease in hand. In the middle of 1981, four years after
our arrival, the Reference Bureau issued her with a
book marked 'Bophuthatswana' on the line that says
'citizenship'! By this time she had become stoical
enough to shrug it off as a fat joke. Citizenship
tags drawn out of a hat!

A novel with a number of time shifts . . . . So I
must go back to part of the process of *my* recycling.
Consider that during 1979, 1980, and 1981 I was a
frequent guest at the WRAB office in New Canada
and at Albert Street, of Co-op-and-develop at 15
Market Street, of Interior at Civitas in Pretoria. I had
come to know the big men who displayed studied,
cold politeness, and small but not-so-weak bureaucrats
who seemed nervously happy that they were giving
me the run-around. Was there a conspiracy to neutralise
me? I kept asking myself. One official said to me at
one stage, 'You should go to Pretoria where you were

born to obtain the 10(1a) and 10(1b) qualifications which can be transferred to Johannesburg.' And then he gave me back my reference book without even looking at me. I had polished enough chairs and benches at Albert Street, New Canada and Market Street not to want to contemplate Pretoria. Why, for instance, would I be given such qualifications in a town which I left when I was 21, before I came to Johannesburg? And so the strong men, big and small, drive the herds this way and that on these wide-wide prairies day after day, year after year, and it's *Move it, move it!* all the time . . . .

Which brings me to Albert Street, the big market place. It is February 1979, just after I'd joined Wits. I have to go to the pass office to be registered for working and residence permits. They call it influx control. It affects every African who comes into an urban area, also called a 'white area'. Only if you have worked for one employer for ten years continuously, or have lived in an urban area for fifteen years continuously, are you exempt from influx control regulations. Theoretically, if you have a profession and a job waiting for you, you are also exempt. It won't matter, though, that you were born in an urban area, for if you leave for only six months you lose your seat in that precious white auditorium, where the performers are white, the stage manager or conductor is white, the ushers are white, the M.C. is white, where either the seats are segregated or there is one night for Africans, another for whites. A poor analogy, but close enough to the truth.

Several people are milling about on the pavements surrounding the building, several are shuffling in and out. They are all carrying papers that determine and run their entire lives. Papers they understand very little about, if anything. White employers have to come here too, to register their workers. To fail to do so is a punishable offence.

Opposite the main building is another which our people call *lesakeng* — a word for any enclosure that keeps livestock at night. Evidently all who come to Albert Street begin here the long process of becoming identifiable as a number in a white area, allowed to hunt for a job, then to work, perhaps to stay. You may be a lodger in a WRAB house in the township or in a single-sex hostel.

Day after day whites come here to announce the jobs they are willing to offer, and each to take his or her pick from those blacks willing to be recruited.

First visit. A white man sits at a high counter in the entrance of the main building. An African male stands in the doorway to usher people in. He makes the necessary enquiries. Then the White man gives the African man a coloured confetti-like piece of paper you have to stick on some part of your garment. This signifies you have come in, so that when you make your exit it will be known that you have been seen by the gateman. The white man does nothing else.

I give the African the letter I have brought from Wits. When he sees the office number I am destined for, he advises me to wait at the main entrance until I see a bus arrive. It is 8.15 a.m., and the office personnel have not yet come. When they have mounted the stairway, I may follow them.

Indeed a bus arrives. It disgorges its human cargo: all white. Ah, sheltered employment, I figure. I follow them up the stairs. A small bearded white clerk reads the letter I have brought from the Staffing Office. It says that I'm being employed as Senior Research Fellow and so on. Tell me all about yourself, invites the little master: where you've been before, what's a research fellow and so on. After I've explained, he goes out with the letter and reference book. He comes back to report that the labour registering officer wants to understand what a research fellow is, and why *I* was especially appointed to do the job. I should bring another letter from Wits spelling out all this.

While I was waiting on a bench in the reception office — such as it was — before being ushered into his office, I had time to feel the texture of the atmosphere, in this market place. Took me back to the old days, some twenty-two years. Greasy, grimy walls and floors, old furniture, disgruntled white workers who run our lives and control our movements. Electric and water pipes running all over on the walls. The subtle smell of officialdom is everywhere, unmistakable.

As I leave the office I find myself on the balcony overlooking a wide area where white workers are milling about, carrying papers, going from one desk to another. I see the up-and-down movements of hands that tell me rubber stamps are making their indelible imprint on documents. Thousands of kilometres in paper must roll through this process in a month . . . . I notice a group of women stop and sit on the edge of desks, some drinking cold drinks out of bottles, others chewing sandwiches, some smoking. Right there, I muse — right there, millions of lives are being thrown into a pipeline with several tributaries. But to these workers we are all mere numbers: we have no faces, no nerves, no longings, no desires, no hungers, no solitudes, no loved ones waiting for us . . . just plain numbers that are passed on between bites and jaw movements and gulps of cold drink and cigarette puffs and pauses for gossip and other noises, just a market place . . . .

As I go out of the depressing building, I stick the confetti on the leaf of a plant in a cluster near the steps. I must remember to stick them all on here, I think to myself.

I bring the required letter. I am told I shall hear from the labour registering officer in three weeks' time. When I tell him that I'm due to go to Rhodes University, the man says I should come and see them when I return. I stick a confetti piece on the leaf that carries the first one. I was to visit Albert Street four more times.

At last my reference book was stamped with a permit to work and stay in Johannesburg until discharged by Wits. When I learned from Personnel at Wits that as a professional I was exempt from the labour regulations, I returned to Albert Street to have the book stamped with a certificate of exemption. But this does not exempt one from regulations determining the 99-year lease. And yet, if one is permitted to be in a 'proclaimed area' to work until discharged, how is it that one may be granted a 99-year lease? There goes the crab moving in a direction you cannot deduce from the shape of its body or the way it is poised . . . .

In February, 1982 I go to New Canada's WRAB office to arrange for the transfer of the house, now that I have the 99-year lease. Mr Marais B., very loud with a rustic manner, 'receives' me in his office. I have learned from past experience that I must simply grab a seat myself, because he is never going to offer it. I'm sure he takes it for granted that you will do so anyhow if you have your head on your shoulders.

On a previous occasion I had told him about the agreements that provide for the transfer of the house from the university to me. He had said, after looking through my file, that he had no knowledge of them. Maybe they were still at the head office downtown. Since 1979! What do you want me to do? I wanted to know. You should bring a letter from Wits saying they are prepared to hand the house over to you.

I stared at him, messages shooting up and down the back of my head and down my spine. 'Shit! Not again — oh no! I've done this up-and-down for far too long — I've gone weary of it. You don't have documents left in the care of your department and so *I* must go back to the university for a letter. Portuguese, Italians, Greeks, they all come into this country and find houses and trading licences immediately. I was born in this country and I've got to wade through all this muck to get even near enough to Pimville to smell the bog around there . . . .'

'I'm not talking politics, I'm doing my duty which has got to do with the housing.'

I stood up and stomped out of the office, choking with the stuff that rises in you when you know damn well that there is no way of passing through that gate if the security won't let you, unless you shoot your way through. By the time my parting shot got off, Mr B. had planted his elbows on the desk to support a rather large head. 'I suppose you don't see this whole outfit and your position in it as politics?'

When I reached the main gate he was already there to head me off. 'Professor,' he called, 'will you please come back with me to the office so we can phone Wits about this thing.'

Silently I followed him. *'God, hierdie werk druk my neer,'* he said. I wasn't going to confirm his belief — whatever it weighed — that he was suffering from strain. He phoned the two most relevant members of staff at Wits without success. 'All right, Professor, I'll keep trying — you may leave.' One man one vote? With us blacks it's one man one Marais B., the genie on my shoulder.

This time around, on a warm February morning, I have come to him in response to his call. All the forms are here for me to sign, and I have to pay 125 rands for these mysterious services. When I give him a cheque he looks at it and says in jest, 'Is this all you're giving me?' and then chuckles good-humoured-ly, which somehow does not become him. 'I can give you more if you want,' I return the gibe. He waves me down with his hand and chuckles again.

Mr. B. calls out to the typist in the next cubicle, '*Maak vir ons tee daar* — or what do you want, Professor — tea or coffee? Or maybe you want brandy or whisky?'

'Whisky.'

I see him open a large cupboard behind me and fish out a whisky bottle from among the alarmingly large supply. There are many brands of booze, various sizes of bottles. He puts it on the table, whereupon I say curtly, 'No thanks, I don't drink except in the evening.' He snorts and takes back the bottle.

Returning to his seat Mr. B. opens a file and pages through it, muttering, '*Waar die moer is dit? Waar's die fokken ding?*' He calls out to the typist for the receipt book. She disappears and returns with a man who is carrying the wanted item and who writes me out a receipt. He takes the book with him when he leaves the room.

When Mr. B. gives me the form Wits must take care of for the transfer to be clinched, I say to him, 'I hope I've finished with you and you with me now, right?' One black, one Mr. B . . . .

'That's correct,' he replies.

As I drive back to the university I ponder the whole recycling process. As I have intimated, the officials at the top display a studied, cold politeness towards blacks. Something new to me. They used to be almost unapproachable before I left the country. Could they be a new breed, and are they being taught a different code on the job, I wonder? Those of the lower ranks are still as tough and sullen as ever. Yes, they are certainly unhappy about something, hostile too. I wonder where they would all go if the whole industry for the control of Africans were to be dismantled . . . .

The day I blew my top in Mr.B.'s presence is the kind of thing that more often occurs in shops when whites are being consciously rude. But wherever it may happen, my attitude to it is always a superior one. I keep reminding myself of Acharya Vinoba Bhave's words from a British colonial prison in India: 'Though action rages without, the heart can be tuned to produce unbroken music.' At the same time I tune into Radhakrishnan's exposition of the Hindu view: 'God's truth, His mercy and justice find their embodiment in the implacable working of the moral law (*karma*).' This principle is a spiritual necessity and not a mechanical law that derives from outside the self — like that which lays down commandments, regulates church-going, baptism and so on. Karma is humanistic and not authoritarian, to use Eric Fromm's distinction.

My attitude then, is that we have come back and are involved in the creation of something bigger and more splendid than the wretched creatures who spend some part of their waking hours debasing and humiliating black people. I fix my sights far ahead of them,

and whatever they may do is but a small particle of a
moment in the context of the huge time span of a
purposeful, creative life, moving inexorably towards
freedom. If they do not become aware of this today
or tomorrow, the greater is their poverty of spirit.
Multiply me by millions and consider how strong,
how intellectually and spiritually superior we shall
always be to those who debase us and thereby debase
themselves. They are busy negating and controlling,
we are busy creating, reaffirming.

I'm flanked on my right by Sekoto's *African Maiden*.
In front of me hangs a new acquisition. Rebecca, during her community work, rediscovered Kwenaeefe
Mohl, the painter, in Soweto. Mohl, in his sixties
today, used to paint landscapes and wild life three
decades ago. He now paints together with his wife,
Rebecca reports.

The painting in front of me is his, and depicts a
Lesotho scene: two men on horseback, in national
dress. In the background is a dark mountain over
which the sun is pouring its yellow light, the fiery
glow washing the backs of the riders and cascading
down the rocks to form a pool at the horse's hooves.
Brazenly but pleasingly representational.

I'm listening to Dollar Brand's piano on disc: his
first recording, *Peace* (1964). Victor Ntoni is on bass,
Nelson Magwaza on drums.

Lanky, with a brooding look on his face that is a
picture of peace, serenity and ease with self, Dollar
(since become Abdullah Ebrahim) came to see us at
our hotel in New York in May 1966. He had heard
that we were arriving from Nairobi and simply came
to visit. Just like that. It was heartwarming.

Already in *Peace* his music had taken on the brooding mood, relieved only by the orchestration that was

to characterise his later work.

His adaptation of 'Just a Song' is an unpretentious rendition, a beauty, followed by 'Little Boy'. The African accent is unmistakable here. In 'Shrimp Boats' the orchestration is subdued, throwing the keyboard up in bold relief. Dollar's having a good time with his variations on the melody. His touch is characteristically light and delicate. So is the African rhythm strong in 'Cherry'. Goes back to the Marabi beat.

The repetitive melody line so true to African tradition has become Dollar's trade mark. The title piece in the album *Bra Joe from Kilimanjaro* takes up the whole side. The line is repeated throughout, with Dollar, Harold Land (sax), Basil Coetzee (flute and tenor), Blue Mitchell (trumpet), Buster Cooper (trombone), Lionel Beukes (bass guitar) extemporising in turns.

Dollar went through the whole gamut of props musicians adopt as a cult — drugs, alcohol, grass and so on. Then he turned to Islam, which he says saved him. He learned karate, studied acupuncture, herbalism and philosophy, which provided him with what he calls 'the energy source.'

After his Newport Jazz appearance in 1964 — an historic moment for him — and his link-up with Duke Ellington who left him his piano seat, he outgrew those humble 1949 beginnings when, as a high-school student in Cape Town, he played with The Tuxedo Slickers, The Streamline Brothers and later with The Willie Max Dance Band. He acknowledges his debt to Kippie Moeketsi's alto sax, which he enlisted for his Jazz Epistles in 1961, together with Hugh Masekela (trumpet), Jonas Gwangwa (trombone), Johnny Gertze (bass) and Makaya Ntshoko (drums).

From then on Dollar was to weave his keyboard music through famous American concert halls and jazz clubs and university campuses. But all the time he has believed it to be folly for young musicians to yearn for fame on the pop-music circuit, saying, 'I could teach them enough in an hour to give them a career — but not to prostitute on pop success. That's a myth. The roots are spiritual, in the traditions.'

Gordon Siwani, a notable sports writer in Soweto today, points up sharply in his liner notes on the *Peace* album the state of mind Dollar has attained, how 'the music projects the man himself. He is at peace with himself.'

While I am listening to Dollar, I open up *The Voice* newspaper of Sunday, March 28, 1982, to see a news item that jolts me out of my reverie about Dollar orchestrated by Sekoto and Mohl. The news item announces the burial of Jacob Moeketsi on March 27.

Jacob, elder brother of Kippie Moeketsi, the alto sax player: his piano goes back to The Harlem Swingsters of the Forties. Music was his life — on stage and radio, in dance halls; a full-time occupation.

In the Fifties, when Khabi and I ran the Syndicate of African Artists, Jacob played piano for us. He was versatile in both jazz and classical music. He invariably provided piano background for my poetry reading, and accompanied Khabi. And this — death's visitation — occurs when he is ready to give me a recorded interview about his music life, his sense of African entertainment history . . . . We had promised ourselves to have fun reminiscing about old times . . . .

There goes a man who, right up to the sudden illness that swept him away like a gale, was teaching piano, employed first by the Johannesburg City Council and then by the West Rand Administration

Board. There goes a man who was the very personifi-
cation of gentility and simplicity, but who also had
the artist's lust for life, a prime actor in Jo'burg's
social history.

Peace, son of Moeketsi, peace.

My mind lingers this night on another death. It
happened on New Year's Day, 1982. Time has had to
pass before I could write about it. Because I have
been struggling in my mind to squeeze a meaning
out of it. A meaning not so readily accessible as that
of Jacob's departure. Its painful ironies baffle poetic
contemplation. Or maybe there's poetry in the event
that sits stubbornly cooped up inside as a state of
mind, refusing release. I cannot delay any longer now.

Sudden stomach pains, the 460-kilometre journey
from Venda to Kalafong hospital in Pretoria, death.

I often stayed with him at his Dube home, Soweto,
when I came from Lebowa during my research trips.
B.M. was robust, heavy-set, with an equally robust
sense of humour. The trouble millions of urban
Africans carry around in their nervous systems
was also his endowment: hypertension.

He was urban representative for Venda before its
'independence'. Then he jumped out of that to form
an opposition party, the Venda Independent Party. It
was dedicated to opposing independence, and he had
a large following in the urban areas.

B.M. often related to me his experiences with the
men from the Bureau of State Security (BOSS) who
called him up frequently to talk to him about Venda
affairs. Kept saying he wanted to quit politics but his
party members wouldn't hear of it. Said BOSS
wanted him to stay in. What was in it for BOSS? I
wanted to know. Couldn't tell. What should I do? he

asked me. Let your own conscience guide you, was
my suggestion. Think what's best for the people — in
the long and short runs. Weigh that against your own
self-interest — I mean your refusal to be corrupted —
and find the meaning in relation to what the South
African government's intentions are in setting up
these homelands. If the principle for which you're
quitting is paramount, you may even find that your
resignation will serve the interests of your supporters
best, though it may be against their own immediate
sense of what's good for them.

B.M. always considered himself an urbanite. Used
to say that whenever he was in Venda his blood
pressure shot up murderously.

How his party won, how the chiefs who supported
his anti-independence position were bought over and
crossed the floor in the House, how his opponents
won the independence motion while some of his own
supporters were in detention — all this is now history.

Any more anti-independence rallies, he was warned,
could cause him to be detained.

Still B.M. seemed to believe that he and his party
had something to sell through its opposition politics.
Perhaps the game of parliamentary participation was
worth it for its own sake.

In the American advertising firm he worked for,
B.M. advised white bosses on copy aimed at the
African market: what would sell, what wouldn't . . . .
He became more and more disgruntled. The white
bosses denied him initiative. Always had to wait for
them to ask him. Organ grinder with his hands tied
behind his back. Marketing management that boasts
black personnel is full of such organ grinders. What
did B.M. have to sell?

The company packed it in. B.M. was left without a

job.

Next thing, after we had not seen each other for about six months, I heard he had gone to Venda to set up a liquor store and a disco-joint. Third World, oh, Third World! Mini-banana republic of Venda . . . .

And then the twister comes and sends him reeling down a bottomless precipice . . . .

I went to Tshakoma, B.M.'s home town, for his funeral. Met other Johannesburgers and some East Randers there too. A family member offered to open the casket (sic) for us to see him. He was dressed up in black, his torso draped with a yellow cloth.

I have never taken easily to corpses dressed up in dinner suits . . . .

I had been asked in the early stages, soon after B.M.'s death, to deliver a funeral speech. I was prepared to speak for not more than ten minutes. A few words of goodbye, a few words of condolence. No personal histories, no victories, no successes . . . . I feel it is vulgar the way our people spend about eight hours mouthing off inflated stuff about the deceased, especially because often the speaker has not even visited the eulogised one during his or her illness or good health. Vultures come to pick the bones of the dead to bolster their own sense of self-importance? Fear-driven creatures come to coax death so as to get used to it against that dreadful visitation when it will be their turn?

Who knows? But I just loathe the way we have deviated from the simple traditional funeral, where the dead are sent off in plain wooden coffins, without any fanfare or gala performance. Quietly, in a way that becomes an occasion for heart-felt mourning, and the serenity of the corpse . . . .

And I loathe the habit people have of stocking up

with liquor when the next-door neighbour has died,
so as to sell to those who come for the wake. Night
after night, the whole week long, drinkers will
commute between the home of the dead and the *ad
hoc* bar, and hymn singing will issue forth more and
more lustily as the night itself waxes foggier and
foggier.

But the Venda government had acted fast. It was
going to be a 'state' funeral! The strong men were in
charge — no fooling. No southerners were going to
speak, it was whispered by those of the inner circle —
B.M.'s southern constituency. They might bring anti-
independence politics into the works . . . we know
these urbanites . . . stuff like that. To further prove
the government's sense of loss, the police were all
over Tshakoma, all along the routes, conducting
traffic, writing down registration numbers, standing
and walking like custodians during a state of emergency.

The day was hot. The lush tropical vegetation, the
red earth, the sun up there, seemed to have prepared
an ambush for us.

The service was held in the Teachers' College hall.
Sweat poured liberally down our faces, necks, down
our chests and backs. All the speakers were govern-
ment people, among them a token representative of
B.M.'s party. The whole service was conducted in
Venda.

The casket was removed from the floor towards
the stage. Going up the stairs from the floor to the
top of the stage it was hemmed in by the wall of
the hall on the right and on the left a timber wall.
Stepping on to the stage the pall-bearers had to negotiate a door frame planted there like an impromptu
gallows. The casket was tilted this way and that, side

to side, back to front, front to back. For one crazy
second I imagined B.M. shouting *what are you doing
to me, you creeps!* The casket had no sooner been
planted on the stage, where the array of frontliners
sat, than I began to to understand the reason for the
performance. TV cameras were rushed to the stage:
SABC. It was set up to be a show of the 'state's' love
for B.M.

And perspiration flowed. And we fanned ourselves
with the programme sheets. And the speeches rolled
on, riding the heat-wave on and on, mindlessly. Tales
of friendship, tales of intimate discussion, tales of
gifts being traded with B.M., tales of love . . . .

The 'state' had lent money to B.M., we were told,
to help him set up his businesses. Five hundred rands
— a donation from the 'state' to the bereaved. Cameras
were trained on the presentation act in which the
chief speaker was handing the cheque to B.M.'s
brother.

The Venda flag was brought on to the stage to
drape the casket. Cameras, words, words, words. And
I knew this was the ultimate triumph of the government, the coup-de-grâce. An act to cancel all acts.
B.M.'s political career — such as it was — was cancelled,
written off, at that moment. The 'state' loved him;
the 'state' buried him, in more ways than one; he was
one of its wards; he had never been in opposition; he
couldn't speak for himself. The cancellation was
complete.

The minister who conducted the service preached
about death. Are you ready for death? he kept re-
peating, like a speaker hopelessly waiting for gems of
wisdom to come in from somewhere, and playing for
time. How does one get ready for death? I kept
puzzling over this in my mind. It was a sermon full of

threats, warnings, denunciations, easy syrupy answers
to all of life's dilemmas and travails.

And poor B.M. lay up there, at last a captive of the
Venda 'state'.

After two-and-a-half hours we left the hall.

On the way to the family graveyard, someone from
B.M.'s constituency told us that the corpse had been
detained at the hospital in the first place, so that it
would go directly to the cemetery from there. As if
the government were not sure for how long the corpse
would be theirs. But someone else prevailed upon the
government to let the corpse go to its original home
in Tshakoma.

The one moment of relief was for me to see the
small graveyard where B.M. was laid to rest. It was in
a wooded spot with tall trees. The idyllic setting, full
of birdsong, an almost uninterrupted cool shade all
around, anticipated autumn leaves that would spread
their carpet over the area — all these seemed finally to
clinch the end of someone's journey in a way that
renders all debts, all claims, and all state funerals
utterly irrelevant.

Death of a salesman? Yes. Except that he had
almost nothing to sell, and the market price on his
head was nothing to talk about.

Funny how it is that no matter what cause an
authority may throw out to be fought over, challengers
are never wanting. No matter how silly or insignificant
the prize, they will appropriate the cause and make it
theirs and live it. Those slave gladiators of ancient
Rome: they knew there were no victories between
one slave contestant and the other. But they appro-
priated the game, to the master's amusement out
there in the faceless pavilion. No victories, not even
for the man the masters saw as winner.

B.M. entered the game of 'homeland' politics. The arena is but a few square metres. Sceptic though he was, hopeful though he was that his party members might become enlightened by the failure of independence, during the debates in the House and party rallies the game did not grow less silly. Instead, his opposite was bent on playing it monstrously rough, armed with weapons like arrest and indefinite detention which his maker had bestowed upon him. And somewhere in the arena someone began to crouch and walk with a menacing stoop and bent knees, and howl at the full moon. And we knew the werewolf was on the prowl . . . . It's not B.M.'s immediate opponent. He's out of it. The werewolf is the system in which he was placed as custodian, so help him God!

B.M. knew all this, I'm sure. But I think he was weary of opposition when he made the final surrender. Let the person who easily classifies territorial top men as two-dimensional clowns — and therefore easily dismisses the millions in the rural areas as a viable constituency — think on B.M.

Exile was exquisite and enriching while I was moving with the momentum Nigeria gave. And then, much later, we decided it had served its purpose. There seemed to be a pattern of inevitability in our return. There wasn't any other sensible thing to do. I know that for some exiles and refugees life hangs, to borrow an image from Tennyson, like a 'broken purpose in air'. Good fortune has carried us on its wings.

Each one of us has finally his or her reason for going into exile, or being forced into it by circumstances to which he or she shapes a unique response. Likewise the decision to stay out or re-enter. A few of our countrymen accused us of selling out. They even

spread stories about a possible deal I might have
made with the government, allowing it to pose as
liberal to the outside world. Speculation that was
passed on from mouth to mouth as fact. The logical
outcome of this was the resolution taken by the
African Literature Association in the United States in
1981 urging a 'cultural boycott' of South Africa. This
was intended to rally Americans for a boycott of
academics and students who have come out to South
Africa with valid passports. Some of the South Africans
in the Association were themselves educated abroad.
What does one say to this, but simply that history will
disclose the truth one day? There are no victories, no
heroes, in this process of resolving the compromise
that exile is, or in the silent refusal to contemplate a
resolution.

Bitterness. Have you tamed that lady now, which you
were pursuing when you went to teach in Lesotho in
1954? someone asked after a lecture I gave at the
1982 summer school, University of Cape Town. Yes,
I have. I feel bitter about things the government is
doing to my people: detentions, arrests, jail sentences,
executions, torture, bannings, poverty, removals of
whole communities for resettlement elsewhere, and
so on. But I can contain the bitterness now. It does
not immobilise me any more. I feel I have the moral
resources to deal with it, to harness it to reinforce my
creative energy. I need never again feel ashamed of
bitterness when white liberals say disparagingly that I
have a chip on my shoulder. When I was younger, I
was constantly warning myself against bitterness,
because I was choking on its poison.

I was an agnostic when I left in 1957. Now I am a

confirmed African humanist. I have said that West Africa gave Africa back to me. The difference between me and western humanists is that I cherish the African's belief in the Supreme Being as a vital force, a dynamic presence in all organic matter and in the elements, in Man, where those of the western world feel uneasy with belief in the supernatural and dismiss African religion as magic. My God is not a product of Hebraic-Christian culture but of African culture. Like Rabindranath Tagore's, my religion is a poet's religion. The poem Tagore wrote at eighteen, after he had been watching the sun at early dawn, was 'The Awakening of the Waterfall'. The waterfall, its spirit dormant in icebound isolation, was touched by the sun. It burst in a cataract of freedom. It found its fulfilment in an unending sacrifice — a continuous union with the sea. As Tagore grew older and was working in the villages, things began to take on a meaning for him. He experienced the unity of a vision. He felt sure that some Being comprehended him and his world, and was seeking expression in his experiences, uniting them in that ever-widening individuality which is a spiritual work of art. To this Being he was responsible, 'for the creation in me is his as well as mine.' When Tagore contemplated this unity between himself and the Supreme Being in a creative comradeship, he felt he had found his religion at last, 'the religion of Man, in which the infinite became defined in humanity and came close to me so as to need my love and co-operation.' The basis of the African's traditional religion lies in the realm of social relationships, in action among other people, in the continued contact between us and the external nature through the spirits of the ancestors.

The image of God is, in the first place, a poetic

creation, a state of mind. We create God according to our needs, our loftiest aspirations, our idealism. Those who create a god that justifies for them the desire and will to shut other people out of their lives in order to establish an exclusive enclave for themselves must be utterly poor in spirit. I find the idea repugnant that we should embrace such a god and pretend that the white intercessor expresses the aspirations of people who are in pursuit of liberty.

African humanism is inclusive, not exclusive. Because those in power in this country have rejected it, I must reserve my humanistic sensibilities for those of my race, yet still leave the door open for others to come in. They must earn their entry. No longer can we, where there is a choice, make ourselves available on the white man's terms.

We sought community, we found it. We sought an identifiable culture, we found it. We sought relevance, we found it. We sought a return to ancestral ground, this is it, and it cuts across all man-made boundaries. We tasted liberty — freedom of association, expression, mobility. We came back to none of these. I said good-bye to asthma as soon as I landed in Nigeria. It has stayed away this long. I continue to jog and skip and do calisthenics alternately throughout the week every week, as I have done since I was fifteen. At 62, I still hold the lease of life God granted me when time released me from my mother's womb. I regard myself as blessed with a wife I have been married to for 37 years; blessed to have been able to extend myself through my children, my art, my teaching; blessed with loyal friends, blessed with the privilege to teach and be involved with the arts, with the literary ambitions of black people, with other activities that I believe make sense only when they are functional for community development.

Soweto. Huge and slummy. Pipes burst and water irrigates the streets for days. Few lavatories work. Water hisses, swooshes and hisses ceaselessly for six months, or the flushing chain jams in a cistern one cannot easily get at, and the West Rand Administration Board couldn't care less. Service payments are hiked periodically: what services? Garbage dumps keep shooting up all over the township, where children and elderly women continue to forage for cast-offs that may come in handy . . . .

They are installing electricity to 'improve the quality of life', as the official jargon goes. Might as well electrify a sewerage bog . . . .

Soweto, home of maggots and rats and cockroaches, what are They doing to us?

The plots They have cut up for home ownership are tiny: a gloryfied slum in the making. An illusion is shared by the oppressor and some of the oppressed — an illusion the size of outer space — that a middle-class is emerging, now that people can own a home on the 99-year lease. Only tiny areas are being opened up in this way. The bureaucrats are seeing to it that the plan stalls several times, lest the urban African begin to feel permanent. Everything must be done to prevent an influx into urban areas.

In certain political camps among the oppressed it is sincerely believed that the Government is creating a middle class in order to encourage antagonisms among us. Those who believe this begin to hurl abuse at the homeowners, whether of new houses or improved housing. They hang on to that and work themselves into an uptight posture. They've begun to believe that the more disadvantaged a person is, the easier it is for activists to draw him or her into the picket lines, the street demonstrations, the rallies.

In reality there is no African middle class. The nearest examples I have seen among blacks generally are the Western Cape 'coloureds' and the Durban and Johannesburg Indian merchants and professionals. Africans in the professions and manual labourers live cheek by jowl, and are all working class, some more miserable than others. We are all in one big slum. Homeowners do not own the land on which they have built; they are in charge of nothing; loud radios and stereos and Zionist services — all these are common throughout in urban areas; so are shebeens and riotous parties; the homeowners don't have the money to invest in the country's economy; nor do the businessmen have such an outlet, so that they resort to buying posh cars, bigger and lavishly furnished houses. Homeowners hardly have a choice of where they can send their children for better schooling. They have no pull in matters of municipal government; the country's legislature has pre-empted that area. We are a colonised people, and it ill behoves any of us to consider it a virtue to live in pokey, over-crowded box dwellings.

Soweto, cave of the grinning skull,

What are They doing to us?

Our black politicians will need to grasp the dialectic of our condition, instead of continually beating the bush for scapegoats. Political and economic impotence — overcrowded slums — physical violence, rape, burglary — increased sense of impotence — unwholesome diversions like drugs, alcohol — increased sense of impotence — political rivalry and uptight doctrinaire positions — and so on.

Soweto — myriad box houses belching smoke from coal stoves. Approaching it from the east of a late afternoon you have a clear if frightening idea of how much smoke Sowetans, from toothless infants to toothless grandpas and grandmas, must be breathing in day after day. And if you care to stretch an image to its limits in this context, you might fancy that you were going to run into an inferno under the pall of smoke. Box houses choking with fat pieces of furniture which by sheer volume push outward beyond the last margin of comfort. The furniture takes over, to hell with the human occupants. But this bullying process has only begun. We own furniture suites, not a mere prosaic assortment of items. Wait till we place the radiogram there, and then the TV box next to it. The gram dominates with its loud boom that makes conversation silly, irrelevant. The new TV stands next to it, commanding attention when it's turned on, both gadgets terrorising us into submission. And let no one complain that he found a TV box in our house and we did not entertain him to it! We are all going to be throwing glances in that direction during the visit, the wayward eyes sometimes resting on a scene without your permission. But if the visitor has any qualms about visiting etiquette, the host is blissfully unruffled, because he is entertaining. So we all begin to feel like children who were told by the teacher to fold their arms and be quiet. The fare unfolds on the screen, and if you have seen TV around the world you can't help but observe that what's given you here has been laundered and sifted and monitored by the moral minority. Expensive TV for the working class in a capitalist society ruled by a moral minority — wow! What next?

Our dear friend Reginald Mbele tells us Sowetans like to hear you talk about your misfortunes and failures, those of your children. Not about your successes or triumphs or those of the child who has gone to

university, here or in another country. They just
enjoy hearing that someone else is in the same mess
they are in.

So we kill and rape one another; so we steal from
one another; so we are constantly on guard against
one another. So we inform on one another to security
men; in any meeting you address you may be sure
there are snoopers it would be futile to try and
identify. So we tell one another that so-and-so is a
snout — informer — pass the word round, and suspicion
has taken on the appearance of fact overnight. So we
begrudge someone else's success or achievement, so
we suddenly run short of praise songs for the hero in
our midst until he's stiff in a coffin and we are about
to drop him into a pit. So we think history began
when we were born and we don't bother to study the
available history of our political struggle and that of
our writers and artists, of our achievers. We are not
neighbours any longer — not in the sense of fellow-
feeling, of functional communal concern. We withdraw
into our individual family circles for self-protection. I
found, when we returned, that families don't
commonly invite people to dinner. Parties, yes: the
only way, it seems, we can socialise — anonymously,
without commitment.

      Soweto, place of the grinning skull,
      — Death in life, life in death —
      What are They doing to us?

We thought we were urban and yet we know full
well that the complete urban life was denied us. It
was just that denial that stimulated our desire for the
things white folks owned. After I had left the country,
I used to think it was not necessary for us to assert
our blackness. We took it for granted. When my dream
of a non-racial society was shattered, dating from

Sharpeville, I realised that the white ruling class and its electorate were in effect rejecting African humanism, which is traditionally inclusive. Away from home, it dawned on me that we had taken our Africanness too much for granted, that we had in fact been assimilating the ways of white folks *on their own terms,* that our immediate need was not to try and win over whites to the side of non-racialism but to strengthen *our* sense of an African identity. Our African consciousness at the deeper levels of culture where it is felt as a spiritual necessity. We would need to defer for now the ideal of non-racialism as a political slogan.

Urban ghetto folks look down on rural folks, because they (urban folks) reject the political concept of 'homelands' — the rural areas. So we write off a whole rural constituency from which we could learn something of the art of living. Because out there may be a culture of poverty, but it is by no means a poverty of culture. I say to our young literary apprentices that they should go out to the rural areas and absorb the landscape and the people's way and rhythm of life. Their response to this is not encouraging. I can read scepticism on their faces.

> Soweto, place of the grinning skull,
> What have They done to us?

Weekend after weekend funeral processions head for the cemeteries. On the roof of a hearse may be a speaker through which a hymn issues . . . . Revolting. A funeral procession files past, the deceased an ex-footballer. At intervals, between cars, are members of his team taking the long strides peculiar to a rickshaw puller. The performance will last the distance to the graveyard. It must be reported after a gala funeral that there were large crowds to bury the deceased — ten or so busloads and a long, long procession of carloads . . . . It must be reported that two oxen or so 'fell' to feed the multitude after the performance . . . .

In the midst of all this I am at pains to extract a meaning. I begin to wonder if the whole show is not an expression of, and at the same time an antidote to despair. So much violence is with us, so much death. To ritualise it, however grotesquely, may be a way of conquering the fear of death, of coaxing it, containing it. I begin to wonder if Soweto, as a paradigm of black South African life, is not striving in its own burlesque fashion to define something of communal experience that the collective memory still cherishes; the disinherited personality trying to salvage something from the collective memory and to give it definition so that people may survive the cruelty of the times. A survival culture, a fugitive culture.

One of the features of this survival culture is popular music in the urban ghettos. Much of it is derivative. Disco. Jazz is dead, has been on the way out since the mid-Sixties. Dead, except when a veteran jazz player has died. Other veterans quickly get together and blow during the procession and at the graveside. That's how antique jazz has become. Music for the dead.

Soweto, place of the grinning skull,
What have They done to us?

Women play a paramount role in this survival culture. Once they have identified a social need they set about the task of forming themselves into a group to deal with the problem — as a voluntary service. The women, more than the men, and sooner, can be seen engaging in services for the physically and mentally handicapped, hospital visits, health programmes, pre-school education, child care, and other voluntary work. Our women are strong. They will always be the ones to keep touching base, no matter what. I pay tribute to them. Here's to the African woman! As also to the equally strong African-American woman.

Soweto children are forever spilling out into the streets. They kick tennis balls, play a game with stones that are going to lie there indefinitely. Like the adults, the children drag their feet when they move to give way to oncoming traffic. Some part of them has already been desensitised and does not respond with the speed demanded by the flow of traffic. Children already learning to live with Soweto danger, from the age of six.

A few weeks ago I was in the north and went to Maupaneng — or what was left of it. I went over the mountain overlooking the valley. Only three houses were left and being lived in, stubborn survivors of soil erosion. My aunt, I was told, had abandoned the house of my childhood. I did not even trouble myself to enquire where she had gone to. She has never needed me, I never needed her. We hardly know each other.

I went into the courtyard to survey the ruins. The rondavel where we used to cook and sleep had no thatching any more. The fireplace was there, described by the bicycle rim. The millstone and the grinder lay there, a dirge in stone. My stern grandmother once on a day in 1930 knelt there, grinding sorghum, and weeping visibly because my mother had come to fetch us.

I left and went to stand in the centre of the valley where the main thoroughfare had been. I listened to the silent dirge. I seemed to hear children's voices as they skipped in groups with the use of a long cord made of tree fibre. I could never think of the skipping without the picture of soft, grey rain. Skipping in the rain also made the rope heavier with the wet earth it collected, and better for the game. I seemed to hear

also the metallic afternoon sound from the women's
pounding as they made small holes on the millstone
with a chunk of iron, to roughen the surface. I thought
my ears caught the lowing of cattle and bleating of
goats for their young as they were driven home.
Soaking wet, I would be driving them home, and my
clothes would dry on my body. Or, on a dry afternoon,
the dust raised by the hooves of the herd against the
red-red sunset — that's how it all comes back to me.

Villages may be harassed to death, but they do not
die in the simple course of nature. This one had been
fighting a rearguard action against the forces of
nature. There was community here. Which is why I
felt something die inside me too. And yet I did not
experience anything like the indignation I felt when
I visited Marabastad. The strong men had begun to
wipe it out in 1940, but nothing significant has taken
its place. Only recently have They started to dig it up
to prepare for a railway station. There have been many
more Marabastads elsewhere since. And They are
promising us still more.

When I climbed the mountain to return home, I
dug out some plants to adorn my rockery.

Glossary

p.56	*ka mmago*	(as true as) your mother
	kea fufulelwa	I'm sweating
p.57	*ke mmago*	it's your mother
	ek sê dis jou ma daai	I say it's your mother
p.69	*basadi!*	women!
p.77	*bana baka*	my children
p.98	*ag jy lieg man*	hey, you're lying, man
p.102	*kak en betaal*	[literally] shit and pay; time to pay up
	mos	in any case
	baba bangmaak	(stories to) frighten children
p.104	*'n moer se skrik, ek sê*	a hell of a fright, I tell you
p.109	*Kenotshi*	I am alone
p.116	*ba tla bona bomma 'bona*	they'll see their mothers (as a threat)
p.124	*kyk hierso, nefie*	look here, cousin (chum or pal)

	jy's a teacher, nie a reporter nie	you're a teacher, not a reporter
	wat kan 'n mens doen in hierdie omstandighede?	what can a fellow do in these circumstances?
p.201	*moenie daai kak taal praat met my, hoor!*	don't talk that shitty (English) language with me, (you) hear!
	lesapa la bosin he le me mong wa lona	[literally] the person who deposits excrement anywhere at night can never be identified
p.202	*jy lieg*	you lie
p.206	*ruiter-in-die-nag*	rider-in-the-night
p.235	*God, hierdie werk druk my neer*	God, this work's getting me down
p.236	*maak vir ons tee daar*	make us tea there
	waar die moer is dit?	where the hell is it?
	waar's die fokken ding?	where's the fucking thing?